over the edge

The Revolution and Evolution of New Rock

ALAN CROSS

PRENTICE HALL CANADA INC.
SCARBOROUGH, ONTARIO

Canadian Cataloguing in Publication Data

Cross, Alan
  Over the edge: the revolution and evolution of new rock

ISBN 0-13-778309-4

1. Rock music - 1981-1990 - History and criticism.
2. Rock music - 1991-2000 - History and criticism.
I. Title.

ML3534.C952 1997 781.66 C97-931683-9

 © 1997 Alan Cross

Prentice Hall Canada Inc.
Scarborough, Ontario
A Division of Simon & Schuster/A Viacom Company

Prentice-Hall, Inc., Upper Saddle River, New Jersey
Prentice-Hall International (UK) Limited, London
Prentice-Hall of Australia, Pty. Limited, Sydney
Prentice-Hall Hispanoamericana, S.A., Mexico City
Prentice-Hall of India Private Limited, New Delhi
Prentice-Hall of Japan, Inc., Tokyo
Simon & Schuster Southeast Asia Private Limited, Singapore
Editora Prentice-Hall do Brasil, Ltda., Rio de Janeiro

ISBN 0-13-778309-4

Managing Editor: Robert Harris
Acquisitions Editor: Jill Lambert
Editor: Sarah Swartz
Editorial Assistant: Joan Whitman
Art Direction: Mary Opper
Production Coordinator: Julie Preston
Cover and Interior Design: Verve Graphic Design Consultants
Cover Photograph: Verve Graphic Design Consultants
Page Layout: Debbie Fleming
Manuscript Processing: Deanne Walle

1 2 3 4 5   W   01 00 99 98 97

Printed and bound in Canada

Visit the Prentice Hall Canada Web site! Send us your comments,
browse our catalogues, and more. **www.phcanada.com**

Over the Edge: The Revolution and Evolution of New Rock

Preface

Back at the beginning, rock'n'roll was a simple proposition: you either liked it or you didn't. But in the forty-some years since Alan Freed coined the term, rock'n'roll has become a lot more complicated, cleaving and stratifying into a seemingly endless series of sub-genres, sub-sub-genres and even sub-sub-sub-genres. And while this is wonderful from a freedom of choice point of view (enabling each of us to find the right musical "scene" for our individual personality), it can be terribly confusing— especially in an age when we are constantly being bombarded with news and trivia about everything.

This book tries to make sense out of the clutter of information constantly being generated by the sub-genre of rock known as alternative. (Don't ask for a definition here; flip to the Preface). Like the rock of the 50s, the whole concept of alternative music was simple: you either got it or you didn't. But the rules suddenly changed in the PN (post Nirvana) Era; what used to be an alternative choice to mainstream rock has become the mainstream! More people than ever are into a form of rock that has its deepest roots in the D.I.Y. aesthetic and of the punk explosion of the 1970s. While Oasis may borrow liberally from the Beatles and Silverchair will cite their Black Sabbath influences, it's the "anything goes" attitude originally demonstrated by the Ramones, the Sex Pistols and the Clash that drives this music forward. And because there are few rules about what is "allowed" in making music, new ideas and new sounds are heard almost daily. In fact, there are so many groups releasing material these days that even the world's largest record stores are having serious trouble managing their inventory.

Managing information about this music is almost as complicated. Even someone like me (who deals with this stuff on a professional basis seven days a week) can find it to be an impossible task. And with the hundreds of information sources available to the average music fan/consumer, where do you start?

One starting point is right in your hands. Having inherited my parents' mania for organization, I have once again tried to collect much of what I have discovered about alternative music in one place. As part of my radio job, I spend hundreds of hours each year writing and researching material for a weekly documentary called *The Ongoing History of New Music*. Using resources ranging from personal interviews, record company bios, the Internet, an out-of-control CD collection, a vast personal library of music books and subscriptions to practically every music magazine in the known universe, I cobble together a one hour radio show every week. Much of the information is used only because it passes my "Oh, COOL!" test. I figure that if a certain bit of trivia or a little-known fact about an artist surprises and enthralls me (a full time and somewhat jaded and cynical music industry professional), then it has to be of at least some interest to the music fan with a real job. The radio program is, thankfully, very popular and I'm constantly being asked for transcripts and tapes of the show. That, however, would be inefficient; it's much smarter and cost-effective to wait until there's sufficient material for another book.

This is not meant to be an all-encompassing encyclopedia on alt-rock; there are many other fine books that feature artist biographies, album reviews, chart positions and scholarly dissertations about What It All Means. I consider myself a "hunter-gatherer" or "pack rat" type of musicologist, the sort that collects information from a wide variety of sources so that it may be presented and preserved in one place. Think of this book as a collection of fun facts and useful information filtered out of the static and packaged almost Reader's Digest-style for easy, bite-sized consumption.

Why go through all this trouble? Because I have this nagging obsession that somebody should preserve this information someplace. I hope you find it interesting. Maybe even to the point where you find yourself going, "Oh—COOL!"

Alan Cross

Waterdown, Ontario, Canada

June 1997

Acknowledgements

Anyone who's even attempted to write a book will tell you that without the support and encouragement of some special people, it's almost an impossible task. The Official Support Team this time around includes my family, all my friends and co-workers at 102.1 The Edge/Toronto (especially Hal and Stu who let me indulge in these writing projects) along with Anne and Jill.

My love and thanks to my wife who put up with all those hours I spent working in the den.

And if you're going to write a book, make sure you have a Strange Little Dog lying under the desk. She'll keep you company and I've found that it's helpful to stop and scratch behind somebody's ears every once in a while.

Introduction:
What's With Music These Days?

DEFINITION 1: Alternative: Existing or functioning outside the established cultural, social or economic system. Offering or expressing a choice.

DEFINITION 2: Alternative music: A catch-all phrase used to describe the genres of rock 'n' roll that originally evolved as an option to the dull mainstream rock of the 80s. Sub-genres include everything from punk, grunge and indie-rock to goth, industrial and electronica.

Sometimes it's tough to get a handle on what's happening with music. It's constantly evolving and mutating, not only in terms of sound but in terms of *perception*. What was praised yesterday may be scorned tomorrow. Paradoxically, what was reviled a few years ago may suddenly and inexplicably be declared retro cool tomorrow. The concept of time is almost non-linear, as sounds and influences from the last half-century are constantly swirling together, forming new bonds while simultaneously being torn apart. Is it any wonder that a lot of people are confused about what's going on with music?

Nowhere is this confusion more acute than in the world of alt-rock. From the mid-80s through to the early 90s, it was perfectly acceptable to use the term "alternative music." While most of the world's attention was fixed upon the corporate rock being churned out by the major labels, another group of music fans was far more interested in the kind of music that *wasn't* being played on the radio. For them, life was too short to listen to normal rock 'n' roll. They knew that if you knew where to look, lots of adventurous non-mainstream music was being made. Of course, you had to go beyond what was being sold at the record store down at the mall.

The Pixies were writing songs using chords no one knew existed. Goth rockers like the Cure and the Sisters of Mercy turned "gloomy" into an art form. My Bloody Valentine showed the world how noise could be beautiful. The Smiths became heroes of the chronically depressed. Finding the state of music boring, if not downright repugnant, these groups intentionally separated themselves from the musical pack, determined not only to do things differently, but to rejoice in this alienation. And since humans have an inherent need to classify things, all this new music was soon being described as "alternative music"—a form of rock 'n' roll that was an alternative to what everybody else was listening to.

Some of this music was unpopular by choice. Many alternative artists worked at being different, rejecting most, if not all, rock 'n' roll conventions. With its emphasis on quirky songwriting, different arrangements and experiments with image and presentation, alternative music definitely wasn't for everybody. Many conventional rock fans found it too esoteric, too cerebral, too *avant-garde*, too different for their tastes; others found beauty in its strangeness and in the music's attempt to subvert traditional rock.

Changes in the modes and rhythms of popular music inevitably lead to changes in society at large.
—*Plato*

For most of the 80s, the alternative scene operated as if it were a separate musical universe. Although some alternative bands crossed over into the mainstream and enjoyed commercial success, they were the exceptions rather than the rule; most alt-rock acts were born, flourished and then died within this separate universe. The same applied to music fans; you tended to be either an alternative supporter (someone who eschewed "normal" rock music) or a mainstream fan (someone who either mocked the alternative scene or was entirely oblivious to its existence). Many alternative fans grew to like this clear delineation of taste and aesthetics.

But by the beginning of the 90s, a number of things created what could be best described as a "market adjustment."[1] Although it was a time of double-digit growth and big profits, mainstream rock had grown stale and bloated. Old music had been constantly regurgitated by the major labels under the banner of "classic rock" for several years with great success. To the majors, it was simple: Why bother investing in the development of new talent when people were still willing to listen to Led Zeppelin and Pink Floyd? And more importantly, why

---

[1] There have been at least two adjustments in the past. The very birth of rock 'n' roll was itself a reaction to the complicated big band music of the 40s and the bland pop of the 50s. The punk revolution of the 70s grew out of a distaste for what mainstream rock had become. Punk wasn't about technical prowess or record sales; it returned rock to the streets, thereby empowering a new generation of musicians.

invest in new acts when the baby boomers were still replacing their old vinyl records with new compact disks?

But then the market crashed. Mainstream rock, tired and vulnerable from too many years of relying on the same artists and the same sound, was quickly overtaken by a new generation of performers who despised everything that conventional rock 'n' roll had to offer. The main force in this *coup d'état* was grunge, a stripped-down, guitar-based form of angst-rock that captured the mood of a new generation, a generation of post-baby boomers (the so-called Generation Xers) who wanted their *own* music, not the music of their parents. Grunge was new and fresh without being too weird. It was alternative rock's commercial face, the bridge between the old and the new. Leading the way were Kurt Cobain and Nirvana[2].

For all of us in the 80s who wanted to hear the Replacements and got Whitesnake and Poison rammed down our throats, the fact that Nirvana exploded didn't make up for that. It didn't mean shit except that Nirvana was a great fluke.
—Butch Vig, producer of Nevermind, *to* Spin.

For millions of people, *Nevermind* was the door to this heretofore unknown universe of exciting underground music. Once Nirvana opened this door a crack (and once they started selling upwards of 300,000 albums a *week*), every major label was sent scouring their rosters for a marketable alt-rock act. That's how bands like Pearl Jam, Soundgarden, Smashing Pumpkins, Nine Inch Nails and Green Day suddenly found themselves in demand, after years of being considered too left-of-center for sensible mainstream tastes.

The media was only too happy to help out. MTV jumped on the bandwagon, first with their late-night *120 Minutes* and then by adding alternative videos to regular rotation. Instead of relying on the local college station for exposure, these artists found that more commercial radio stations (referring to their format as "modern rock" or "new rock") were devoting a growing percentage of their playlist to their music. As the alt-rock movement gathered strength, ratings rose and the number of new rock stations increased tenfold in just a couple of years. And a quick glance at the newsstand for the number of *Entertainment Weekly* covers devoted to new music made it very obvious that alt-rock had hit the big time.

---

[2] Although Nirvana was the major force behind the popularization of grunge, they did not invent it. Consider the dictum of German naturalist Alexander von Humboldt (1769-1859) on the three stages of popular attitude toward a great discovery: (1) Everyone doubts its existence. (2) Everyone denies its importance. (3) Everyone gives credit to the wrong person.

By the mid 90s, alternative rock had supplanted virtually all of the old rock 'n' roll war horses. Pearl Jam sold a million records in a week. The Smashing Pumpkins released a double album that was certified seven times platinum. More than 10 million people bought an Offspring album, even though they recorded for a independent label. *Nevermind* generated $50 million in gross revenues. Courtney Love was a presenter at the Academy Awards. And the Butthole Surfers were guests on *The Larry Sanders Show*. So much for being an "alternative" to the mainstream.

DEFINITION 3: Death By Mainstream: A situation where an artist is considered to lose any claim to credibility and authenticity as a result of commercial success.

Yeah, I think my music is mainstream. You can't sell that many records and still think that you're in the underground. I'm not saying you can't have that underground or alternative element to it, but the underground has infiltrated, to some degree, into the mainstream. But the reason I sleep well at night is because I know I didn't try to cater to the mainstream. Then "Closer" takes off, and the fucking record sells two or three million copies. It surprised me because—not to sound lofty, but I didn't think people would get it, you know?
—Trent Reznor of Nine Inch Nails to Rolling Stone.

Today the alt-rock scene is so big that it has *become the mainstream*—which begs the question: What's so alternative about alternative music these days?

This question has caused considerable angst among people who consider themselves to be "true" alternative music fans. They are angry and disillusioned with what's happened to "their" music. This explosion of popularity in alt-rock has been a complete disaster for them, leaching away all the art, integrity and exclusivity that this music scene once possessed—some of the very attributes that made it so attractive and enticing in the first place. What's so alternative about being into the same music that every kid on the block is listening to on his Walkman? This music—a treasured secret that could only be revealed to the privileged few who "understood"—is now available to the unwashed, unschooled, undedicated masses. The secret's out—and somehow, that's tainted the whole experience of being an alternative music fan.

And at whom are alt-rock fans directing their anger? The media and the corporate whores who run the music industry take the brunt of it—but so do many performers. Despite honest efforts to maintain grass roots contacts with their fans, some of these performers are now seen as traitors to the cause simply by virtue of their popularity and commercial success. To longtime supporters, these artists have become as bad as the old regime of classic rockers!

The problem with success
Is you become what you detest.
How 'bout that?
—"The Right Decision," Jesus Jones

The Alternative Music Life Cycle

There is a theory of societal evolution that goes like this: Barbarians invent a new culture. A middle class emerges to manage and help perpetuate the culture. An aristocracy eventually develops out of the middle class and they devote their energies to making things comfortable for themselves. Finally, a new set of barbarians smash everything apart and destroy the status quo so that the process must start all over again. If the culture in question is rock 'n' roll, then alternative musicians and fans are the barbarians.

A similar type of four-stage evolution goes on within the community of alternative music fans.

Stage One: A new, unknown band with an interesting and unique sound emerges and begins to tour in an old van or station wagon. After playing a number of small clubs and parties, they attract a few enthusiastic supporters. These are the first level of alternative music fans, the early adopters, people who pride themselves on being the first to know about a new group or a new type of music. They support the band in whatever way they can, buying the band's indie cassettes off the stage at the end of the night and maybe dropping ten bucks on a T-shirt. These fans are extremely loyal and very protective of their new, secret discovery.

A word about the value of obscurity: To some people, the only good music is the music made by groups who are almost totally unknown outside a small circle of fans. The assumption is that these performers are not in it for the money but the art of making music. Seen as untainted by the evils and temptations of the music industry, they are often assigned more integrity, authenticity and credibility than a similar group which has achieved wider fame and greater commercial success. These music fans also tend to feel more comfortable in this pocket environment, because it allows them to know a great deal about what surrounds them. This in turn spawns an intense feeling of community among the people who populate this environment.

Stage Two: As word of the new group spreads, their popularity reaches a second level of fans, some of whom support certain groups because they love to pull for the underdog. Smaller magazines write stories on the group, college radio plays their indie releases and a major record label or two might show some interest. They begin to play larger clubs and attract a new, larger circle of fans. The Stage One fans are still there, but they're beginning to feel a little squeezed by the new fans who are invading their territory. A few may also be starting to wonder about the group, perhaps questioning their integrity when it comes to music versus fame and fortune.

Stage Three: If the music is good and the market conditions are right, the band is signed to a major label. They may begin to sell records in significant quantities to a third circle of alternative music fans. These fans rarely buy indie releases and only occasionally go to small club shows—but they know what they like and usually buy a fair number of alternative records each year. Stage One fans are definitely feeling claustrophobic by now and even worried that their group has "sold out." Even a few Stage Two fans are uncomfortable.

Stage Four: In very rare cases, the band may go on to become extremely popular and might even invade the mainstream, attracting a fourth level of fans— the casual music fan who likes whatever is big at the moment. The Smashing Pumpkins, Nirvana, Pearl Jam and Stone Temple Pilots fall into this category. At this point, the group is virtually abandoned by Stage One fans—the people who liked them when they were small and unknown. Stage One fans start looking for something new and the process starts all over again.[3]

This life cycle is crucial to the health of the entire scene because alternative music *depends on constant change in order to survive.*

In sociological terms, this is called "the acceptance curve," which occurs in any situation that involves introducing something new into society which eventually achieves widespread acceptance. Innovators are the first to adopt what is being offered. They are the opinion leaders. They are followed by early fans, a larger group of users who help disseminate information a little more. Finally, there is the late majority, the people who ultimately sustain the concept. But when the majority has embraced the situation, chances are that the innovators have started looking for something new again. To them, authenticity declines in direct proportion to social acceptance.

---

[3] In many ways, the experience of the dedicated alt-rock fan parallels that of the hardcore jazz fan who sees a brilliant but obscure performer become a commercial success.

REM is the perfect example of how this life cycle works. In 1981 and 1982, they were known only to a small group of dedicated fans who heard their indie songs on campus stations like WUOG in Athens, Georgia—Stage One. Through the 80s (on the strength of their music), they attracted more and more attention, started selling more and more albums, and started playing in bigger and bigger venues—Stage Two. Beginning in about 1987, they began to play large venues and sell half a million copies per album, all without the benefit of widespread radio airplay or exposure through videos—Stage Three. Now they are full blown Stage Four—so big that the whole world knows about them and they signed a record deal for $80 million in 1996. The truth is they've maintained most of their original sense of integrity and credibility and continue to stick by the principles they held dear in 1982, but they just happen to be very, very big. However, the kind of people who were inclined to search out and support a young band from a little college town in Georgia have long since lost interest. They're probably out there in some small club, giving their support to a new, hungry young band. And thank goodness for them for they are the prospectors of the new music of the future. This is how one generation's underground becomes the pop of the next.

I get so tired of this attitude that if you're on an indie label, it's better than being on a major. People can say whatever they want, but, ultimately, you'll just have to hear the record. Besides, a lot of early punk bands were all on major labels. When the Sex Pistols first came out and got all that money without putting out a record, everybody was like "Take the money! Stick it to them!" If a band did that today, people would be going, "That's not very cool, man, that's not very PC." Fuck 'em all.
—David Yow of Jesus Lizard to Rolling Stone.

One of the realities of this alternative music life cycle is that it results in the occasional crisis of faith among alt-rock fans—occasions where "their" music was being corrupted and co-opted by the mainstream. In fact, we seem to run into this sort of thing every 15 years or so.

If 1965 is Year Zero for alternative music (this was the year of the birth of the Velvet Underground and the rise of American garage bands like The Barbarians, ? and the Mysterians and The Seeds), the first major crisis hit about 1978. The original punk movement had run out of gas at exactly the same instant that mainstream forces had finally found a way to market at least a portion of this music. Virtually every major label succeeded in packaging and marketing some of the less-threatening and pop-sounding performers under the banner of New

Wave.[4] By signing groups such as the Talking Heads, Blondie, Duran Duran and the B52s, the majors injected some new life into their rock and pop divisions, softening the financial meltdown that came with the end of the disco era and the recession of 1979 to 1981. As New Wave caught on (thanks in large part to MTV), radical techno-pop bands like OMD and the Human League were signed to worldwide deals and started having Top 40 hits.

The original punks recognized this for what it was: a co-opting of their music by the mainstream. Then came the Great Confidence Crisis of 1982. It had been bad enough in 1977 when the Clash, the band thought to have more credibility and integrity than all punk bands put together, signed a deal with CBS Records for £100,000. But when they agreed to open for the Who on their 1982 farewell world tour, it seemed like the end of the world. If the Clash could sell out like this, what hope was there for "real" music? To the original punks this made it official: Punk was dead.

Despite enthusiastic support from the video channels, New Wave eventually burned out on over-exposure and faded away. Any gains the underground had made in overtaking the mainstream were surrendered to Michael Jackson, Madonna and Whitney Houston. Pop fans also soon found themselves inundated with Huey Lewis and the News, Phil Collins, Lionel Ritchie and similar lightweight corporate fare. Mainstream rock fans drifted towards hair-and-spandex bands with a heavy metal-ish bent: Poison, Ratt, Van Halen and Bon Jovi.

Happy to be ignored by the mainstream once again, alternative music merely returned to the underground. Out of sight and unsupervised, all kinds of new and exciting music was created. Punk and its offspring weren't dead; they had just returned to the environment from whence they came. This music had once again become the dangerous, radical stuff of the streets, *real* music, full of an energy and sense of style that wasn't found anywhere else. Like the music of the original punk era, it was again the "alternative" to regular rock 'n' roll.

But what, exactly, qualified as "alternative music"? At first, it was defined by what it was *not*. It was not the Rolling Stones or Styx or REO Speedwagon. It was not the kind of music you heard on the local Top 40 radio station or the local album rock station. It was a type of rock 'n' roll, but it was an alternative to everything else that was out there. From there, this idea of "definition by exclusion" expanded to include all the weird stuff that you never saw on MTV or

---

[4] "New Wave" was nothing more than a marketing term conceived by some record company executive. It's based on the French film term *nouvelle vague*.

heard on the radio unless you were listening to some whacko campus station. This music wasn't for everybody—especially the rockheads who, when confronted with a Smiths album or a new 12-inch remix from Depeche Mode, would more often than not dismiss it as "fag music" or "weird shit that didn't rock." It was the stuff of cults, indie record labels, campus radio stations, strange record stores staffed by fanatics, and small clubs where the weird went to hang out.

The alternative scene was left alone for several years. Although most of the major labels thought it was good policy to carry at least a few of these fringe bands on their roster (or at least on some minor subsidiary label), they considered this music to be too weird and too radical to be marketed to the masses. At best, the majors gave these acts token attention and were happy to sell a few records to a small group of hard-core fans. Those performers who were not picked up by a major found a home at any of a growing number of small, do-it-yourself, non-aligned independent record labels.

This allowed the cycle to start anew. Disenfranchised and alienated by the state of mainstream rock 'n' roll, alternative performers continued to rebel against the status quo, just like their punk forebears of the 70s. Because these new approaches to music were left to gestate undisturbed, a new generation of musicians began to develop interesting hybrid sounds. Since synthesizers and keyboards were too expensive and complicated, many young performers turned once again to the guitar—which in turn led to the rise of new forms of rock with names like "grunge" and "hardcore punk."

Meanwhile, some of the old techno-pop kids who could afford new gear were learning new tricks. New Order made it cool to dance again, while others created computer-driven music that was so fast, hard and angry that it could only be called "industrial." You had to know where to look—but it was there: a growing backlash against complicated, pretentious and mainstream corporate rock. The new guitar heroes were found in the Pixies and Sonic Youth; Morrissey became a poet laureate to a generation; cool DJs packed the floor with New Order and then went home to chill out with Joy Division. Iggy Pop was revered as a Founding Father, while Patti Smith was our queen. It was a fully self-contained and completely separate musical universe that enjoyed its blissful isolation from the mainstream.

But then, starting in about 1989, a subtle but very fundamental shift began to occur—a shift that would end up changing everything in the rock world. For the first time since the beginning of New Wave era, the alternative underground began to bubble up into the mainstream again—only this time, the assault was much stronger.

We hate it when our friends become successful.
— *"We Hate It When Our Friends Become Successful,"* Morrissey

The Overthrow of Mainstream Rock

How did alternative music manage to overthrow mainstream rock? There are a number of explanations.

The Death of the Spandex-and-Hair Bands The 80s were a great time for bands like Warrant, Trixter, Ratt, White Lion, Poison, Cinderella and hundreds of other groups that played riff-heavy melodic metal—but then they all became the victims of their own success, especially after they all discovered the economic benefits of the "power ballad." By the end of the decade, these hair metal bands were everywhere: on every type of radio station, on MTV a dozen times a day, on movie soundtracks. It was a simple case of overexposure. People got sick of them.

Record companies tend to be much more fashion-conscious than the average music consumer. Realizing that the melodic metal thing had been almost tapped out, A&R reps were sent looking for The Next Big Thing. They found it in Seattle.

The Nirvana Factor The grunge scene of the Pacific Northwest was a major label's wet dream. Here were all these groups that played a melodic form of guitar-based rock but with a completely different twist. At the same time, the music wasn't too different, incorporating such familiar influences as Neil Young, Black Sabbath and Kiss—but without spandex, poodle haircuts and the tedious rock star posing. The only thing missing for everything to move to the next economic level was a group that exemplified all that was great about the Seattle scene in a form that made it easy for the rest of the world to understand. That group was Nirvana.

Make no mistake, Nirvana was expertly marketed to the masses using all the vast publicity resources of the recording industry. Yet at the same time, this music was *different*. Unlike the fluffy metal of the 80s, this music really seemed to mean something to the post-baby boom generation—and they responded by stampeding to the record stores. The huge success of Nirvana was a watershed event for all music. *Nevermind* showed the world, including the major record labels, commercial radio stations and all the music video channels, that alternative music could have broad appeal; it wasn't just for weird people out on the fringes of pop and rock. Plus, this brand of alternative music attacked the old guard on their own terms. In the early 80s, the New Wave bands launched their assault with fancy haircuts and synthesizers. In the 90s, the weapons were flannel shirts, Doc Martens and guitars.

Once Nirvana broke big, it was inevitable that capitalist interests would start mining the entire alternative scene, hoping to find another group or artist who would prove as profitable as Cobain and Co. There was a sudden flurry of interest in other Seattle groups like Pearl Jam, Soundgarden and Alice in Chains. Once the Pacific Northwest had been thoroughly scoured, the major labels started signing virtually any group that sounded even vaguely grunge. Say hello to Stone Temple Pilots, Sugar, the Smashing Pumpkins and dozens of others.

The Classic Rock Factor In the 80s and early 90s, mainstream rock radio relied heavily on classic rock artists such as Led Zeppelin, Aerosmith, Van Halen and the Eagles. Stations all over North American spent the better part of a decade re-hashing the same songs from the same old bands. For a while, this strategy worked and many stations with a classic rock format enjoyed high ratings and fat revenues. Record companies did well, too, making millions by re-issuing old inventory again and again.

But this maneuver turned out to be very shortsighted and eventually led to the "market correction" of the early 90s. Since so much time was spent on selling and promoting old rock music, very little emphasis was placed on developing new rock talent. Any bands that did break through were of the lightweight variety: Poison, Warrant, Ratt—groups that didn't have any real longevity mainly due to severe overexposure. In other words, old resources were being used up and new ones weren't becoming available. You can only survive on the past for so long before you stagnate and burn out.

Realizing that they had to find some new talent in a hurry (and intrigued by the success of Nirvana), mainstream rock stations started looking to the music scene where new talent was still a cherished thing—alternative music. What they found was a gold mine. The alternative scene provided them with dozens of well-developed, highly skilled guitar-based groups which didn't sound too out of place alongside mainstream groups. This is how Nirvana, Pearl Jam, Stone Temple Pilots, Soundgarden, Green Day and the Offspring found themselves being played alongside Eric Clapton and Metallica. The result was more public exposure and thus greater penetration into the mainstream.

The Demographic Factor With the dawn of the 90s came a whole new generation of music fans—kids that might not have even been born when the original punk movement hit in the 70s. These kids did not want to listen to their parents' music. They had wants, needs and concerns of their own—and they wanted their own music. The situation was very similar to what faced the punks of the mid-70s. Unable to identify with Mick Jagger or David Lee Roth, the new generation latched onto artists with whom they felt something in common: Kurt Cobain, Eddie Vedder, Tori Amos.

And don't underestimate global economics in this youth equation. The brutal recession of the early 90s hit young people particularly hard, creating a general sense of pessimism and gloom. Grunge was the soundtrack for this recession, reflecting the mood of Gen Xers and connecting with them on a specific spiritual level.

The Nomenclature Factor As alternative music occupied a growing chunk of the mainstream through the 90s, dozens of formerly cult-like bands were becoming multi-platinum artists. Even small indie bands were receiving more attention than they ever dreamed as more people were turned on to this new music. "Alternative" became synonymous with "cool." Some bands couldn't be bothered with this sophistry; others were only too happy to label themselves as "alternative," seeing this as a good career move.

Fans also began using the word as a kind of cultural shorthand. By referring to a specific group as "alternative," you automatically conveyed a large amount of information about that group: their non-traditional sound, their attitude, their fashion sense, their stage presence. To a certain extent, the term helped codify a widespread musical movement. By calling a band alternative, you communicated that there was a modicum of coolness to them. Even if you had never heard of this band before, if they were described as alternative, you at least had some idea what they were about.

The Good Music Factor The music created by the alternative mindset was too good and too exciting to be kept a secret forever. Maybe it was just a matter of time before the rest of the world caught on.

But let's get back to this business of trying to define what is "alternative." By 1992, it was obvious that the old definition of "alternative music" was in danger, simply because the music was no longer an alternative to anything—it was virtually the only new rock 'n' roll being made. Longtime fans were very conscious of the fact that *their* alternative music choices were now the *main* choices of greater numbers of casual music fans.

At the same time, many newer fans were uncomfortable with the word "alternative." To them, the word evoked images of weirdos festooned with tattoos and mohawks. Commercial radio stations experimenting with new formats involving this music invented euphemisms like "new rock" or "modern rock" to get around using the word "alternative." In the end, however, there was no fighting it. More and more, bands were classified as "alternative" simply because no one knew what else to call them. Today the media, the music industry, record stores and just about everyone else have relented and have begun using the "a" word. What would have been called simply "rock 'n' roll" in another era past has become the center of an ongoing debate over nomenclature.

The upshot of all this is that the original spirit of the word "alternative" has been rendered meaningless. Guided By Voices and Prolapse obviously fit the old definition—but what about groups like the Smashing Pumpkins, Bush and others who have ascended to multi-platinum status? Bands like this are now the mainstream! What are they an "alternative" to?

It's no longer enough to define something by what it is not. Alternative is no longer the stuff out on the fringe. And with all the different types of new music out there, it can no longer be applied to a specific sound or look. So what exactly are we talking about?

Maybe it all comes down to a combination of history, influences, inspiration, a common mindset and a common attitude about how music can be made. So, for the purposes of the rest of this book, the following definition is the one we'll use.

DEFINITION 4: Alternative music (revised): A useful and accepted musical term as recognizable and as flexible as "blues" or "jazz." It's a form of rock music, based on the aesthetics of the punk movement of the mid-70s, made by people who aren't afraid to take chances with musical self-expression. It's passionate music that flirts with conventional approaches to song writing without ever really embracing them. There's an emphasis on experimentation with not only music but sounds and the novel combinations of music and sounds. This music is also often infused with a do-it-yourself (i.e. I'm gonna do it my way) work ethic. And some of it just happens to be wildly popular.

The Future of Alternative Music

Here are some general points to think about when you're contemplating the state of music and wondering where things are going:

Fame and Commercial Success Every band in the world makes music with the idea of playing it for other people. This music is a performer's life work. In most cases, therefore, it is only natural that they would want as many people as possible to participate in their art. What would be the value in intentionally languishing in obscurity? Why spend years creating great music while at the same time preventing people from hearing it?

Success is not a bad thing. However, some fans believe that a band forfeits their right to call themselves "alternative" once they sell enough records to quit their day jobs. Success is something that everyone should strive for—but not at the expense of integrity and a sense of self. If a band like Nine Inch Nails or the Smashing Pumpkins can sell five million albums while being true to their ideals, what's the problem?

However, it is also perfectly acceptable for bands to intentionally *limit* their appeal and commercial success. If, for example, a certain group wishes to stick to an agenda of releasing low-priced indie records and playing exclusively for all-ages crowds (Fugazi comes to mind), that's great. If a performer wants to shake things up by making difficult and deliberately unpopular music (think Japanese noise bands like the Boredoms, or European noise terrorists like Atari Teenage Riot), that's fine, too. For some performers, being different is more important than anything else.

And while we're on the topic, let's keep the concept of success in perspective. If the Offspring sell ten million copies of *S*M*A*S*H** and only three million *of Ixnay on the Hombre*, does this mean that the latter is a "failure" or is "disappointing"? Be reasonable!

Out with the Old, In with the New There will be a periodic changing of the guard. If an established superstar starts to slip, don't panic. You may be bummed out if you're a fan, but the spotlight eventually runs out for everyone, no matter how big you are. All music goes through a continuous winnowing process. Time screens out the mediocre and allows only the truly brilliant to survive.

The Cyclical Nature of the Quality of Music There are periodic downward cycles in the quality of music, but this has always been the case. How many times has rock been declared dead over the last 40 years? Funny how it always seems to make a comeback, though.

And yes, the major record labels must share some of the blame when music takes a dive. Too many bands are releasing too many albums (close to 30,000 releases in 1996). Not enough time is spent developing young acts and the result is far too many one-hit wonders. Musical trends are beaten to death or new trends invented. What happened with grunge is a prime example. The major labels seized grunge in 1992, marketing it to death and increasing U.S. gross sales from $4 billion to $11 billion. The huge emphasis on a certain sound ends up with a marketplace that's saturated and homogenized, squeezing the life out of what was once a unique and exciting musical movement.

To complicate matters, the entire music industry is enduring an ongoing shake-up from a financial point of view. After years of artificially high profits (as fans were buying shiny new CD copies to replace their old vinyl albums), growth has decreased and the guys in the suits are worried. And they've only begun to properly contemplate the growing competition for the public's attention by other forms of entertainment, such as video games, computers and the Internet. Back in the bad old days of the record industry recession of 1979 to 1981, it was the music video that helped get people excited about music again. Now the video is old hat, over-hyped and hugely expensive. The question in many executive offices these days is "Now what?"

The Cost of Music The price of compact disks is still, in the eyes of many people, too high. With money always being a concern for young people (who constitute the greatest percentage of music consumers), is it any wonder that they are buying more and more compilation CDs rather than individual albums? To them, compilations provide more bang for their limited spending buck. They are also savvy shoppers: with many record stores offering listening posts or listening centers, music fans can now listen to a record before they buy it, instead of purchasing it on good faith.

The Future Role of Technology Technology is playing a greater role in music. You could hear the technological revolution that took place in the late 70s and early 80s, as synthesizers became cheaper and more versatile. Now, with computers and samplers and MIDI interfaces becoming cheaper and more powerful all the time, it's possible to make extremely sophisticated music in your own bedroom. This offers artists an incredible amount of power because it puts more of the necessary tools than ever directly in their hands. If you can make an album in your room, why spend thousands of dollars from your advance on renting a recording studio at hundreds of dollars an hour? To many artists (especially in dance and techno genres), this technological empowerment means less indentured servitude to the big labels. Many an indie label is now born on the kitchen table.

Speaking of technology, we haven't even touched on the potential of the Internet. Some people are predicting that the Net will be the death of the record store and the retailing sector as we know it. Why go out to purchase new music when you can sample it and then download what you want on your home computer? And if you're an artist, why bother with a label? New songs, updates, revisions and remixes could be downloaded by fans as easy as the newest shareware version of *Doom*. Believe me, this has them sweating in the corporate offices.

But what of our original question? What is alternative music? Is alternative dead? Some people have already had the funeral and scattered the ashes, but I think that's premature. Crises in confidence are cyclical. Things always turn around eventually. Punk was declared dead in 1977—but try telling that to the thousands of great punk bands out there right now. The term "alternative" may be passé, but there will always be a kid who wants to change the world with music, whether with guitars or computers. If you get discouraged about the state of music from time to time, all you have to do is go deeper underground. There's nothing quite like the feeling that comes with the serendipitous discovery of a new sound. You're always going to find something that excites you; it just takes a little prospecting.

In fact, it's actually *good* for music to get a little stale and boring from time to time. All the best music results when new young artists are moved to find *new* alternatives. In order for there to be musical rebellion, there must be something to rebel against and some traditions to subvert. It's safe to say that as you're reading this, The Next Big Thing is down in a basement somewhere holding their very first practice.

Besides, haven't we all complained that regular mainstream music is mush? The alternative music of the last few years has ripped a huge hole in the fabric of the pre-fab crap to which the world has been subjected over the last 15 years. At least the masses are listening to Green Day and Offspring instead of Huey Lewis and Billy Joel. And that's a good thing.

Part 1

The New Rock Timeline

The 1920s

More people begin to take notice of the musical contributions of non-mainstream cultures. Boogie-woogie, gospel, blues, hillbilly and jazz (originally known as "jass") enter the margins of pop music. Much of this material comes from areas outside the mainstream music centers of New York and Los Angeles—such as Chicago, New Orleans and Memphis—as well as from many rural areas.

The 1930s

Adolf Rickenbacker, Paul Barth and George Beauchamp build the world's first electric guitar in 1932—a lap steel guitar called "the Frying Pan." T-Bone Walker and Charlie Christian use it to bring electricity to the blues and jazz.

The 1940s

Les Paul invents the first solid body electric guitar in 1941. Post-World War II prosperity creates a new class of consumers with a wide range of tastes and needs. One of those needs is a music to call their own.

Early 1950s

Rock 'n' roll is born. White teenagers embrace black rhythm 'n' blues, mainly because no other form of music captures the same excitement. Listening to "race records" becomes an alternative to the sugary pop and "good music" of the era.

Late 1950s

Even the r 'n' b of the late 50s has its extreme performers. Billy Lee Riley (who recorded for the Sun label in Memphis) makes some records by screaming into a microphone as he literally hangs upside down from the ceiling. Gene Vincent sneers while wearing his black leather jacket. Eddie Cochrane cranks out rough-edged teenage anthems, such as "Summertime Blues." Rockabilly performers pound their pianos to splinters.

1963-65

The rise of the American "garage band" begins. Surf acts such as the Ventures and Dick Dale emerge out of California. The Kingsmen record their slop-rock classic "Louie Louie" for $50. Rumors that the unintelligible lyrics are hiding something pornographic attract the attention of the FBI. In Britain, "bad boy" bands such as the Rolling Stones, the Kinks and the High Numbers (later the Who) gain popularity among "mods" and "rockers."

1965

July: Lou Reed, John Cale and Sterling Morrison begin taping their rehearsals for the first time. They call their group "The Velvet Underground" after the title of a trashy S & M novel by Michael Leigh.

December 11: The Velvet Underground play their first paying gig at Summit Park High School in Summit, New Jersey. They're paid $75.

1966

January: David Jones changes his name to David Bowie.

Spring: The Velvet Underground begin residency at Café Bizarre in Greenwich Village and soon attract the attention of artist Andy Warhol. He becomes their manager and chief patron.

Summer: Some tough-looking American garage bands are being referred to as "punks." These include Count Five, the Seeds, the Barbarians, the Standells, ? and the Mysterians and the Shadows of Knight. The images of some of these groups conjure up visions of a leather-clad James Dean.

1967

February 20: Kurt Donald Cobain is born in Aberdeen, Washington.

March: The Andy Warhol-produced *The Velvet Underground and Nico* is released. Many consider this to be the first true "alternative" album.

Spring: The MC5 are formed in Lincoln Park, a suburb of Detroit. Aspiring poets Patti Smith, Tom Verlaine and Richard Hell move to New York.

June: David Bowie releases his self-titled debut solo album.

October 31: Iggy Pop and the Stooges make their debut at a Halloween party in Ann Arbor, Michigan.

1968

January: The Velvets' second album *White Light, White Heat* reaches number 199 on the *Billboard* album charts. Songs like "Heroin" and "Sister Ray" are considered harsh and weird by the vast majority who hear the album. Others are inspired.

Summer: Iggy Pop is busted for indecent exposure as the result of his extreme stage antics. The MC5 record their debut album after going to the Democratic National Convention in Chicago. They are signed by Elektra Records.

1969

Early spring: Elektra signs the Stooges for $25,000.

June: Bowie auditions for RCA by performing "Space Oddity." The song becomes a hit after it's used during television coverage of the Apollo 11 moon landing.

August: *The Stooges*, produced by John Cale, is released.

October: Captain Beefheart releases *Trout Mask Replica*, an album that's embraced by people who are into weird and disagreeable music. Early Beefheart fans in England include Johnny Lydon.

1970

Spring: Lou Reed leaves the Velvet Underground.

August: The Stooges release *Fun House*.

November: Bowie releases *The Man Who Sold the World*.

1971

Early spring: Patti Smith, already accepted as a hip, avant-garde poet, gives readings at St. Mark's Place in New York.

Summer: Anti-hippie Jonathan Richman forms the Modern Lovers in Boston. The group features Jerry Harrison (soon to be with the Talking Heads) and drummer David Robinson (who will later leave to join the Cars).

Fall: Proto-punk glam band the New York Dolls are formed in Queens, New York, evolving out of a group called Actress.

1972

Spring: David Bowie releases *The Rise and Fall of Ziggy Stardust and the Spiders from Mars*, one of the most important and influential albums of his career.

June 13: The New York Dolls, dressed in spandex, combat boots and lipstick, begin a long residency at the Mercer Arts Center in Manhattan.

Summer: Jonathan Richman and the Modern Lovers record a series of demos in California with John Cale of the Velvet Underground producing.

Fall: "Pub rock," a form of sweaty American influenced British r 'n' b, causes a buzz around England, thanks to groups like Brinsley Schwartz and Ducks Deluxe.

October: The New York Dolls meet Malcolm McLaren while shopping in his outrageous clothing shop "Let It Rock." He will eventually become the band's manager.

1973

March: After scouting the New York Dolls close to a hundred times, Mercury Records signs the group. Kraftwerk marks their U.K. debut.
Spring: Tom Verlaine and Richard Hell join with drummer Billy Ficca and form the Neon Boys. By December, they will change their name to Television.
October: The New York Dolls release their self-titled debut album. Meanwhile, more and more young people begin to express their disillusionment with the "peace and love" approach of the 60s. They consider the hippie movement to change the world a miserable failure. Some of this disillusionment begins to be manifested in a new, angry form of music.

1974

January 27: The Ramones hold their first rehearsal. They're a trio at this point, featuring a tall guy named Jeff Hyman (later Joey Ramone) on drums.
May: The New York Dolls release their second album *Too Much, Too Soon*.
June 5: The Patti Smith group records what could be the first-ever punk single. Side one features a version of "Hey Joe," while the B-side is a reading of Patti's poem, "Piss Factory."
August 16: Now a four-piece, the Ramones play their first show at CBGBs in Manhattan.
Fall: The Stranglers are formed in Guildford, England.
December: After Television proves the viability of their Sunday "new music nights," CBGBs institutes a "rock only" policy.

1975

August: A green-haired Johnny Lydon auditions for the band Malcolm McLaren is putting together in "Sex," his London clothing shop. Lydon impresses McLaren when he sings along with the jukebox, which is playing "I'm Eighteen" by Alice Cooper.
September: Cleveland legends Pere Ubu release "30 Seconds Over Tokyo," one of the first American underground indie 7-inch singles.
Fall: People seem to be referring to the new music of the CBGBs scene as "punk." Some of the credit for this label must go to a local fanzine called *Sniffin' Glue*.
November 6: The Sex Pistols play their first-ever gig at St. Martin's College of Art. The show lasts five songs before the power is cut.
November: *Horses*, the debut album from Patti Smith, is released.

1976

April 23: Sire releases *The Ramones*. The album was recorded for $6,400 and was allegedly so loud that it damaged the mastering equipment at the pressing plant.

May: Patti Smith makes her U.K. debut in London.

June 4: The Sex Pistols play the Lesser Free Trade Hall in Manchester. They so impress the crowd with their attitude that several members of the audience are inspired to form their own groups. Included in this number are future members of Joy Division/New Order, the Buzzcocks and the Pet Shop Boys, as well as Manchester's biggest New York Dolls fan, Stephen Patrick Morrissey.

July 4: The Ramones play the Roundhouse in London. Their appearance helps kick the entire British punk scene into high gear. In Sheffield, the Clash play their first public show.

September 20-21: The 100 Club hosts one of the most important events of the punk era: the two-day Punk Festival. Hundreds of early punk fans show up to see the Sex Pistols, the Clash, Subway Sect and an early incarnation of Siouxsie and the Banshees.

October 8: The Sex Pistols sign with EMI for £40,000.

October 22: The Damned release "New Rose," the first British punk single.

November 19: The Sex Pistols release their first single, "Anarchy in the UK."

December 1: The Sex Pistols create a national scandal after a foul-mouthed appearance on the ITV chat program, *Today*, with Bill Grundy. By the following morning, all of Britain is talking about this terrible new thing called "punk rock."

December 28: The Buzzcocks issue a four-track EP called *Spiral Scratch* on their own New Hormones label, becoming the first British punk band to release an independent record.

1977

January: Robert Smith forms the Easy Cure.

January 28: The Sex Pistols are booted off EMI for their lewd behavior in a settlement that nets them an extra £50,000 in a buy-out.

February 17: The Saints, one of Australia's punk pioneers, release *I'm Stranded*, their debut album. It's the first of many recorded debuts this year, setting the stage for the Year of Punk. The Damned, Television, the Clash, the Dead Boys, the Vibrators and the Sex Pistols will all have albums in the stores by the end of the year. Other groups to release debuts in 1977 include the Jam, Elvis Costello, Blondie and Television.

March 10: The Sex Pistols sign with A&M. They're fired six days later—but not until after they cash that A&M cheque for £75,000.

April: Kraftwerk release their hugely influential *Trans-Europe Express* album. The album will ultimately have an impact on everything from techno-pop and industrial music to disco and hip-hop.

May 27: Two weeks after signing with Virgin, the Sex Pistols release "God Save the Queen." The song goes to number one in Britain, despite being banned just about everywhere.

November 17: The Ramones release *Rocket to Russia*, two days before the Clash hit the stores with *The Clash*.

December 8: The Talking Heads give everyone a taste of what to expect during the coming New Wave era with their first single "Psycho Killer."

1978

January 5: The Sex Pistols start their ill-fated North American tour in Atlanta. It will end with the break-up of the band on January 14.

Early spring: As the novelty of punk begins to wear off, the No Wave/Noise scene begins to take root in New York City. New Wave begins to catch on with successful releases from the Cars, Blondie, Devo, the Police and the Talking Heads.

Spring: Post-punk music begins to fracture in every direction all at once. Although inspired by the original punks, new groups like the Fall, the Cure, the Cramps, Joy Division and XTC take this music to the next level. Others, such as 18-year-old Kate Bush, have a gentler sound.

March: The Normal (Daniel Miller, soon to be the head of Mute Records) picks up on the electronic sensibilities of Kraftwerk and releases the electro hit, "Warm Leatherette." Thanks to the declining price of synthesizers and a growing boredom with the anger of punk, many others soon follow, including Orchestral Maneouvres in the Dark, Gary Numan and the Human League.

Summer: The Specials begin to attract serious attention with their punked-up ska sound. Reggae influences are heard in the Clash, the Police and others.

Fall: Black Flag creates a home for punks in Southern California with the creation of their indie label, SST.

November: U2 begin work on their first demo tapes.

1979

March: Having enjoyed such a positive reaction to their music, the Specials set up 2 Tone Records, their own ska label. In addition to the Specials, the company will become home to Madness, the Selecter, the (English) Beat and the Bodysnatchers.

Spring: M releases "Pop Music," another important milestone in the rise of techno-pop.

Summer: New Wave is hot, thanks to XTC, the B52s and Blondie. The Cars play in front of half a million people in New York's Central Park. Numerous New Wave festivals are held across North America.

Fall: Some people are fascinated by the deconstructionist and atonal approach to music championed by Teenage Jesus and the Jerks, DNA and Mars. They are part of the No Wave scene of Lower Manhattan.

November: Public Image, Ltd. releases *Metal Box*, an intentionally harsh-sounding record that will have an impact on the future industrial scene as do new releases from Throbbing Gristle.

1980

January: *London Calling* from the Clash (which was actually released in the previous December) is hailed as a punk masterpiece. Meanwhile, the Pretenders self-titled debut is described as a fine mix of punk, New Wave and pop.

Early spring: The English "Goth" scene begins to gather momentum, thanks to the musical theatrics of such bands as UK Decay, and Australian imports the Birthday Party.

Summer: The Talking Heads raise the standard of post-punk musicianship with their incorporation of complex African rhythms.

Fall: British music fans benefit from the boom in new indie labels. Rough Trade, Mute, 4AD, Stiff, Factory, Beggar's Banquet and others spend time developing acts and distributing music that the major labels won't touch. Some underground American bands find their homes on indie labels like SST and Alternative Tentacles, the San Francisco label founded by the Dead Kennedys.

1981

Spring: Synthesizer prices continue to decline, while the machines themselves become more powerful and infinitely versatile. Performers incorporate more electronics into their sounds, while others ditch their guitars and drums entirely.

Summer: Frustrated by the fact that they can't find a label to distribute their brand of Southern California punk, Bad Religion opt for the Black Flag solution: they form their own independent record label. Epitaph will eventually become one of the most successful indie operations in the world.

August 1: The moribund music industry starts to be lifted out of the post-disco recession with the debut of MTV. New Wave bands, with their telegenic images (especially those from England where they've been accustomed to TV performances for years), are among the first to benefit from the added exposure.

September: Depeche Mode release their debut album, *Speak and Spell*.

1982

Spring: New Wave and techno-pop groups make serious infiltrations into mainstream music, thanks to releases by Duran Duran, ABC, A Flock of Seagulls, Dexy's Midnight Runners and many others. Rock radio stations find room for albums by Roxy Music, Simple Minds, the Clash and U2.

Summer: Goth reaches its peak in England with groups like Alien Sex Fiend and Sex Gang Children. Ska is declared dead by the British music media who turn their attention to rockabilly bands like the Stray Cats.

Fall: Record companies begin to acknowledge the power and influence of campus radio stations. More attention is paid to the potential of "college rock" bands (like REM) with their more basic guitar-bass-drums approach.

1983

January: *Combat Rock* from the Clash sells more than a million copies in the U.S. and yields the Top-10 single, "Rock the Casbah." The band will be invited to play the US Festival in May.

March: Using new sampling and sequencing technologies, New Order records "Blue Monday," an innovative eight-minute 12-inch single. During a time when the big dance tracks are from Olivia Newton-John and Joan Jett, "Blue Monday" makes it cool to dance again. The single will go on to sell more than three million copies.

March 23: Michael Jackson performs his famous "moonwalk" on the nationally televised *Motown 25th Anniversary Special* and people stampede to record stores to buy copies of *Thriller*. This gives the entire music industry a huge boost and many techno-pop and college rock bands benefit from the fact that there are now more consumers going through the racks in record stores.

Summer: The Clash, Billy Idol and the Police, all former fringe acts, have major hit singles, while Tears for Fears, the Talking Heads and U2 have become staples on mainstream rock radio. Back in the underground, Echo and the Bunnymen and others are exploring a new neo-psychedelic sound while groups like Cabaret Voltaire are churning out heavy, aggressive dance music.

Fall: Campus radio stations across North America offer a wonderfully eclectic fare during the fall semester: REM, Kate Bush, Psychic TV and Einsturzende Neubauten. In the U.K., the Jesus and Mary Chain shake up the indie scene with their new approach to noise and feedback.

1984

January: "Frankie Mania" hits the U.K. with the spectacular rise of Frankie Goes to Hollywood.

February: The Smiths release their self-titled debut album. The group's simple guitar sound and eloquent lyrics create a sharp contrast with the rest of England's synthesizer-happy sound. The group will eventually become one of the most influential British acts of the decade.

Spring: Minneapolis' Husker Du releases *Zen Arcade*, highlighting the group's ability to merge hardcore punk with pop melodies. Other groups (including several in the Pacific Northwest) soon pick up the thread. Meanwhile, the Minneapolis scene thrives, thanks to groups like Soul Asylum and the Replacements.

September: Depeche Mode issue *Construction Time Again*. The album's heavy, clanking rhythms contribute to the evolution of industrial music.

Fall: While Belgium's Front 242 work on what they call "electric body music," and tour with Chicago's re-born Ministry, Vancouver's Skinny Puppy experiment with heavy dance beats, aggressive keyboards, grinding guitars and samples, laying some of the foundations for late 80s industrial music.

October 1: U2 release *The Unforgettable Fire*, one of the best-selling rock albums of the year.

1985

Spring: A new sludgy guitar sound takes shape in the Seattle area, incorporating influences ranging from Sonic Youth, Husker Du and California punk bands such as Black Flag, to Neil Young, Black Sabbath, Led Zeppelin and Kiss. Several of these new groups (such as Soundgarden, the Melvins, Skin Yard, and Green River) turn up on a locally successful compilation entitled *Deep Six*.

Summer: Sonic Youth begin to hit their stride as the top American indie band with the release of *Bad Moon Rising*. Husker Du continue to contribute fresh ideas combining melodies and hardcore with *New Day Rising* and *Flip Your Wig*.

November: Big Audio Dynamite's "E=MC^2" becomes the first rock hit to make extensive use of sampling.

1986

March: Jane's Addiction play their first show.

May: The Cure issue their singles collection, *Standing on a Beach*.

June: The Smiths release *The Queen is Dead*, which is considered by many to be their masterpiece.

Summer: In the back room of Muzak headquarters in Seattle, Bruce Pavitt spends his coffee breaks establishing an independent record label designed to show off some of the new local talent. He calls his label Sub Pop. On the spine of Sub Pop 100, the company's first release, is the message: "The new thing, the big thing, the God thing: A multi-national conglomerate based in the Pacific Northwest."

September: Kate Bush sets a new standard for alternative dream-pop with *Hounds of Love*.

Fall: New Order continues to change the sound of dance music with the multitude of remixes from their *Brotherhood* album, including "Bizarre Love Triangle." They and several other British bands (Psychedelic Furs, OMD) receive a lot of exposure thanks to the soundtrack of the John Hughes film *Pretty in Pink*.

Winter: Johnny Lydon records his impressions of the local scene in Seattle with a song called "Seattle." Local musicians agree Lydon understands what's going on in the city.

1987

March 1: U2 release *The Joshua Tree*. Out of all the "alternative-type" albums to date, it becomes the biggest-selling of all time (15 million plus copies) and establishes U2 as a worldwide superstar act.

Spring: Nirvana play their first public gig in front of 13 people at the World Theater in Tacoma, Washington.

September: After months of uncertainty, the Smiths announce their breakup. Meanwhile, REM issues *Document* and finds further support beyond the "college rock" crowd. In Seattle, Sub Pop releases Soundgarden's *Ultramega OK* EP.

October: Boston-based band the Pixies find a home on England's 4AD label.

Fall: "Pump Up the Volume" from M/A/R/R/S, a song stitched together from dozens of separately sampled parts, gives an indication of where sampling technology is headed—and shows how a computer can be used as a musical instrument. The Pet Shop Boys record their entire *Actually* album using a Fairlight computer keyboard.

1988

Spring: Guitars continue to make a big comeback, thanks to groups such as Jane's Addiction. The grunge movement gathers strength in Seattle, while fans of the hardcore punk scene buy new releases from indie labels such as SST, Epitaph and Dischord.

Summer: Sonic Youth's double album, *Daydream Nation*, becomes a landmark in American indie music, blending noise with punk and pop. At about the same time, *Surfer Rosa* becomes an underground classic for the Pixies and Dinosaur Jr. finds fans with *Bug*.

1989

May: The Stone Roses issue their debut album, solidifying their position as one-third of "Madchester's" Holy Trinity with the Happy Mondays and the Inspiral

Carpets (who, by the way, have just hired a new guitar roadie on a salary of five pounds a night. His name is Noel Gallagher). The Roses' album will also set some of the foundations for the upcoming Britpop movement.

June: Nirvana's *Bleach* album (recorded for $606.17) is released on Sub Pop.

July: Depeche Mode performs in front of nearly 70,000 people at the Rose Bowl in Pasadena, California.

Summer: My Bloody Valentine's droning noise receives serious attention.

November: REM issues *Green* and is declared by *Rolling Stone* to be "America's Best Rock 'n' Roll Band."

November 29: *Pretty Hate Machine* from Nine Inch Nails is released. Together with *The Land of Rape and Honey* (1988) and *A Mind Is a Terrible Thing to Taste* (1989) from Ministry, American industrial music enters a new era.

1990

March 20: Demand for Depeche Mode's *Violator* album is so intense that a riot breaks out at an autograph session at a record store in Los Angeles. The album's subsequent success forces the major labels to take a closer look at the so-called "fringe" bands on their rosters.

March 27: The whole Manchester scene peaks when 30,000 people attend a Stone Roses concert at Spike Island in England.

Summer: Techno emerges out of the basements of Detroit, where it was born in the 80s, and takes hold of the rave scene in England as well as on the U.S. West Coast. Earlier techno stars include 808 State and the Orb.

Fall: Tired of baby boomer bands and classic rock (especially after a Summer featuring mega-tours by the Rolling Stones, Pink Floyd and Paul McCartney), members of Generation X are restless and search for a music to call their own. Meanwhile, on the recommendation of Sonic Youth (who have just stunned the indie world by releasing *Goo* on a major label), Nirvana and Sub Pop negotiate with DGC.

December 22: Pearl Jam, under their original name, Mookie Blaylock, play their first show.

1991

March: REM releases *Out of Time*, their major commercial breakthrough. It will hit number one on North American album charts.

Spring: A series of indie acts (Blur, Jesus Jones, James, Ned's Automatic Dustbin) make major gains in the U.K. and overseas.

July 18: The first Lollapalooza tour starts outside of Phoenix, Arizona. Despite predictions that the concept is doomed to failure, the tour is a success and will become an annual event.

September 24: Nirvana issues *Nevermind* and the grunge assault on mainstream rock 'n' roll begins. The album becomes one of the first "alternative" records to make it big on mainstream radio and to sell in mega-large numbers. Gross revenues from the album will eventually top $50 million.

1992

January 11: *Nevermind* hits number one on *Billboard* charts, displacing Michael Jackson.

February: U2 begin a two-year Zoo TV tour. Its sheer scope and magnitude will make it not only one of the most well-attended tours of all time, but also one of the most expensive, costing the band more than $125,000 a day just to keep it on the road. In the end, U2 nearly goes bankrupt.

Spring: At the corporate level, the power has begun to shift from those who favor mainstream acts like Bon Jovi and Warrant to those who have been following the indie scene. Hundreds of groups enjoy the residual effects of Nirvana's popularity, including the Lemonheads, Sugar, Sonic Youth, the Pixies, Pearl Jam, the Smashing Pumpkins and Soundgarden.

Summer: The rave scene continues to build throughout the U.K., the U.S. and Canada. Moby, Orbital and Prodigy emerge as techno stars. Offshoot sounds include "ambient" and "trance."

November: The coolness of grunge takes a major hit, when *Vogue* runs a feature on grunge fashion.

1993

Spring: Alt-rock is all over the mainstream media. *Entertainment Weekly*, *Time*, *Newsweek* and even the *New York Times* devote space to the new trends in music. Concerned with acquiring street level indie credibility, all six major labels begin to set up "faux indie" labels, companies which have the look and feel of real indie labels, but are actually owned and operated by one of the majors.

July: The Smashing Pumpkins issue *Siamese Dream*, making the band a major force in alt-rock. Several other alt-rock groups have mainstream breakthroughs: Rage Against the Machine, Tool, the Breeders, Soul Asylum, Alice in Chains and the Stone Temple Pilots.

Summer: Radiohead and the Cranberries manage to crack the tough American market. Several American indie acts have good summers, including the Breeders and Belly.

September: Nirvana releases *In Utero*.

October 11: At about the same time Pearl Jam appears on the cover of *Time*, they set an all-time first week sales record as 950,378 copies of *Vs* are purchased.

1994

April 5: Kurt Cobain commits suicide. In England, Britpop gets underway with the release of *Definitely Maybe* from Oasis.

Spring: Hip-hop flavored acts such as the Beastie Boys and Luscious Jackson begin to gain wider acceptance. Portishead, Massive Attack and Tricky are categorized as trip-hop. Lo-fi sounds from Pavement, Sebadoh and others find a niche in the underground. Deeper underground, the Riot Grrl movement finds fans.

June 29: Despite being one of the hardest and most intense albums of the year, *The Downward Spiral* from Nine Inch Nails debuts at number one on *Billboard* charts. Three NIN shows in Los Angeles sell out in less than 20 minutes.

Summer: Southern California hardcore punk dominates. Offspring's *S*M*A*S*H** becomes the biggest-selling independently-released album of all time with more than seven million copies sold. Green Day's *Dookie* eventually sells ten million. Even Bad Religion release an album on a major label.

Fall: A new type of radio format called AAA is appearing in more major cities. Adult Album Alternative stations feature the softer side of alt-rock, such as Sarah McLachlan and Crash Test Dummies.

1995

Early Spring: Bush releases *Sixteen Stone*.

May: Remade teenage dance queen Alanis re-emerges as Alanis Morissette and is marketed as an "alternative" artist with unprecedented results. *Jagged Little Pill* goes on to sell close to 20 million copies worldwide. Labels scramble to sign tough-minded, attitude-driven female solo artists.

Summer: Guitar-based bands continue to rule, even though the grunge phenomenon has faded. Mainstream rock radio stations capitulate and begin playing more artists who are associated with the alternative scene.

August: The fifth annual Lollapalooza tour breaks all previous attendance records.

Late Summer: Britpop is in high gear, culminating in the bitter Blur-versus-Oasis feud. Music from the 80s makes a big comeback with more "retro 80s" nights at dance clubs along with the release of a growing number of 80s compilations.

Fall: Some music fans begin to notice a disturbing increase in one-hit-wonder acts. Major labels are accused of throwing anything against the wall to see what might stick.

October: The Smashing Pumpkins release *Mellon Collie and the Infinite Sadness*, soon to become the biggest selling double album of the decade. In England, Oasis issue *(What's the Story) Morning Glory?*

1996

Spring: More artists set up their own vanity labels as a condition of their insistence on total creative control—or as a way of putting their new-found wealth back into the indie scene. Examples of the former include Trent Reznor's Nothing Records, while the Offspring's Nitro Records is an example of the latter.

June: The Sex Pistols reunite for a live album and tour. A startling number of older alt-rock acts try it again: Lou Reed, Patti Smith, the Damned, the Buzzcocks, Stiff Little Fingers, Heaven 17, Iggy Pop, the Specials, Madness, Devo, Modern English, the Strangers, the Talking Heads and more.

Summer: U.K. fans bored with Britpop are turned on to jungle and other various flavors of techno in the dance clubs.

September: REM signs a new record deal worth an estimated $80 million. Oasis nearly self-destructs on their American tour. The Ramones retire after 22 years.

Fall: An interesting re-evaluation begins to take place. Artists such as Silverchair, Soundgarden and the Smashing Pumpkins admit they were influenced by 70s groups such as Kiss, Judas Priest and Black Sabbath, signalling to some that it's now okay to like those bands again. Meanwhile, high-profile releases from REM and Pearl Jam fail to sell as well as expected. Labels and retailers remain concerned about stagnant revenues and flat sales.

Late Fall: More concern over the growing number of one-hit-wonder acts.

Winter: A new computer-driven form of electronic music (dubbed "electronica") begins to attract attention outside U.K. dance clubs.

1997:

Late Winter: Jungle and techno are thrust into the spotlight, when U2 and David Bowie experiment with those sounds on their new albums. The Prodigy signs to Madonna's Maverick label, while the Chemical Brothers score an international hit with the single "Setting Sun." The subsequent album *Dig Your Own Hole* sells in the millions.

January 8: David Bowie turns 50.

Spring: Protesters across the U.S., Canada and the U.K. attempt to ban Marilyn Manson from their cities, recalling similar hysteria generated in the 70s by Alice Cooper, Kiss and the Sex Pistols.

April 9: Soundgarden breaks up.

April 26: U2 starts their PopMart world tour in Las Vegas.

May 26: The Prodigy begins their first North American tour in Toronto. Five weeks later, their *Fat of the Land* album debuts at Number One on *Billboard*.

August 21: Oasis sells one million copies of *Be Here Now* in the U.K. in one week.

Part 2
366 Days of New Rock

January
1st
1977: At the London Film-Makers Co-op, the North London Invaders play their last gig. All three members of the band have decided to start fresh and, after adding a few new members, make their debut as Madness a few weeks later.

2nd
1979: The Sid Vicious trial begins in New York. The previous October, Sid was charged with the murder of his girlfriend after she was stabbed to death in Room 100 of the Chelsea Hotel. The case will remain unsolved because Sid will die of a heroin overdose on February 2.

3rd
1996: While walking through the streets of Paris, singer John Power and drummer Keith O'Neill of Cast are attacked by a knife-wielding mugger. Both escape unharmed but when a gendarme stumbles upon the scene, he gives O'Neill a good whack on the arm, thinking that he is the mugger.

4th
1991: After several months of intense negotiations, Geffen Records announces that they have signed Nirvana, a virtually unknown band from Aberdeen, Washington, to a two-album deal. Geffen gives Nirvana an advance for $287,000 along with the rights to full mechanical royalties, in the unlikely event that the next album goes gold. Nirvana's contract with Sub Pop is bought out for $75,000 plus 2 percent of the sales on the next two albums.

5th
1978: The Sex Pistols start their tour of America at the Great SouthEast Music Hall in Atlanta. More than 500 punks and curiosity-seekers show up to see what

all the fuss is about. The subsequent tour is such a disaster that, nine days later in San Francisco, the band breaks up. They will not play together again for another 18 years.

6th
1983: At Manhattan Sound in Manchester, England, the Smiths play their first headlining gig. Three hundred fans see the band perform eight songs, although some of their attention is reserved for the maraca-playing, stiletto-wearing gay go-go dancer hired by the group's manager.

7th
1996: A huge blizzard shuts down roads and airports along the U.S. eastern seaboard, stranding thousands of people. The guests that night at the Hilton in Allentown, Pennsylvania include the Orlando Magic, the cast of *Sesame Street Live* and Marilyn Manson. With nowhere else to go, everyone gathers in the bar to wait out the storm and have a few drinks. By the end of the night, the Magic, the Sesame Street actors and the Marilyn Manson crew become great friends, eventually joining together to sing the theme to *Sesame Street*. Magic center Jon Koncak calls it the most surreal bar scene since the first *Star Wars* movie.

8th
1991: Sixteen-year-old Jeremy Wade Delle kills himself in front of his English class in Richardson, Texas. Upset at being reprimanded for skipping school, he steals his father's .357, smuggles it into school and shoots himself in the head. Saddened by Delle's obvious inability to come to terms with his situation, Eddie Vedder and Pearl Jam are moved to write a song called "Jeremy."

9th
1996: With previous musical targets that include Sinead O'Connor (1991), Mr. Blackwell names Courtney Love to his annual "Worst Dressed List."

10th
1979: The Ramones release "I Wanna Be Sedated." The lyrics came to Joey in Canterbury, England during a long, difficult tour and after a backstage accident with a humidifier that left him with a third-degree scald on his face and neck. The song becomes an anthem for the Ramones.

11th
1997: The Smashing Pumpkins announce that they have filed a lawsuit for $10 million against Chrysalis Music, their song publishing company. The band contends that the four album deal they signed in 1992 is unenforceable.

12th
1981: The Recording Industry Association of America (RIAA) thoughtfully donates more than 800 albums to the White House as an inauguration gift to President Ronald Reagan. Included in the shipment is a copy of *Never Mind the Bollocks* by the Sex Pistols.

13th
1996: Reports from Britain say that original Oasis drummer Tony McCarroll is suing the band for damages and lost royalties from the group's *(What's the Story) Morning Glory* album. He contends that his firing stemmed from the fact that he didn't get along with Noel Gallagher, rather than his playing ability. On the same day, it's revealed that Creation Records was very generous with Christmas gifts. Noel received a chocolate brown Rolls-Royce—despite the fact that he doesn't have a driver's license.

14th
1993: Stating that he is tired of being pressured by his record company and management to come up with a new album and worn out from continuing disagreements with bassist Kim Deal, Black Francis announces that he is disbanding the Pixies.

15th
1997: There's an announcement that Sinead O'Connor has been cast to play the Virgin Mary in the movie *The Butcher Boy*. Remembering that O'Connor once tore up a picture of the Pope on *Saturday Night Live*, religious groups around the world express their outrage and the Catholic Church states that someone else should have been cast in the role.

16th
1996: News reports say that the Smashing Pumpkins have run into trouble while filming a video for their song "1979." Following a long shoot in California's Santa Clarita Valley, the crew member in charge of the raw footage puts four beta tapes of footage on the roof of his car and drives away. The tapes fall off and are never found, despite an offer of a thousand dollar reward from Virgin Records. As a result, the band and the crew have to go back and shoot the video all over again.

17th

1996: Bono and Adam Clayton of U2 have a close call when their seaplane is strafed by gunfire from Jamaican police who believed that the plane was piloted by drug smugglers trying to land at Negril. No one is hurt in the incident.

18th

1978: Johnny Rotten announces in an interview with the *New York Post* that the Sex Pistols have broken up, adding that he's sick of working with the band. The group officially fires him the following day for "not being weird enough." Johnny resurfaces in London later in the year with a new group called Public Image Ltd.

19th

1988: The Sugarcubes are asked to re-edit their "Cold Sweat" video after British TV refuses to air the clip. They contend that the shot of one of the members having his throat cut is too intense. The revamped video features a shot of some monkeys at play.

20th

1995: Courtney Love complains that her private e-mail is being intercepted by teenage hackers. At the same time, her postings to various Internet sites (including alt.fan.c-love) become required reading for Hole fans. Her prolific raves and rants are eventually used as the basis for an off-Broadway play (at a space called Here in SoHo) entitled *Love in the Void,* starring Carolyn Baeumler as Love and directed by Elyse Singer. One day later, the real Courtney is arrested and strip searched by Australian police after creating a disturbance on a Qantas flight from Melbourne to Brisbane.

21st

1996: "Spaceman" by Babylon Zoo hits number one in Britain, becoming the fastest-selling U.K. debut single of all time. Much of the song's success had to do with the fact that it was used in a popular Levi's Jeans commercial before it was officially released.

22nd

1972: David Bowie makes a frank confession to *Melody Maker* writer Michael Watts about his sexuality: "I'm gay and I always have been, even when I was David Jones." Bowie later admits that this confession wasn't true, but that it seemed like a good thing to say at the time. Bowie's comments cause a media storm in Britain.

23rd

1977: In the middle of "Ain't It Strange" at a concert in Tampa, Florida, punk priestess and poet Patti Smith falls fifteen feet off the edge of the stage. She suffers a 22-stitch cut and even more seriously, a cracked vertebra in her neck. She's taken away in an ambulance and subsequent medical examinations reveal that there's no paralysis. She needs a couple of weeks in a neck brace.

24th

1979: After enduring two years of indifference by the American branch of their record company, the Clash finally officially release a single in the U.S. It's a cover of "I Fought the Law" by the Bobby Fuller Four.

25th

1980: British ska makes it to America as the Specials play their first U.S. concert at Hurrah in New York.

26th

1978: There's a crisis at the EMI pressing plant in Britain. Workers refuse to press copies of the Buzzcocks single "What Do I Get," because the B-side is entitled "Oh, Shit."

27th

1994: A new band from Manchester called Oasis make their London debut at Water Rats in Kings Cross. The club is jammed and more than 200 people are turned away.

28th

1996: As part of a long overdue crackdown, officials in the southern Chinese province of Guangdong destroy more than 400,000 packages of pirated CDs, laser disks and CD-ROMs. Despite these efforts, China remains one of the world's biggest sources of counterfeit audio and video recordings, as well as computer software.

29th

1979: Brenda Spencer of San Diego, California, leans out of her bedroom window and opens fire on people at her school across the street, killing two. A journalist manages to get through to Brenda on the phone and asks why she's shooting people. She replies, "Something to do. I don't like Mondays." The incident becomes the basis for the Boomtown Rats song, "I Don't Like Mondays."

30th

1997: According to several published reports out today, the "What's the Frequency, Kenneth" mystery is finally solved. In October 1994, CBS news anchor Dan Rather was beaten by a man as he walked to work along Park Avenue in New York. As Rather ran for cover, his attacker kept asking "Kenneth, what's the frequency?" One theory was a KGB agent had mistaken Dan for Kenneth Schaffer, an electronics expert who had built a system for intercepting Soviet satellite transmissions. But now Rather discovers the real truth. The attacker was William Tager, a mentally ill man who believed that the media was beaming hostile messages into his brain. He wanted Dan to give him the frequency, so he could shut it off. REM bases their song "What's the Frequency Kenneth" on the incident. Tager is eventually sent to prison for murdering an NBC technician in 1994.

31st

1976: David Bowie releases *Station to Station*. Years later, he will confess that he was doing so many drugs at the time that he doesn't remember *anything* about 1976.

February

1st

1995: The Richey Manic mystery begins. Just before the Manic Street Preachers were supposed to leave for a big North American tour, guitarist Richey Edwards checks out of room 516 of the London Embassy Hotel at 7 a.m., withdraws some money from his bank account and drives off into the countryside. Although his car will be found abandoned two weeks later on a bridge over the Bristol Channel, he will never be seen again.

2nd

1979: After a spaghetti dinner at the apartment of a friend, Sid Vicious takes some heroin from his mother's purse and ODs for the last time. At the time of his death, Sid was still awaiting trial in connection with the murder of his girlfriend Nancy Spungen the previous October. All the facts of the case never came out and as a result, no one really knows if Sid was responsible.

3rd

1997: Some concerned citizens of Anchorage, Alaska, think they've come up with a way of preventing Marilyn Manson from playing there in March. Several church groups have suggested they buy up all the tickets to the show and destroy them, thereby ensuring that no one can go. The mayor points out the possibility of a lawsuit, and the concert proceeds as scheduled—although the disappearance of a vital piece of computer equipment delays the start of the show. An 11 p.m. curfew means that the band only gets to play for about 45 minutes. An interesting rumor circulates after the show. Some claim that the concert ended early after Mr. Manson was hit with a T-shirt with the word "God" written on it. Rumor has it that the spiritual power contained in the shirt sapped Mr. Manson's strength to the point where he could no longer continue the performance.

4th

1996: The city council of Johnson City, Tennessee cancels a White Zombie concert, revoking the contract after a Baptist minister complains about the group's lyrics and charges White Zombie with being advocates of Satan.

5th

1993: Computer hackers on Prodigy post bootleg sound files from *Songs of Faith and Devotion*, Depeche Mode's still unreleased new album. Several radio stations are blamed for the initial leaks.

6th

1979: The Cure re-issue their first single on a new label run by the group's manager Chris Parry. "Killing An Arab" originally came out on Small Wonder Records three months ago, but now all subsequent copies (and every future Cure release) will bear the imprint of Fiction Records. Despite Robert Smith's assertions that the song is anti-racist (having based it on the Albert Camus novel *L'Etranger*), the track creates enormous problems for the band over the next ten years when various Arab groups in England, the U.S. and Canada take issue with the lyrics.

7th

1987: The Smiths play their last live concert at a festival in San Remo, Italy. They perform six songs, the last of which is "Panic." The band will officially dissolve in September.

8th

1997: An 18-year-old is arrested in Laval, Quebec and is charged with the attempted murder of his father. The teenager claims that he was listening to a Nirvana song when he heard a voice telling him to commit a crime. Meanwhile, the night before, the NBC show *Unsolved Mysteries* ran a segment suggesting that Kurt Cobain was murdered rather than having committed suicide.

9th

1996: After four years together, Sugar breaks up. Bassist Dave Barbe says that he wants to spent more time with his three children and less time touring and recording with the group. Leader Bob Mould can't find an adequate replacement, so he decides to kill off the group. Mould continues as a solo artist, while Barbe concentrates on a part-time project called "Buzz Hungry."

10th

1997: The wedding for Oasis singer Liam Gallagher and actress Patsy Kensit is called off at the last second. The official explanation is that the media attention has been too intrusive, despite the fact that the couple had taken out six different marriage licenses in six different locations for the ceremony. The decision to cancel the wedding costs Liam and Patsy thousands of dollars as flowers (exotic French lilies) had been ordered, limos had been booked and security had been hired—not to mention that the caterer had arranged for 25 crates of French champagne and wine for the reception (the flowers were handed out in bouquets to fans who had gathered). The couple will eventually be married on April 7 in a ceremony so secret that not even their parents will attend.

11th

1994: Some 20 years after their first show, The Ramones play gig number 2,000 of their career in Tokyo.

12th

1997: David Bowie finally gets a star on the Hollywood Walk of Fame: star number 2,083 and right in front of the Galaxy Theater on Hollywood Boulevard. "It's always nice to be lying flat on the pavement at three in the morning," says Bowie. "It brings back old memories. If I make any more bad albums, come over here and walk all over me, all right?"

13th

1981: Island Records creates a storm within the British music industry when they introduce their One Plus One cassette tapes. One side features pre-recorded music, while the other side is blank. Some members of the industry see this as a way of promoting home taping.

14th

1977: On the campus of the University of Georgia in Athens, the B52s play their first gig at a party in one of the greenhouses.

15th

1972: Three years after the first rock bootleg record appears on the streets, the U.S. Congress finally gets around to passing the Anti-Bootlegging Bill which gives formal copyright protection to sound recordings.

16th

1991: Disgusted at the state of the music industry, Sinead O'Connor says she will refuse to accept anything she wins at the Grammy Awards, even though she's been nominated in four categories.

17th

1979: The Clash begin their first American tour at the Palladium in New York. Calling the tour "Pearl Harbor '79," their first song of the evening is "I'm So Bored with the U.S.A." A photo of Paul Simonon smashing his bass during the show becomes the infamous cover shot of *London Calling*.

18th

1978: *Sniffin' Glue*, the original punk fanzine, folds for good. Music fan Legs McNeil started publishing the 'zine in 1975 and is credited by many as being the first to use the word "punk" in conjunction with the new stripped-down underground music of the day played by bands like the Ramones. Legs later becomes senior editor at *Spin*.

19th

1996: Pulp lead singer Jarvis Cocker is accused of assaulting three children when he crashes Michael Jackson's pompous performance at the Brit Music Awards. He denies doing anything wrong, but admits to jumping onstage uninvited "as a kind of protest at the way Michael Jackson sees himself as some Christ-like figure with the power of healing." A video of the event clearly shows Cocker being roughly escorted offstage by security and he is exonerated of all charges. He briefly considers suing Jackson for defamation of character. Later in the year, Cocker begins to fear retribution from angry bands of vigilante Michael Jackson fans during Pulp's brief North American tour.

20th

1995: Blur wins four Brit Music Awards, including Best Band. They celebrate by tossing dinner rolls at "The Artist Formerly Known As Prince" during dinner.

21st

1992: Pearl Jam is robbed in Manchester, England. Their tour bus is held up by a gang armed with knives. One gang member holds manager Kelly Curtis, while the rest of them grab everything they can.

22nd

1978: As part of their make-up for a Wrigley's Chewing Gum TV commercial, all three members of the Police agree to bleach their hair. It's a look that will stay with them for years.

23rd

1985: The Smiths pull a major coup when their album *Meat Is Murder* knocks Bruce Springsteen's *Born in the USA* out of the number one position on the U.K. album charts.

24th

1992: On a cliff overlooking Waikiki Beach in Hawaii, Kurt Cobain marries Courtney Love. The ceremony is performed by a non-denominational female minister whom Courtney found through the Hawaiian wedding bureau. The groom wears green-and-white check pyjamas, a lei and a strong heroin buzz. Witnesses include three Nirvana employees and a passing drug dealer.

25th

1995: Elastica gets nicked for appropriating material from the Stranglers. A judge orders the group to give up almost half the publishing rights from their song "Waking Up," because it sounds a little too much like the Stranglers' "No More Heroes."

26th

1996: After a long flight from London, Bjork gets off a plane at Don Muang Airport in Bangkok and promptly slugs a local TV reporter who had come to welcome her to Thailand. The scuffle is caught on video and Bjork later apologizes to the woman.

27th

1992: The Recording Industry Association of America (RIAA) announces that in response to environmental concerns, they plan to phase out the CD packaging known as the "longbox." As of 1993, all CDs will be sold in shrink-wrapped jewel boxes. Retailers are not happy. The longbox was designed to fit CDs neatly into store displays that once held vinyl albums, thereby removing the need to invest in new shelves. Stores had also insisted that longboxes cut down on shoplifting.

28th

1979: In the middle of a Cure concert in Bournemouth, England, a girl gets into a fight with her boyfriend and manages to pull off his ear.

29th

1992: U2 open their Zoo TV tour in Lakeland, Florida. It will go on to become one of the ten highest-grossing tours in music history. But that achievement won't come cheap; during the later stages of the tour, it's reported that it costs $125,000 a day just to keep the production on the road.

March

1st

1995: Just before launching into the falsetto section of the song "Tongue" during a concert in Lausanne, Switzerland, REM drummer Bill Berry is suddenly hit with what he thinks is a bad migraine headache. The pain is so excruciating—he compares it to a bowling ball being dropped on his head—that he has to leave the stage. After being examined by a doctor the following morning, it's discovered that he has a brain aneurysm and he is rushed into surgery. Bill makes a full recovery and REM is back on the road by May with what they called the Aneurysm Tour. Some of the official programs feature Berry's actual CAT scan pictures, showing the locations of the two aneurysms.

2nd

1988: It's U2 night at the Grammy Music Awards. *The Joshua Tree* wins two awards, including Best Album.

3rd

1987: A London newspaper carries a report saying that Sinead O'Connor has been cast in the role of Cathy in a Paramount Pictures remake of the Emily Bronte classic *Wuthering Heights*. It never happens.

4th

1994: In Room 541 of the Excelsior Hotel in Rome, Kurt Cobain attempts suicide with an overdose on the prescription drug Rohypnol and champagne. Courtney Love finds him on the floor in a coma at 6:15 a.m. and has an ambulance take him to Umberto I Hospital where doctors pump his stomach. Kurt is then transferred to American Hospital, a private luxury facility. The official word at the time is that this was an accidental overdose.

5th

1997: Foo Fighters drummer William Goldsmith leaves the band after completing his parts on the album *The Colour and the Shape*. His replacement is Taylor Hawkins, formerly of Alanis Morissette's band.

6th

1970: Charles Manson releases an independent album that he calls *Lie* to finance his defense in the Tate-LaBianca murders.

7th

1987: The Beastie Boys make history as *Licensed to Ill* becomes the first rap album to hit number one on the American album charts. Critics charge that the reason the Beasties are first is because they're white. The album's big hit, "Fight for Your Right to Party," was written after a drunken evening at the Palladium in 1986.

8th

1965: David Bowie's British TV debut (as Davey Jones, lead singer for the Mannish Boys) is almost canceled because the producers *of Gadzooks! It's All Happening* feel his hair is too long. Bowie had already been in the papers, defending his long hair and speaking out on behalf of the International League for the Preservation of Animal Filament, a group formed to protect the rights of long-haired pop musicians.

9th

1987: U2 release *The Joshua Tree*. It will go on to sell more than 15 million copies and will become the first release to sell a million as a compact disk.

10th

1977: The Sex Pistols sign a deal with A&M Records in a much-hyped ceremony outside Buckingham Palace. Their anti-monarchist stance and reputation for outrageous behavior creates so much controversy within the A&M organization (everyone from label executives to A&M artists like Peter Frampton and Karen Carpenter call to complain) that the label drops them in less than a week—but not before paying them £75,000 to go away.

11th

1977: It's a big day for Omaha's 311, because their third album (*311*) has been on the *Billboard 200* album charts for 52 consecutive weeks. The band celebrates by going into the studio to start work on their fourth album.

12th

1984: Before a gig at the Hammersmith Palais, Smiths singer Morrissey grants an interview to *Rolling Stone* and offers these comments about British Prime Minister Margaret Thatcher: "She's only one person and she can be destroyed. I just pray that there is a Sirhan Sirhan somewhere. It's the only remedy for this country at the moment."

13th

1984: Sometimes the show *can't* go on. Simple Minds have to bail out in mid-concert in Birmingham, England, when singer Jim Kerr becomes too ill to continue. He is not only suffering from the flu, but also from a chest infection complicated by an allergic reaction to antibiotics.

14th

1997: U2 announce their intentions to play Kocevo Stadium in Sarajevo as part of their PopMart tour. Bono has wanted to play there ever since he spent New Year's Eve 1995 in the city. Proceeds from the concert will go towards rebuilding a local hospital that was destroyed in the civil war.

15th

1987: After several glorious years of hype and controversy, Frankie Goes to Hollywood announce that they're breaking up.

16th

1995: Celtic-punk fiddler Ashley MacIsaac marks St. Patrick's Day by playing in front of the home that formerly belonged to the late Nicole Brown Simpson in the Brentwood area of Los Angeles.

17th

1978: Elvis Costello releases his second album in the U.K. He calls it *This Year's Model.*

18th

1995: A 17-year-old from Orlando, Florida files a misdemeanor battery charge against Courtney Love, alleging that she punched him in the chest when she dove into the mosh pit during a Hole concert earlier in the week. When the case goes to court, Courtney is cleared. The judge points out that when a person consents to going into a mosh pit, there is a reasonable expectation that the person might get hurt. Courtney later exercises her right under Florida law to try and recoup the $27,000 she spent defending herself. (Some of that money was spent on transcripts, photocopies, phone calls, and the expert testimony of a psychiatrist who analyzed the meaning and emotion of Hole songs. Courtney did, however, drop the $38 charges for the limousine ride between her hotel and the courthouse.)

19th

1990: Andrew Wood, lead singer for the glamorous and flamboyant Seattle band Mother Love Bone, dies of a drug overdose. A couple of the members eventually re-group with a new lead singer named Eddie Vedder and change their name to Pearl Jam.

20th

1990: During a Depeche Mode autograph session at a record store in Los Angeles, a near-riot develops when more than the expected number of fans show up. Seven kids are injured and the promoters of the event are sent a bill for $25,000 to cover the costs of fire and police services.

21st

1988: The Pixies release *Surfer Rosa*, one of the most important and influential independent albums of the 80s.

22nd

1997: The London *Times* reports on the richest musicians in Britain, concluding that Oasis have made £40 million since they released their first single in April 1994—60 percent of which was made outside the U.K. INXS singer Michael Hutchence is said to have a net worth of $30 million.

23rd

1993: Depeche Mode officially issues *Songs of Faith and Devotion.* The subsequent tour in support of the album will almost see the band fall apart, as singer Dave Gahan's heroin habit escalates and keyboardist Andrew Fletcher suffers a nervous breakdown. Things get even worse when Martin Gore is hit with a brain seizure and chief programmer Alan Wilder quits.

24th

1973: During a performance of "Waiting for the Man" in Buffalo, New York, a man leaps out of the audience, screams "LEATHER!" and proceeds to bite Lou Reed on the ass.

25th

1995: Eddie Vedder of Pearl Jam almost gets swept out to sea, while swimming with Tim Finn of Crowded House. Eddie is sucked a few hundred feet offshore by a riptide and is in serious danger of drowning before he's rescued by lifeguards.

26th

1993: Original drummer Jack Sherman sues the Red Hot Chili Peppers for a greater share of royalties. Court documents show Jack alleges that he was fired without reason in 1985—and, what's more, Anthony Kiedis and Flea giggled while they told him he was out. A judge eventually tosses out the lawsuit, ruling that Sherman waited too long before filing a complaint.

27th

1987: U2 create havoc in downtown Los Angeles when they decide to film the video for "Where the Streets Have No Name" on the roof of a liquor store at 7th and Main. The original plan is to lip-sync for the cameras, but when a local radio station breaks the news, a huge crowd gathers in the street below, encouraging the band to play a quick set that lasts until the LAPD breaks things up.

28th

1994: Riot police move in when 2,000 people without tickets try to force their way into a Pearl Jam concert in Miami. As the mob moves forward, rocks and bottles are tossed. Five people are hurt and four taken into custody.

29th

1995: In a move seen as progressive by concert fans, seven New York state legislators propose a bill to limit the amount of service charge ticket agencies can add to the cost of a ticket.

30th

1974: The Ramones play their very first gig. Playing as a trio with Joey on drums, about 30 people paid a cover of $2 see them play. Dee Dee is so nervous that he accidentally steps on his bass and breaks it.

31st

1994: Morrissey manages to sell out a show at the Olympic in Los Angeles in a record two minutes and 32 seconds. He is playing in the area for the first time in a decade.

April
1st
1988: With a $20,000 loan, Bruce Pavitt and Jonathan Poneman officially establish Sub Pop Records in Seattle. Seven years later, they will sell a 49 percent stake to Warner Brothers for $20 million.

2nd
1994: Courtney Love is frantic because she can't find her husband. Kurt Cobain walked away from the Exodus Recovery Center in Marina del Rey, California on March 30 and hasn't been heard from since. She hires private detective Tom Grant and orders him to find Kurt. After Kurt's death, Grant becomes a leading proponent of the "Kurt was murdered" conspiracy.

3rd
1997: Fans of groups such as Elastica and Oasis are talking about a symposium in Britpop that's being offered by Leeds University. Calling the genre a "post-grunge reaction to American music," academicians from all over the U.K. meet for a week for *Britpop: Towards a Musicological Perspective.* They discuss papers like "Our Cellophane Sounds: Suede and the Concept of Trash" and "Oasis: What's the Copy (Pop Gone Sloppy)?" The event conveniently features a field trip to a local nightclub.

4th
1977: The Clash prepare to release their self-titled debut album in Britain where it becomes a major success. It also becomes one of the most in-demand imports around the world. The demand is especially strong in the United States because the Clash's record company, caught up in the throes of disco, says that the album is too intense for American audiences. That doesn't stop music fans from snapping up more than 100,000 import copies. An American domestic release is still two years away and, when it is released, the track listing is significantly different from the original British version.

5th
1980: REM play their first gig together in an old church on Oconee St. in Athens, Georgia. The occasion is a birthday party for their friend Kathleen O'Brien. More than 300 people see the group stumble through a two-hour, beer-powered set featuring a mix of hastily conceived originals and covers by the Sex Pistols, the Monkees and Them.

6th

1997: It's announced that charges of heroin possession against Screaming Trees singer Mark Lanegan have been dropped. He had been arrested on March 26 in the Tenderloin district of San Francisco and faced up to six months in jail if convicted.

7th

1996: Two years after his death, Kurt Cobain's ashes are on their way to their final resting place. Courtney Love has chosen a cemetery in Olympia, Washington, halfway between Seattle and Kurt's hometown of Aberdeen. Since his death, Courtney has been lugging some of Cobain's ashes around the country in a backpack shaped like a teddy bear.

8th

1994: At 8:40 a.m., PDT, an electrician finds Kurt Cobain's body in the room above the garage at his Seattle house. The electrician calls his boss who then calls a Seattle radio station with the news. By 11:45, police confirm that they have found a body. A positive identification is announced at 7:05 p.m. Courtney Love hears the news as she watches MTV in her Hollywood hotel room. By mid-afternoon, virtually every record store in the city reports that they are sold out of every Nirvana album.

9th

1997: A&M Records shocks everyone when they issue a short press release: "After twelve years, the members of Soundgarden have amicably and mutually decided to disband to pursue other interests. There is no word at this time on any of the members' future plans."

10th

1981: The Cure finally make it to North America, kicking off a tour in Cherry Hill, New Jersey.

11th

1988: David Byrne (who's still with the Talking Heads at this point) and two collaborators win an Academy Award for scoring the Bernardo Bertolucci film *The Last Emperor*.

12th

1997: U2 announces that they have recorded their first TV theme. Big fans of director Robert Altman, they recorded a version of the Beatles' "Happiness is a Warm Gun" for Altman's six-episode ABC series called *Gun*.

13th

1995: Green Day's *Dookie* album is certified sextuple platinum, signifying sales of more than six million copies.

14th

1983: Former Pretenders bassist Pete Farndon dies of a drug overdose at age 30. He had been fired from the band about a year before.

15th

1986: Dead Kennedys singer Jello Biafra awakens to find his apartment being raided by both the San Francisco Police Department and the Los Angeles Police Department. The cops are looking for "harmful material" related to *Frankenchrist*, the Dead Kennedys 1985 album. Several copies of the album along with posters by Swiss surrealist H.R. Giger, the *real* target of the bust, are seized. It's the beginning of an ordeal that cost the band $80,000 and stretched out over almost two years. The trial started in August 1987 and ended with the jury hopelessly deadlocked at 7–5 in favor of acquittal on June 2, 1988. A motion for a re-trial was denied and all charges were dropped.

16th

1996: Rumors abound about an Oasis breakup after the group cancels a show in Phoenix, Arizona, the group's second canceled show in three days. The band's doctor issues a statement saying that everything is all right. Noel just has a bad case of the flu along with a nasty throat infection.

17th

1995: Courtney Love becomes the first subscriber in the history of America Online to be shut down by the company. The problem? "A huge number of violations in terms of service, including a death threat."

18th

1996: Singer Scott Weiland is in trouble with the law again. Newspaper reports reveal he spent two days in jail earlier that week for a drunk driving conviction that was handed down in Santa Barbara, California, on January 5. When he was stopped back in November, authorities say that his blood alcohol level was measured at .18, three times the legal limit.

19th

1995: The Cult play one last gig in Rio de Janeiro, Brazil. After the show, the group announces that they're breaking up.

20th

1979: Jerry Dammers establishes 2 Tone Records. It will become the premiere ska label in the U.K. for the next several years, releasing material from the Specials, the Selecter, Madness and others.

21st

1997: *Newsweek* names Beck, Billy Corgan and Ani DiFranco as three people who will make a huge impact on the world of entertainment in the 21st century.

22nd

1997: The Pretenders announce that they have to cancel their co-headlining tour with Sinead O'Connor because singer Chrissie Hynde requires surgery to repair an old knee injury.

23rd

1991: Legendary punk guitarist Johnny Thunders is found dead of a suspected drug overdose in New Orleans.

24th

1992: David Bowie and supermodel Iman get married in a private ceremony in a small town in Switzerland. They soon move to the sixth floor of a Central Park apartment that comes complete with bulletproof windows, because Bowie is terrified of a possible sniper attack.

25th

1979: Roger Corman's *Rock 'n' Roll High School* has its premiere in Los Angeles. The movie was originally going to be about the disco scene, but Corman was talked out of it. The Ramones are hired to star in the film and will get great reviews.

26th

1996: The Stone Temple Pilots are talking about replacing singer Scott Weiland. Weiland's substance abuse problems have spiralled out of control over the past couple of years, making it difficult for the band to get anything done. Sources say Weiland was the subject of an intervention two nights ago. While the rest of the band records a secret back-up album with a new singer under the name *Talk Show* just in case Weiland proves unable to continue, the group eventually pulls together.

27th

1990: David Bowie begins the North American leg of his Sound and Vision tour. He vows that this will be the last tour where fans will hear him sing all the old hits like "Young Americans," "Let's Dance" and "Ziggy Stardust."

28th

1994: A California band called the Sleestacks release a single called "Cobain's Dead." It is sung to the tune of the Smiths' "Girlfriend in a Coma."

29th

1977: The Jam release "In the City," their first single. Although the song doesn't reach any higher than number 40, it marks the beginning of a long string of Jam singles over the next few years, as well as the start of the mod revival in the U.K. The Jam's trademark suits, skinny ties and short hair will eventually have a big influence on the look of the coming New Wave era.

30th

1994: The Cranberries cancel more concert dates, this time in the U.K. Singer Dolores O'Riordan fell while skiing two weeks earlier and her knee is just not up to a performance. Because it does not heal properly, the injury will be blamed for many more cancellations in the future.

May
1st

1995: Many performers have admitted to using drugs while writing music but there's never been a confession like this one. New Order and Electronic guitarist/singer Bernard Sumner announces that the upcoming album *Raise the Pressure* was written under the influence of Prozac. Suffering from a bad case of writer's block, Sumner had heard how the drug seems to stimulate creativity in some people. His progress is charted in a British TV special called *Prozac Diaries*.

2nd

1995: A British woman's magazine called *For Women*, still feeling a little stung after being refused permission to take nude centerfold shots of Oasis, issues a wish list featuring musicians that they'd like to see naked. Michael Hutchence of INXS is offered $48,000 to pose, while ex-Pogue Shane MacGowan is offered only $500. The very next day, Courtney Love turns down a cool $1 million to pose for *Playboy*. She says she doesn't need the money or the publicity.

3rd

1995: Police in Michigan City, Indiana, have been called in to investigate a case of missing CDs. An employee of the Smashing Pumpkins organization reports that ten CDs of unreleased material were taken from a band member's vacation home. A local radio station reports that bootleg copies have already begun to circulate.

4th

1996: Dolores O'Riordan finally gets the apology she has been looking for. A newspaper called *Sport* had alleged that she appeared onstage without panties at a concert in Hamburg, Germany, the previous July and exposed herself to the audience. O'Riordan insisted that this was untrue and sued the paper, eventually winning a public apology and a $7,500 donation to the WarChild charity.

5th

1984: Chrissie Hynde of the Pretenders marries Jim Kerr of Simple Minds in a romantic ceremony in New York's Central Park. They will file for divorce in a couple of years. Kerr will then marry actress Patsy Kensit. That marriage doesn't last, either.

6th

1994: Adam Horowitz of the Beastie Boys is sentenced to two years probation and 200 hours of community service when he is found guilty of assaulting a *Hard Copy* cameraman at the funeral for River Phoenix.

7th

1994: The British band Verve is forced to modify their name after a complaint by the American jazz label Verve. From now on, the U.K. band will be known worldwide as The Verve.

8th

1978: An unknown group called the Nosebleeds play their second and final gig, featuring original songs with titles like "(I Think) I'm Ready for the Electric Chair." The band features a Manchester singer named Stephen Morrissey.

9th

1990: Sinead O'Connor makes it known that if comedian Andrew Dice Clay is the guest host for this weekend's *Saturday Night Live*, she will not appear as the musical guest. Dice stays, O'Connor cancels and a group called the Spanic Boys fill in at the last moment.

10th

1991: Malcolm McLaren has been busy since the breakup of the Sex Pistols, moving on to produce TV commercials. Today, his new dance-oriented chocolate bar spot appears on British TV for the first time. Malcolm can't resist including a quick cameo appearance in the ad.

11th

1979: The The, featuring leader Matt Johnson, debut at the Africa Center in London.

12th

1977: Two months after they were dumped by A&M, the Sex Pistols are signed by Virgin Records. They've been with the label ever since.

13th

1983: The Smiths release "Hand in Glove," their first single.

14th

1982: The Clash release their *Combat Rock* album, a record that includes a brief appearance by poet Allen Ginsberg.

15th

1995: On the same day that REM resumes their Monster tour following Bill Berry's brain surgery, Stone Temple Pilots singer Scott Weiland is busted for allegedly trying to buy cocaine in the parking lot of a hotel in Pasadena, California. It's the beginning of a long public ordeal for Weiland. The following night, Courtney Love phones a local radio station and reads a statement on his behalf.

16th

1996: A mysterious new version of a Hole song surfaces in Seattle. It's a previously unknown studio quality recording of "Asking for It," featuring a duet between Courtney Love and the late Kurt Cobain. Cobain can be clearly heard in the background during the second verse, the bridge and over the fadeout. Courtney's publicist confirms that the voice is that of Cobain, but will not elaborate. The recording fuels rumors that Cobain wrote all or part of *Live Through This* for his wife.

17th

1986: Self Aid, the largest musical ever staged in Ireland, arrives in Dublin. The show features performances by U2, the Pogues and Elvis Costello, as well as

Bob Geldof, who will play his final gig with the Boomtown Rats. More than 30,000 fans help raise money to create jobs across the country.

18th

1980: Joy Division singer Ian Curtis commits suicide at his home in Manchester. He hangs himself in the kitchen with a length of clothesline.

19th

1994: Oasis find themselves in trouble with the Coca-Cola Corporation. Coke threatens to sue unless Liam Gallagher promises to stop inserting the lyrics "I'd like to buy the world a Coke" whenever he sings "Shaker Maker"—which, oddly enough, sounds suspiciously like the old "I'd Like to Teach the World to Sing" Coke jingle from the early 70s.

20th

1996: Stories of the Church of Kurt Cobain begin to circulate in Portland, Oregon. The founder calls himself the Reverend Jim Dillion and he announces that he'll start signing up members next week, saying that his new religion will honor Cobain and the "alienated tribe" of Generation X. The Reverend is quick to point out that he and his followers don't worship Kurt. They merely seek guidance and inspiration from his lyrics, theorizing that Nirvana's self-absorbed and brooding music contains a deeper spiritual meaning. He promises sermons based on Nirvana songs. Within a few months, the Reverend Jim confesses that the whole thing is a hoax and this real name is Jerry Ketel. When the *New York Times* asked how Ketel thought Cobain might have reacted to the stunt, he replied "I like to think that he'd punch me in the face."

21st

1993: Hugh Whitaker, former drummer with the Housemartins, is sentenced to six years in jail for attacking his former business partner with an axe. Whitaker was upset with the way partner James Hewitt invested his life savings in an auto dealership that failed.

22nd

1996: Pulp cuts short a concert in Los Angeles, because Jarvis Cocker is just too sick to finish the show. He contracted a strange bug in Hawaii that left him with fever blisters on the inside of his mouth. It was obvious from the start that Jarvis wasn't feeling well, as he kept mopping his brow with an oversized bra some fan threw onstage.

23rd
1996: As an experiment, computer nerd Perry Farrell makes the new Porno For Pyros album available on the Internet before it can be purchased in the stores. Fans all over the world spend the day downloading soundfiles featuring material from *Good God's Urge.*

24th
1982: Drummer Topper Headon leaves the Clash. The band's original drummer Terry Chimes is his replacement.

25th
1978: Paul McGuinness sees U2 for the first time at the Project Arts Center in Dublin, when they open for a group called the Gamblers. He watches carefully as they perform several originals along with covers from Neil Young and the Bay City Rollers. Even though he would prefer they had more experience, he's nevertheless impressed by their energy and ambition and decides to become their manager. McGuinness has been with the band ever since, earning an estimated 20 percent share of the profits.

26th
1977: After three record deals and dozens of delays, the Sex Pistols finally release "God Save the Queen" for Virgin, just in time for Queen Elizabeth's Silver Jubilee. Even though the song is promptly banned on the BBC and by every chain store in the U.K., it still sells 150,000 copies in just five days.

27th
1982: Robert Smith and Simon Gallup of the Cure get into a fist fight following a concert in Strasbourg, France. After the fight breaks up, both declare that they've had enough and they're leaving the band. Both return to play a show a week later in Aix-en-Provence.

28th
1983: David Bowie is paid $1 million to co-headline the US Festival in Devore, near San Bernardino, California. The event is sponsored by Steve Wozniak, one of the founders of Apple Computers, who loses millions of dollars, partly because of the high fees paid to some of the performers. Some estimates say the crowd peaked at 700,000.

29th
1977: A band called Warsaw opens a show for the Buzzcocks at Electric Circus in Manchester. Until showtime, they were known as Stiff Kittens, but decided on a name change at the last second. There will be one more change in a few

months when the band discovers that they're being confused with a metal band called Warsaw Pakt. That's when they decide to go with Joy Division.

30th
1987: A Beastie Boys concert in Liverpool, England gets out of hand when tear gas is lobbed into the theatre. Adam Horowitz is arrested when he's accused of hitting a female fan. He's later acquitted.

31st
1992: During a Zoo TV show at Earl's Court in London, Bono calls a sex line from a cell phone onstage in the midst of the encore.

June
1st
1974: A letter written by an opinionated 15-year-old from Manchester appears in the *NME*. Stephen Patrick Morrissey wants everyone to know that the best band in the world is Sparks.

2nd
1995: Tori Amos is honored with the 1994 Visionary Award by a rape crisis clinic in Washington, D.C. As a former rape victim herself, Tori remains committed to helping other victims through organizations such as the Rape, Abuse and Incest National Network (RAINN).

3rd
1977: Despite the fact that it has been officially banned by the BBC, other British radio stations (who won't even play commercials advertising it) and virtually every major department store, "God Save the Queen" by the Sex Pistols enters the British singles charts at number eleven. In its second week of release, the song officially hits number one.

4th
1994: Alan McGee's Creation Records celebrates its tenth birthday with a concert called "Undrugged" featuring Oasis, the Boo Radleys and other acts on the Creation roster.

5th
1996: Rumors spread that Liam Gallagher and Patsy Kensit are about to break up. He says that he has no intention of buying her the $240,000 Aston Martin sports car that he promised her after weeks of bad behavior. Meanwhile, Patsy says that she likes her BMW just fine.

6th

1976: Joe Strummer quits the 101ers and agrees to join Paul Simonon, Mick Jones and Terry Chimes in forming a new band. After considering names such the Psycho Negatives, the Weak Heartdrops and the Outsiders, they eventually decide on the Clash.

7th

1992: The parents of a Sioux Indian boy from South Dakota file a lawsuit against the Cult and their record label. They contend that the boy's picture was used for the cover of the Cult's *Ceremony* album without his parents' permission. They ask for $61 million in damages.

8th

1986: The Sugarcubes, featuring lead singer and former child star Bjork Gudmundsdottir, are founded in Reykjavik, Iceland. It's the same day that Bjork gives birth to her son Sindri.

9th

1990: Pixies bassist Kim Deal decides to launch a side project with her sister Kelley called the Breeders. Ironically, they end up selling way more records than the Pixies ever did.

10th

1996: Blur frontman Damon Albarn turns down an offer from *Cosmopolitan* to pose nude. The magazine had approached close to 50 different celebrities, including British Prime Minister John Major.

11th

1995: Pearl Jam cancels two shows at the Del Marr Fairgrounds in San Diego after the sheriff's department issues a statement saying that they're worried about crowd safety. Eddie Vedder calls their concerns ridiculous, saying that they over-reacted and created an impossible situation. Things get even more confusing when it's reported that the band is about to call off their long-running feud with Ticketmaster over high service charges on concert tickets. Pearl Jam denies those reports.

12th

1982: The Banshees are forced to postpone another upcoming tour because singer Siouxsie Sioux needs to rest her throat. She's once again suffering from severely strained vocal chords.

13th

1994: A fire destroys the stage at the site of the Glastonbury Festival in England. Work immediately begins on a new temporary stage that will be ready when the concerts start on June 24.

14th

1989: Original Echo and the Bunnymen drummer Pete de Freitas is killed in a motorcycle accident near Liverpool, England. He is 28.

15th

1994: Hole bassist Kristen Pfaff is found dead of a heroin overdose in her bathtub in Seattle. She had been getting ready to move back to Minneapolis, away from the heroin scene in the city.

16th

1982: Pretenders guitarist James Honeyman-Scott goes to a party in London and ends up dying of a cocaine overdose. He is 25.

17th

1994: Perry Farrell of Porno for Pyros wins a big trademark infringement case against the Ford Motor Co. after they featured the word "lollapalooza" in an ad for the Ford Escort. The company settles by donating money to Farrell's favorite rainforest charity.

18th

1986: The Cure make a crucial appearance on French TV, but only after Robert Smith is promised that everything will be over in time for him to see a World Cup match featuring England.

19th

1994: Johnny Marr (ex Smiths) and Ian McCulloch (ex Echo and the Bunnymen) announce that they will not be able to release the album on which they had been working, because someone has stolen the master tapes from all the recording sessions. The tapes are never found.

20th

1992: In defiance of a court order, members of U2 take part in an anti-nuclear protest against the Sellafield reprocessing plant in North England. The protesters storm the beach after coming ashore in inflatable dinghies.

21st

1996: Eighteen years after what was supposed to be their final show together, the reunited Sex Pistols start a world tour in front of 15,000 people in Messila, Finland, 100 kilometers north of Helsinki. Instead of receiving a hero's welcome, they are barraged with rocks and bottles—but they still manage to finish the set.

22nd

1995: During soundcheck before a show at Madison Square Gardens in New York, CBS news anchor Dan Rather jams with REM on "What's the Frequency, Kenneth?" The song is based on a 1986 incident in which Rather was beaten by a mysterious stranger.

23rd

1979: The Cure release a single called "Boys Don't Cry," a song that doesn't appear on their *Three Imaginary Boys* album. The track will eventually become a fan favorite.

24th

1994: Seven songs into a highly anticipated concert in San Francisco, Eddie Vedder tells thousands of Pearl Jam fans that he can't go on because he's too sick (the result of food poisoning from a bad tuna sandwich). Neil Young takes over for the rest of the show.

25th

1992: While Pearl Jam is onstage performing a three-hour set before a packed house in Stockholm, Sweden, someone breaks into their dressing room and steals the band's clothes, money—and Eddie's journal, the place where he writes all his ideas for songs and lyrics. He never let the thing out of his sight, leaving it alone only when the band was performing. Eddie is so rattled by the loss that he punches out a security guard during a show the next night. The next two gigs are canceled, supposedly because Eddie is suffering from exhaustion.

26th

1996: Stone Temple Pilots singer Scott Weiland walks away from a drug rehab center in Pasadena, California. Since he is there on a court order, a warrant is issued for his arrest. However, Weiland reappears the following day, saying that he left the clinic for personal reasons and had to speak to his wife. At a court appearance the next day, prosecutors argue that Weiland should be sent to jail, but the judge rules that a return to the clinic is enough.

27th

1978: Peter Gabriel releases his second solo album and like the first, this one is called *Peter Gabriel*, too. He will release a total of four consecutive albums with the title *Peter Gabriel* (the fourth of which was issued in America under the title *Security*, a move not sanctioned by Gabriel), until he comes out with *So* in 1986.

28th

1993: Bjork releases an album called *Debut*. While it *is* her first album since the breakup of the Sugarcubes, it's not her first solo record. She recorded an Icelandic jazz album in 1990, and released an album full of songs for kids when she was a child star back in the late 70s and early 80s.

29th

1985: For the first time in their career, U2 headline a concert at a football stadium. The venue is Croke Park in Dublin in front of a sellout crowd of 57,000. In a gesture of thanks, the band donates the proceeds of the show to the building of rehearsal space and for the purchase of equipment to be used by young bands. The City Center officially opens in June, 1989.

30th

1995: The Meat Puppets' Curt Kirkwood, Gavin Rossdale of Bush and the Beastie Boys' Adam Horowitz all make *Playgirl's* annual list of "The 10 Sexiest Men in Rock 'n' Roll."

July

1st

1984: Caught up in the mania of the music video, a company called Music Theater Network announces their plans for Concert Cinema. The idea is to show videos in 600 movie theaters across the U.S. The concept is soon proven to be a total failure, as music fans find it much easier to stay home and watch MTV for free.

2nd

1992: Pearl Jam open for U2 in Verona, Italy, during the Zooropa tour.

3rd

1973: At the end of a two night stand at the Hammersmith Odeon in London, David Bowie shocks everyone by announcing his retirement. "Of all the shows on this tour," he says, "this particular show will remain with us the longest—because not only is it the last show of the tour, it's the last show we'll ever do. Thank you." Although Bowie seems adamant in the weeks following the announcement, he's back by the following June, minus the Ziggy Stardust character.

4th

1995: The fifth annual Lollapalooza tour opens at The Gorge, Washington, with a bang. Courtney Love punches Kathleen Hanna of Bikini Kill in the face after she allegedly made some derogatory comments about Courtney and her daughter being on drugs. According to Courtney, Hanna snapped "Where's the baby? In a closet with an IV?" An assault charge is filed and Courtney is ordered to attend an "anger management" seminar.

5th

1993: U2 surprise everyone by unexpectedly releasing an album called *Zooropa*, just 17 months after *Achtung Baby*. The band was so inspired by how well things had been going on the Zoo TV tour that they knocked off the record during a break in the schedule.

6th

1976: Punk pioneers the Damned play their first real gig when they open for the Sex Pistols at the 100 Club in London. Despite the fact that the Pistols were formed first, the Damned end up being the first British punk act to release a record the following October.

7th

1989: It's announced that for the first time in history, compact disks are outselling vinyl records. This comes just seven years after the introduction of the CD and far ahead of all industry predictions.

8th

1996: Prosecutors in Los Angeles charge Dave Gahan of Depeche Mode with one count of possession of cocaine and another of being under the influence of cocaine, after an overdose at the Sunset Marquis Hotel on May 28. Paramedics are called to the hotel at 1:15 a.m. and find Gahan in full cardiac arrest. He is clinically dead for two minutes before he is revived. When he regains consciousness, police tell him that if he's convicted on the two cocaine charges, he could be sentenced to four years in prison. He pleads not guilty and is set free on $10,000 bail.

9th

1977: Two days after the release of "(Angels Wanna Wear My) Red Shoes," his third single for Stiff, Elvis Costello finally quits his day job as a computer programmer for Elizabeth Arden Cosmetics. Up until now, he has been using his accumulated sick days in order to tour and record.

10th

1983: After Johnny Marr and Andy Rourke corner Rough Trade boss Geoff Travis in the kitchen at the label's offices, demanding that he listen to the band's demo tape, the Smiths get their first record deal. It calls for four Rough Trade albums through to 1986.

11th

1995: Reports surface that the Ramones are about to retire. Joey Ramone says that after 21 years, too many people are taking the band for granted. Meanwhile, REM bassist Mike Mills undergoes abdominal surgery in Germany to correct a problem resulting from an appendectomy years earlier. This comes less than two months after the Monster tour resumed, following Bill Berry's brain surgery.

12th

1996: Jonathan Melvoin, touring keyboardist with the Smashing Pumpkins, dies of a drug overdose at the Regency Hotel in New York City. Pumpkins drummer Jimmy Chamberlain also ODs but survives. Fed up after dealing with Chamberlain's addictions for the last nine years, the group fire him a few days later.

13th

1985: At 12:01 p.m. in front of 72,000 people at Wembley Stadium in London (and billions more on TV), Live Aid gets underway. Over the next 16 hours, the world sees performances from U2, the Style Council, Elvis Costello, the Boomtown Rats, David Bowie, Bryan Ferry and many more. The show ends up raising $70 million for Ethiopian famine relief. Rats singer Bob Geldof (who organized the event) is later knighted by Queen Elizabeth.

14th

1979: U2 is given a big boost. They receive a positive review when they're featured as part of a profile on new unsigned bands in *Sounds* magazine. They spend a good part of their summer playing strong, hour-long sets to all-ages crowds in places such as youth clubs in suburban Dublin.

15th

1994: The Wonder Stuff call it quits after playing one last show at the Phoenix Festival in Britain. Singer Miles Hunt goes on to work with MTV for a while.

16th

1996: The New York Police Department report a huge rise in demand for Red Rum heroin, the variety that killed Smashing Pumpkins touring keyboardist Jonathan Melvoin four days earlier. According to the commanding officer at New York's Downtown Narcotics, "Whether it's people looking for the ultimate high, whether it's because of the name or because he used it, the fact is there is greater demand than last week."

17th

1995: Complaining that she's not feeling well, Sinead O'Connor suddenly pulls out of the Lollapalooza tour after just a couple of dates. It turns out she's pregnant.

18th

1991: The very first Lollapalooza tour begins at Compton Terrace, just outside Phoenix. Despite desert temperatures of more than a hundred degrees Fahrenheit, more than 15,000 people turn out to see headliners Jane's Addiction, plus Siouxsie and the Banshees, Living Color, Nine Inch Nails, the Butthole Surfers and the Rollins Band.

19th

1979: The Flying Lizards (David Cunningham and Deborah Evans) release their version of Barret Strong's 1960 hit "Money." Using an upright piano filled with rubber toys and phone books and several pots and pans for percussion, everything was recorded at their house for a grand total of $14. The result becomes a worldwide hit single, grossing millions.

20th

1994: Three years to the day after EMF scores a number one hit with "Unbelievable," keyboardist Derry Brownson is arrested for making crop circles in a French corn field with his rental car. He's hit with a £2,000 fine. The car is a write-off.

21st

1995: H.R. (Paul Hudson), lead singer of Bad Brains, is charged with assault after attacking two fans during a concert in Lawrence, Kansas.

22nd

1984: The Beastie Boys get a big break: they go on tour as the opening act for Madonna.

23rd

1996: On his way back to the studio after a few drinks at a local pub, Charlatans keyboardist Rob Collins dies in a car crash when his BMW clips the curb and hits a ditch. An autopsy later reveals that he had twice the legal limit of alcohol in his blood, and would have probably survived the crash if he had been wearing his seat belt.

24th

1996: An American theater chain decides to run the Primus video "Wynona's Big Brown Beaver" as a short subject for the regular showing of *Clueless*. Some people in the audience complain about the video's double entendres.

25th

1978: Ex-Sex Pistols singer Johnny Rotten reverts to his old name, John Lydon, and announces the formation of his new band Public Image, Ltd.

26th

1986: "Sledgehammer" by Peter Gabriel becomes a number one single in America. A good part of the song's success can be attributed to its state-of-the-art claymation video.

27th

1986: A Cure concert in Los Angeles is interrupted when a fan runs towards the stage and begins to stab himself with a hunting knife before being carried away by security guards. The man later tells police that he wanted to make a point with his ex-girlfriend.

28th

1977: Just before they open for the Clash, the Automatics decide to change their name to the Specials AKA to avoid any further confusion with another band called the Automatics.

29th

1980: The surviving members of Joy Division re-emerge as New Order at the Beach Club in Manchester.

30th

1983: Recognizing that the post-punk ska scene has lost momentum, the English Beat officially break up. Dave Wakeling and Ranking Roger form General Public, while Andy Cox and David Steele join Roland Gift in Fine Young Cannibals.

31st

1969: It's getting tougher to find a working public phone in Moscow, as more and more phone booths are being mysteriously stripped of their electronic parts. Reports from the Soviet Union say authorities blame the rise in popularity of rock music because the missing phone components can be used as pickups in homemade electric guitars.

August
1st

1981: With only 250 videos available (including 30 from Rod Stewart alone), MTV makes its debut on American cable television at 12:01AM EDT. The first video is, appropriately, "Video Killed the Radio Star" from the Buggles.

2nd

1991: Perry Farrell makes it official: Jane's Addiction are about to break up. They finish up the Lollapalooza tour on August 28 and play one final show in Honolulu on September 26.

3rd

1996: Reports begin to surface that Courtney Love has entered a drug rehab facility outside of Philadelphia following the end of filming for *The People Vs. Larry Flynt*. A spokesperson denies this, saying that Courtney has simply gone on vacation.

4th

1996: Denying rumors that Red Hot Chili Peppers drummer Chad Smith will be joining the band, the Smashing Pumpkins continue to hold top-secret auditions in New York. They do, however, announce that Dennis Fleming of the Milwaukee band the Frogs has been hired as the group's new touring keyboardist. Matt Walker of Filter becomes the Pumpkins' temporary drummer on August 8.

5th

1991: Hole releases "Teenage Whore," the first single from their debut album *Pretty in the Inside*.

6th

1990: Flea and Chad Smith of the Red Hot Chili Peppers are ordered by a Daytona Beach judge to pay $1,000 in fines, $300 in court costs and $5,000 each to the Volusia County Rape Crisis Center and issue written apologies to a 20-year-old college student. At issue are events that took place during a spring break party on March 16 and were televised on MTV, where the woman was spanked by Smith as Flea spun her around on his shoulders. At an earlier separate trial, Anthony Kiedis had also been fined $2,000 for indecent exposure and sexual battery. The woman later sued the band for $4 million.

7th

1995: Reports out of Elastica say that original bassist Annie Holland is about to leave the group because she is exhausted and tired of touring. She is not with the band when they appear at several Lollapalooza shows. Her departure is made official on August 23.

8th

1996: Morrissey signs a long-term worldwide record deal with Mercury Records.

9th

1996: The Sex Pistols appear on *The Late Show with David Letterman*.

10th

1996: All 2,300-plus Wal-Mart stores in the U.S. announce that they will refuse to stock the upcoming album by Sheryl Crow because the lyrics of the song "Love is a Good Thing" imply that the chain sells guns to children.

11th

1995: An Internet pop music gossip page features several pictures from *Playgirl* showing nude rock stars, including Billie Joe Armstrong of Green Day.

12th

1993: The Red Hot Chili Peppers announce that Jesse Tobias will replace guitarist Arik Marshall. He lasts three months before ex-Jane's Addiction guitarist Dave Navarro is brought in.

13th

1976: A five-member Clash (Joe Strummer, Mick Jones, Paul Simonon, Terry Chimes and Keith Levine) hold a private performance for friends and invited members of the press in an old British Rail warehouse in Camden that serves as their practice space.

14th

1995: Six Soul Asylum fans are treated for injuries they received while moshing and body-surfing at a concert in Lincoln, Nebraska.

15th

1983: At four in the morning, Johnny Ramone gets into a fight over a girl with Sub Zero Construction's Seth Macklin in New York and ends up with a fractured skull. After emergency brain surgery, Johnny can't remember anything about what happened.

16th

1974: The Ramones era at CBGBs in New York begins when the band plays their first gig at the club. Less than a dozen people see them burn through about ten songs in less than 20 minutes. At the end of the night, club owner Hilly Kristal says "Nobody's gonna like you guys, but I'll have you back."

17th

1995: After checking out of a rehab center in Arizona, Depeche Mode singer Dave Gahan returns to his house in Los Angeles to find it completely looted. Everything, from all the cutlery to his gym equipment, has been taken. Depressed and angry, he checks into the Sunset Marquis Hotel with some heroin, and ends up in the bathroom with a razor blade, cutting a two-inch gash into his left forearm. The suicide attempt lands him in a psychiatric ward for a week.

18th

1992: At 7:40 a.m., a seven pound, one ounce girl named Frances Bean is born to Courtney Love and Kurt Cobain. Kurt is with Courtney in the delivery room— but passes out on the floor.

19th

1996: Pearl Jam guitarist Mike McCready, manager Kelly Curtis and three other investors open The Garage, an upscale pool hall in Seattle.

20th

1977: After driving 400 miles up to Edinburgh, Scotland, to play at a club called Clouds, Generation X is told by police that the concert has been canceled because the club doesn't have a music license. Rather than heading back to London, the group arranges to have the 300 fans who showed up for the gig bussed across the city to another club where the show proceeds as scheduled.

21st

1990: A music store in Royal Oak, Michigan, is ticketed by police for displaying what they call an "obscene" poster in the window. It's a poster for the Jane's Addiction album *Ritual de lo Habitual*.

22nd

1995: Skinny Puppy drummer Dwayne Goettel is found dead in his parents' home in Edmonton, Alberta. Upset about the demise of the band, he accidentally overdosed on heroin.

23rd

1994: Stumped in their hunt for a new guitarist to replace Bernard Butler, Suede run an ad in *Melody Maker*. Out of the hundreds of people who respond, 17-year-old Richard Oakes gets the job.

24th

1995: Microsoft launches Windows 95 with a huge media campaign that includes a TV commercial featuring the Rolling Stones song "Start Me Up." Even though the company pays a rumored $12 million for the rights to the song, it wasn't their first choice. They had asked REM for permission to use "It's the End of the World as We Know It," but the band refused.

25th

1994: Soundgarden is forced to cancel a big European tour because Chris Cornell's voice is suffering. After his doctor discovered nodules on his vocal chords, he orders Cornell to get some serious rest.

26th

1994: Hole appears at the Reading Festival with new bassist Melissa Auf der Maur. She replaces Kristen Pfaff, who had died of a drug overdose in June. Melissa gets the job after she's recommended for the position by Billy Corgan of the Smashing Pumpkins.

27th

1996: Pearl Jam releases *No Code*. The album sells about 367,000 copies in its first week, a far cry from the numbers generated by the previous two albums. More than 877,000 copies of *Vs* were sold in its first week in 1994, while *Vitalogy* sold close to a million in five days.

28th
1972: David Bowie and the Spiders from Mars play Carnegie Hall in New York.

29th
1995: In a solemn press release, the Verve announce that they're breaking up following singer Richard Ashcroft's decision to leave the group. The band reunites two years later on the advice of Ashcroft's spiritual advisor.

30th
1995: Sterling Morrison, guitarist for the Velvet Underground, university lecturer and former tugboat captain, dies of non-Hodgkin's lymphoma at age 53.

31st
1983: MuchMusic, Canada's answer to MTV, debuts from its studios in Toronto.

September
1st
1994: While driving on a country road in Scotland, Alan Wilder of Depeche Mode is nearly killed when a Royal Air Force jet plane on a training flight narrowly misses his car and crashes into a nearby hill.

2nd
1992: Having purchased the rights to the entire Smiths catalog, WEA decides to re-release "How Soon Is Now?" in connection with its use in a TV commercial for Levi's.

3rd
1982: Living a dream to finance a major rock concert event, Steve Wozniak of Apple computers oversees the start of the first US Festival in San Bernardino, California. More than 400,000 people see sets from the Talking Heads, the Cars and the Police over the next three days.

4th
1995: Hole, Veruca Salt, Metallica and Moist play a special Labor Day concert in Tuktoyaktuk, a small town north of the Arctic Circle in Canada's Northwest Territories. The whole thing is a publicity stunt staged by Molson breweries to promote their ice beer. Reports state Metallica has been paid $1 million, while Hole gets $500,000.

5th

1993: About halfway through a Pearl Jam show at The Gorge in Washington State, angry fans without tickets crash through two metal fences and try to rush the stage. Five people are hospitalized and more than a hundred others are treated for injuries. Exactly three years later, Pearl Jam's *No Code* debuts at number one on the *Billboard* charts after selling 367,000 copies in its first week. Some people see this as cause for concern since *Vitalogy* sold 877,001 copies in its first week in 1994, while *Vs* sold 950,378 in 1993.

6th

1996: Anne Beverly, mother of the Sex Pistols' Sid Vicious and a registered drug addict, is found dead at her home in Swadlincote, Derbyshire. Before intentionally overdosing, she wrote letters to her friends explaining that she was going to kill herself. When police were alerted, they arrived to find all her clothes neatly packed in bags and all her credit cards carefully cut in half.

7th

1979: Just before Siouxsie and the Banshees take the stage for a concert in Aberdeen, Scotland, guitarist John McKay and drummer Kenny Morris leave town, upset over events at an autograph signing session at a local record store earlier in the day. Their set is canceled, but not before Siouxsie addresses the crowd, saying that "You have my blessings to beat the shit out of them."

8th

1984: During a U2 show at the Entertainment Center in Sydney, Australia, a girl jumps onstage and hides behind the drums until security guards find her. Bono rescues her from the guards and ends up dancing with her.

9th

1995: At an outdoor Green Day concert in Boston, some of the 65,000 fans rush the stage, crushing those at the front. More than a hundred people are hurt and 24 others are sent to hospital.

10th

1974: The New York Dolls, one of the most important and influential groups of the pre-punk scene, break up for good.

11th

1977: David Bowie is Bing Crosby's guest for a taping of a Christmas TV special. Bowie and Crosby sing a duet on "The Little Drummer Boy."

12th

1987: Weeks of rumors and speculation come to an end when the *NME* announces that the Smiths have definitely broken up.

13th

1996: Stories about the breakup of Oasis are everywhere. Noel Gallagher abruptly flew home yesterday, abandoning the band in the middle of an American tour. So far, Creation Records have issued one brief statement: "Oasis have hit internal differences on their ninth tour of America, resulting in the tour being pulled two-thirds of the way through. It is unlikely that immediate tour commitments will be fulfilled."

14th

1977: Peter O'Toole, singer for the Easy Cure, quits the band to join a kibbutz in Israel. His departure forces guitarist Robert Smith to step forward to take his place. The group soon shortens their name to the Cure.

15th

1990: In a move they will later regret, the Stone Roses sign a 30-year deal with Silvertone Records. It states that Silvertone and Zomba (their publishing company) own the band and everything they do, from albums to T-shirts. The contract states that the company can drop the band at any time and prohibits the band from recording for any other label. The Stone Roses are the property of Silvertone for "the entire world and the solar system." This contract becomes the central issue in a dispute that takes months to resolve, delaying work on the band's second album. Later in May 1991, a judge calls the agreement unreasonable and unfair, and orders it dissolved. Silvertone is also ordered to pick up the legal costs, estimated by some people to be as high as £500,000.

16th

1994: The Cure win a long legal battle brought against them by founding member Lol Tolhurst, who sued the band for a greater share of royalties. Tolhurst is left with a legal bill of more than one million pounds.

17th

1995: During the last song of a concert in Santa Monica, Silverchair singer Daniel Johns is hit in the head by a bottle thrown from the audience. Even though he has blood streaming down his face (the cut requires five stitches to close), the band finishes the set.

18th

1995: In an effort to avoid battles between rival groups of fans, Oasis cancels tonight's show at the Bournemouth International Center and reschedules it for September 20. Why? Because Blur has a show at another venue right down the street tonight. Police are relieved that they won't have to deal with fights between Blur and Oasis fans, especially since competitive tensions between the two bands are at an all-time high.

19th

1975: The Ramones record a quick demo tape featuring some of their first original songs. One of the songs that catches the ear of Seymour Stein of Sire Records is a rough version of "Judy is a Punk," probably the first song to ever use the word "punk" to describe a specific type of music fan.

20th

1995: Live wrap up a tour in Philadelphia, not far from their hometown of York, Pennsylvania. The band jokes that they want the key to the city so they can "burn it down."

21st

1996: After 17 years, IRS Records calls it quits. Founder Miles Copeland (brother of Police drummer Stewart Copeland), says that the label has been having problems ever since REM and Concrete Blonde jumped ship for better deals with other companies.

22nd

1995: After six hours without a cigarette on a transatlantic flight between London and Atlanta, Charlatans keyboardist Rob Collins tries to sneak a smoke in the lavatory. Even though he puts a water-soaked towel over the smoke detector, it goes off. He's met at Hartsfield Airport by two cops who arrest him for the federal violation of disabling a smoke detector. Collins is later released after paying a hefty fine.

23rd

1996: Members of Weezer are hit with a temporary restraining order over the title of their new album *Pinkerton*. Although leader Rivers Cuomo tries to explain that the title is taken from the name of a character in the Puccini opera "Madame Butterfly," the Pinkerton Security and Investigation Service is not amused. They have asked for $2 million in a lawsuit alleging the band has infringed upon their registered trademark. A week later, a judge dissolves the order and the album is released as scheduled.

24th

1991: Sub Pop Records releases *Nevermind*, shipping exactly 46,251 copies to record stores in the U.S. and another 40,000 to the U.K. By Christmas, it is selling more than 300,000 copies a *week*.

25th

1995: Supergrass are offered a big contract to help re-launch Hai Karate aftershave. They decline, saying that none of them really shaves all that often.

26th

1991: Following up on an earlier promise, Perry Farrell and Jane's Addiction play one final show together in Hawaii. In celebration of the event, Farrell performs part of the set in the nude.

27th

1990: Ex-Ramones guitarist Dee Dee Ramone is arrested with 25 others on a marijuana charge after police conduct a drug sweep of Greenwich Village in New York City.

28th

1987: *Strangeways, Here We Come*, the Smiths' final album, is released.

29th

1995: "Closer" from Nine Inch Nails is named Top Mood Song by an Australian radio station in their "Big Bonking Poll." Listeners say it's the best song to have on while having sex.

30th

1993: Kate Pierson of the B52s is arrested during a sit-in at the offices of *Vogue* magazine in New York City. She's part of an animal rights group protesting the magazine's policy of running ads for fur coats.

October

1st

1984: U2 start their European tour in Rotterdam, the Netherlands, on the same day they release *The Unforgettable Fire*.

2nd

1995: XFM, London's private alternative radio station (financed in part by Robert Smith of the Cure) begins operating with its fifth and last restricted broadcast license. The station is finally given a permanent license in 1997.

3rd

1996: Reports say that an Irish consortium, led by U2 manager Paul McGuinness, wants to buy the Wimbledon football club and move it to a new stadium in Dublin. The deal is worth close to $42 million.

4th

1994: In an interesting gesture of generosity, Bono appears on an Irish radio show and offers to pay for a stranger's vasectomy after hearing that a couple didn't want any more children but couldn't afford to pay for the operation.

5th

1995: In *Out* magazine, REM's Michael Stipe talks about his sexuality, saying that he's neither 100 percent homosexual nor 100 percent heterosexual. He also doesn't appreciate the word "bisexual." As for Courtney Love's recent suggestion that he and Kurt Cobain spent a wild weekend together, Stipe laughs it off, saying that the baby and the nanny were there the whole time.

6th

1980: Johnny Lydon of Public Image, Ltd. is arrested after a brawl breaks out at a club in Dublin, Ireland. At his first trial, he's sentenced to three years in jail. An appeal gets him acquitted.

7th

1995: One year to the day after Suede introduced new guitarist Richard Oakes to the press in Paris, drummer Simon Gilbert is hit in the head by a bunch of gay bashers in Stratford-upon-Avon.

8th

1980: Reggae king Bob Marley collapses on stage in Pittsburgh. He's flown to New York where doctors discover he is suffering from advanced lung and brain cancer. All efforts to treat him fail and he dies the following May at age 36.

9th

1977: A show by the Clash in Orebro, Sweden is delayed when someone phones in a bomb threat to the club where they're scheduled to play. When they finally take the stage, a local gang tries to disrupt the show by throwing things at the band. The Clash respond by throwing things right back at the gang, who are so shocked that they behave for the rest of the night.

10th

1993: While a guest on Howard Stern's nationally syndicated radio show, Eddie Vedder gives out his home phone number and tells the audience that if they have any questions, they can call him. His phone rings almost constantly for weeks.

11th

1996: Reports from the current Pearl Jam tour say guitarist Stone Gossard is frantic, because someone managed to steal one of his favorite guitars right off the stage at a show in Miami a couple of nights ago. Two weeks later, the guitar shows up at the offices of Pearl Jam's record label. The thief was a really drunk 18-year-old kid who took the guitar on a dare. No charges are filed.

12th

1981: U2 releases their *October* album. Bono was forced to ad-lib most of the words in the studio, because someone had stolen his briefcase containing his notebook of song ideas and lyrics after a show in Portland, Oregon back on March 22.

13th

1985: Ricky Wilson, guitarist and founding member with the B52s, dies from complications resulting from AIDS.

14th

1996: There's a weird report out of Russia. Victor Vlasov of Moscow died this past weekend when he doused himself in gasoline and set himself on fire in front of his wife and daughter. He was angry because his wife was totally fascinated by Liam Gallagher of Oasis and every square inch of their apartment was covered with Oasis posters. Nina Vlasov and the couple's 7-year-old daughter suffered slight burns in the incident.

15th

1979: American Express issues an injunction against the Sex Pistols over the sleeve of one of its singles which features a parody of the American Express card. Virgin Records is also hit with various copyright and trademark infringement charges.

16th

1991: Pearl Jam start their first full-blown American tour as the opening band for the Red Hot Chili Peppers. They are joined for some shows by a new Chicago band called the Smashing Pumpkins.

17th

1996: Lush drummer Chris Acland hangs himself at his parents' house in England. He was apparently depressed about earning $250 a week after eight years in the music business and was living in a friend's back room after a breakup with his girlfriend.

18th

1995: Oasis appear on *The Late Show with David Letterman* without a regular bass player. Bonehead is forced to switch from guitar to bass for the appearance. Scott McLeod, who had been filling in for the ailing Paul McGuigan, had abruptly quit the day before the appearance.

19th

1991: Oasis play their first real show together at the Boardwalk in Manchester.

20th

1978: The Police begin their first-ever tour of North America with a show at CBGBs in New York. They're planning to travel from gig to gig with everything packed into a beat-up station wagon.

21st

1995: Blind Melon singer Shannon Hoon is found dead in the band's tour bus in New Orleans. The coroner rules that he died of a cocaine overdose.

22nd

1976: Five months after their first show and after spending a grand total of £50 on a recording studio, the Damned becomes the first British punk band to issue a single when they release "New Rose." The B-side is their version of the Beatles' "Help."

23rd

1996: Three months after the signing of a new contract worth more than $80 million, there are concerns about REM's first album under that deal. *New Adventures in Hi-Fi* has not sold well, falling out of the Top 20 on album charts in both the U.S. and Britain just one month after its release.

24th

1995: Chrissie Hynde of the Pretenders sings the American national anthem before a World Series game in Cleveland.

25th

1996: Gossip reporters say that Hole guitarist Eric Erlandson has broken up with actress Drew Barrymore.

26th

1981: David Bowie and the members of Queen are neighbors in Switzerland. Together they write and release "Under Pressure."

27th

1986: When Morrissey is hit in the head by either a coin or a drumstick, the Smiths shut down a show at the Guildwood in Preston, England, after just one song ("The Queen is Dead"). The event goes down in history as the shortest Smiths gig ever.

28th

1977: The Sex Pistols' *Never Mind the Bollocks* is released in America. It's immediately banned by several record chains (including Woolworth's) and never makes it higher that 106 on the album charts. The album eventually sells a million copies—but it takes more than ten years.

29th

1996: The Stone Roses break up. They make it official with a short statement from singer Ian Brown: "Having spent the last ten years in the filthiest business in the universe, it's a pleasure to announce the end of the Stone Roses. May God bless all who gave us their love and supported us throughout this time. Special thanks to the people of Manchester who sent us on our way. Peace be upon you."

30th

1996: Oasis releases "Wonderwall," the single that establishes the group as worldwide superstars.

31st

1996: Despite rampant rumors that he was going to kill himself on stage this Halloween, Marilyn Manson disappoints the crowd at a show at the New Jersey Convention Center in Asbury Park by remaining alive for the entire show.

November

1st

1980: The Pretenders release their self-titled debut album. It will go on to become an important and influential record, building new bridges between punk, New Wave and pop.

2nd

1981: After several years together, the Specials announce that they're breaking up. Leader Jerry Dammers's 2 Tone Records will survive for a few more years before he sells the company. Three of the members form Fun Boy Three with Terry Hall, eventually departing to form the Colourfield. Guitarist Lynval Golding re-forms the Specials in 1995.

3rd

1988: *Rattle and Hum*, the U2 concert film of their 1987 Joshua Tree tour directed by Phil Joanou, has its North American premiere in New York. The band had planned to play live in Times Square, but are denied permission by the city, which is worried about a riot.

4th

1995: During a sellout show in London, 60 Oasis fans have to be treated for "emotional exhaustion."

5th

1994: Fred Smith, guitarist with the legendary MC5 and husband of punk poet Patti Smith, dies of a heart attack at age 47.

6th

1995: *Mellon Collie and the Infinite Sadness*, the double album from the Smashing Pumpkins, debuts at number one on the *Billboard* album chart. It will eventually become the biggest selling double album of the 90s, with four million copies sold in the U.S.

7th

1991: Backstage at a Bryan Adams concert at Wembley Arena, Gavin Rossdale meets Nigel Pulsford. Within a few months, they are playing together in a new band they call Bush.

8th

1980: There's a big change in the Human League as Craig Marsh and Martyn Ware leave the group to form a new band called Heaven 17.

9th

1995: The Red Hot Chili Peppers postpone their North American tour after drummer Chad Smith breaks his wrist during a baseball game. Opening act Silverchair decides to tour on their own, simply because they're out of school and have the time.

10th

1994: Seattle's Sky Cries Mary becomes the first professional band to broadcast a concert live over the Internet. Earlier in the year, a group of computer engineers had gotten together to become the first band ever to do a netcast.

11th

1986: Smiths guitarist Johnny Marr crashes his BMW into a wall after spending an evening drinking tequila and wine. The crash is so bad that he's lucky not to lose both his legs. A cover story says that his wife Angie was driving at the time. Johnny was driving without a license.

12th

1994: Boris Williams quits as the Cure's drummer to take a job with Peter Gabriel. The band finds his replacement, Jason Cooper, by placing ads in British music magazines.

13th

1993: Kate Bush's short film *The Line, The Cross and the Curve* premieres in London. She not only stars in the film, but also wrote the screenplay and directed it.

14th

1996: Gibby Haynes of the Butthole Surfers is ordered off the road when he is diagnosed with a punctured eardrum. His doctors tell him to take it easy for a few months or risk even worse damage.

15th

1987: After two members of the audience are bashed in the head with a mike stand at a concert in Toronto, Jim Reid of the Jesus and Mary Chain is arrested and charged with assault. Reid was upset because some people in the crowd kept yelling that the show was boring. When he appeared in court the following spring, he pleaded guilty and was given a conditional discharge after making a $1,000 donation to the Salvation Army.

16th
1985: U2 launch their own record label with the altruistic intention of helping young Irish bands. Mother Records will give new groups a leg up and then will allow them to sign elsewhere (with no strings attached) when they reach a certain level. Mother signings include the Hothouse Flowers and Cactus World News.

17th
1995: The surviving members of Nirvana, along with Courtney Love, settle a lawsuit launched by a German promoter. He has complained about spending hundreds of thousands of dollars rescheduling Nirvana shows following Kurt Cobain's OD in Rome in March 1994—and then spending even more money when Kurt committed suicide. The terms are not disclosed.

18th
1993: Eddie Vedder is booked for public drunkenness and disturbing the peace after he and his friend, Chicago White Sox pitcher Jack McDowell, got into a bar room brawl in New Orleans. Eddie is accused of starting the fight by spitting in a waiter's face. The charges are later dropped.

19th
1990: A riot erupts outside the Tower Theater in Philadelphia after Jane's Addiction cuts short their set. Perry Farrell has decided that the crowd just isn't into the music enough. The crowd pours out into the streets and fights with police before taking on the band's tour bus, which is parked out back. Twenty-three people are arrested and dozens are injured.

20th
1995: Alice in Chains' eponymous album debuts at number one on the *Billboard* Top 200 album chart. It sells a respectable 190,000 copies in its first week.

21st
1995: Billie Joe Armstrong moons the audience during a Green Day concert in Milwaukee. He's charged with indecent exposure and fined $141.85. Charges are later dropped and Billie Joe gets a full refund, when the district attorney decides that the audience wasn't shocked.

22nd
1994: Pearl Jam releases a limited edition vinyl version of *Vitalogy*.

23rd
1978: Two 19-year-olds working under the name Orchestral Maneouvres in the Dark make their debut at Eric's in Liverpool, England. Inspired by Kraftwerk, not the Sex Pistols, OMD is an all-electronic affair whose line-up is augmented by a reel-to-reel tape recorder named "Winston."

24th
1977: The owner of a record store in Nottingham, England, appears in court. He is charged with contravening the 1889 Indecent Advertising Act by displaying a six-by-nine foot display of the Sex Pistols album *Never Mind the Bollocks* in his shop window. The issue is whether or not the word "bollocks" is obscene. Following the defense testimony of an English professor about the origins and meaning of the word, the judge deliberates for 20 minutes and throws the case out.

25th
1984: Band Aid records "Do They Know It's Christmas" at SARM Studios in London. It is written by Boomtown Rats singer Bob Geldof and Ultravox singer Midge Ure on a cheap Casio keyboard, and they convince 36 artists to participate for free, including U2, Frankie Goes to Hollywood and Sting. All proceeds from the project go to Ethiopian famine relief efforts.

26th
1979: Joy Division records four more tracks for another John Peel session to be aired on BBC Radio. One of the new songs they record is called "Love Will Tear Us Apart."

27th
1987: The Cowboy Junkies record their second album in a church in downtown Toronto. They spend about 12 hours recording tracks with a single overhead microphone plugged into a DAT player. The resulting album is called *The Trinity Session* and sells more than a million copies around the world. Total recording costs: $162.

28th
1995: The Stone Roses do their first U.K. tour in nearly six years with a show at Bridlington Spa.

29th

1995: Morrissey abruptly drops out as the opener for David Bowie's U.K. tour, leaving it to a roadie to tell the audience that he won't be appearing. He later checks into a private clinic, the official explanation being "exhaustion."

30th

1994: Kelley Deal of the Breeders accepts a courier package full of heroin at her home in Dayton, Ohio, and is promptly arrested and charged with possession.

December

1st

1981: Vince Clarke announces that he is leaving Depeche Mode to form a group called Yazoo with singer Alison Moyet. Once they break up, he joins the Assembly before finding long-term work with Andy Bell in Erasure. Meanwhile, Martin Gore assumes the role of chief songwriter in Depeche Mode.

2nd

1996: Green Day denies rumors that they've broken up and that Billie Joe Armstrong has left the band to work on a new project. A spokesman reports: "The band is taking a brief break before recording a new album, but they're still very much together. The rumor is total nonsense." *Nimrod* is released on October 14, 1997.

3rd

1995: The members of Cast are thrown in jail after trashing their room and throwing a TV out the window at a Holiday Inn in Nantes, France.

4th

1979: A misunderstanding by the promoter results in U2 being billed as "The U2s" for their first English appearance at the Hope and Anchor in London. Bono manages to get dozens of record company people and journalists to come out, but only nine paying customers are in the crowd that night. The group is so discouraged that when the Edge breaks a string in the middle of the set, the band walks off the stage and doesn't come back.

5th

1994: More than five years after the release of their debut album, the Stone Roses finally come through with their second, calling it *Second Coming*. Unfortunately, many people are disappointed by the record and the band decides to break up.

6th

1996: Silverchair's Daniel Johns is arrested in Malibu Beach, California, for reckless driving. Johns and his passengers (Ben Gilles and Chris Joannou of Silverchair, along with Dave Navarro of the Red Hot Chili Peppers) are taken into custody and soon released without any charges being filed.

7th

1995: Ministry announces a chance for fans to get involved with the new album "Filth Pig." The group invites submissions for the cover artwork with the winner getting a brahma bull skull autographed by Al Jourgensen.

8th

1995: Oasis is ordered to pay royalties for their song "Whatever" to composer Neil Innes. A judge rules that the Oasis song sounds too much like "How Sweet to be an Idiot," a song Innes wrote for Monty Python's Flying Circus.

9th

1996: *The Wall Street Journal* reports that people will be able to buy investment bonds backed by future royalties on David Bowie's back catalogue. Bowie will get $50 million up front instead of waiting for the cheques to come in. Prudential Life Insurance likes the idea and underwrites the bond issue, guaranteeing investors an annual return of 7.9 percent.

10th

1984: Band Aid's "Do They Know It's Christmas" debuts at number one on the British charts and eventually becomes the biggest selling single of all time in the U.K.

11th

1982: After six years together and with 20 Top 40 U.K. singles, including four number one songs, the Jam perform their last gig together in Brighton, England.

12th

1996: Marilyn Manson take heat from American Senator Joseph Lieberman who calls the band "perhaps the sickest group ever promoted by a mainstream record company." Seagram, the parent company of Marilyn Manson's record label, is also targeted by various family values crusaders.

13th

1980: The Clash release a triple album called *Sandinista!* one year less a day after they issued their double album *London Calling*.

14th

1996: Director Milos Forman announces that Courtney Love has won the role of Althea Flynt in his new movie *The People Vs Larry Flynt*. On December 12, 1996, the New York Film Critics Circle name her the year's best supporting actress. Despite a push to have her nominated for an Academy Award, she doesn't make the cut.

15th

1992: Nirvana issues a rarities and B-sides collection called *Incesticide*. Kurt Cobain's liner notes are left out for legal reasons.

16th

1982: Japan play their final concert in (appropriately enough) Nagoya, Japan.

17th

1977: Unable to appear because they've been denied visas, the Sex Pistols do not appear as scheduled on *Saturday Night Live*. In their place is Elvis Costello, who annoys NBC by reneging on a promise to perform "Less Than Zero" and going with "Radio Radio," a song that takes a shot at radio station owners—like NBC.

18th

1996: A year after Perry Farrell quits the Lollapalooza organization over philosophical differences, reports out of Los Angeles say that he has rejoined the company. He'll be involved mostly with non-musical events, such as the midway attractions and the sideshows.

19th

1991: On their way home from the grocery store in Venice, California, Henry Rollins and Rollins Band roadie Joe Cole are held up by a gang. They are marched back to the house and ordered to lie on the floor. In the confusion, something goes wrong and Joe is shot dead.

20th

1987: U2 end the eight-month Joshua Tree tour with two sold-out shows where it began: Sun Devil Stadium in Tempe, Arizona. They use the opportunity to shoot more footage for their concert film *Rattle and Hum*. To make sure both shows sell out, all tickets are priced at $5.

21st

1979: The English Beat sign a major record deal with Arista. Their contract stipulates that they will be able to offer advice on signing other groups to the label.

22nd

1990: Mookie Blaylock celebrate their lead singer's birthday by playing their first public show, opening for Alice in Chains at the Moore Theater in Seattle. Within a few months, the group change their name to Pearl Jam.

23rd

1978: Punk fans display the power of the pogo at an Ian Dury gig at the Ilford Odeon. They stomp the floor so hard that it gives way. The only thing that stops the audience from falling into the basement is the carpet.

24th

1995: The K Foundation, a "charity" backed by the KLF, dumps a truckload of canned beer in front of the British Parliament. They want to give beer to the homeless for Christmas—but they couldn't find any homeless people. So they dropped off 6,237 cans, just in case they should happen to come by.

25th

1972: Robert Smith gets his first guitar as a Christmas present.

26th

1988: Shane McGowan of the Pogues spends the day drinking and decides to kick in a shop window. He's arrested and fined £250.

27th

1995: On the same day the Throwing Muses leave Warner Brothers, Ride breaks up after seven years when vocalist/guitarist Mark Gardener quits.

28th

1976: With a £250 loan from Pete Shelley's dad, the Buzzcocks record the four-track *Spiral Scratch* EP on their own New Hormones label, becoming the first punk band to issue an indie release.

29th

1988: Nirvana continue work on their debut album *Bleach*, often under the influence of a strong codeine cough syrup. By the time they wrap things up next month, they will have spent a grand total of $606.17 on recording costs. The album has since sold more than a million copies.

30th

1995: The *Times of London* and the BBC publish their list of the top songs for the first half of the decade. Pulp's "Common People" finishes first, followed by "Smells Like Teen Spirit" by Nirvana, "Live Forever" from Oasis and Blur's "Girls And Boys."

31st

1978: Ultra-goth pioneers Bauhaus are born when they play their first gig in a Wellingborough pub under the name "Bauhaus 1919."

Part 3

Spin the Black Circle: Records & Videos

The Format Wars:
A Brief History of Recorded Music

July 1876
Using some of the newly discovered principles of sound from his experiments with the telegraph and telephone (and looking to invent, essentially, a telephone answering machine), Thomas Edison rigs up a device consisting of a brass cylinder wrapped in tin foil. Resting on the tin foil is a needle connected to a diaphragm. As Edison rotates the cylinder with a crank, he shouts "Mary Had a Little Lamb" in the direction of the diaphragm. When the needle is repositioned at the beginning of the groove it dug and the crank is again turned, a scratchy but very intelligible recording of Edison's voice is heard. A demonstration at the offices of *Scientific American* on December 6 creates a sensation. The U.S. patent office is notified of the new invention on Christmas Eve.

February 17, 1877
Edison is awarded a U.S. patent for his "phonograph." Other recording formats (the flat rotating disk and strip recording) have been dismissed as not worth the effort.

c.1880-85
Engineers at Alexander Graham Bell's lab modify Edison's invention by substituting a wax-coated cardboard cylinder for the tin foil-wrapped brass cylinder. They also conduct experiments with something called a Photophone which can transmit speech over a beam of light.

1888
Emile Berliner demonstrates his gramophone in Philadelphia on May 18. Using a diaphragm-and-needle principle similar to the one invented by Edison, Berliner's machine inscribes spiraling lateral grooves onto a flat rotating disk. The advantage of the flat disk is that a "master" disk can be used as a mold to press up an unlimited number of copies, while each copy made of the Edison cylinder

must be made in a slower "real time" process. Despite the manufacturing advantages of the disk, Edison dismisses the invention as being technically inferior to his rotating cylinder. Berliner presses ahead with his format and is selling pre-recorded disks by 1893.

1889

On November 29, the Pacific Phonograph Company installs the world's first jukebox at the Palais Royal Saloon in San Francisco. For a nickel, a person can hear it play an Edison cylinder.

1889

Oberlin Smith describes a process whereby sound can be recorded on long, magnetized strips of metal. By 1890, Denmark's Valdemar Poulson is able to demonstrate the "telegraphone," a metal strip recorder and playback unit that looks remarkably like a modern reel-to-reel tape machine.

1890s

The "talking machine" industry explodes, as many new companies try to take advantage of the new technology. Unfortunately, there are no uniform standards and the public is faced with a series of incompatible machines competing against one another. Depending on the disk, it may require speeds of 50 to 120 RPM. By the turn of the century, the big battle is between Edison's phonograph and Berliner's gramophone. Each format can record approximately two minutes of material on each disk or cylinder.

1891

George W. Johnson, an ex-slave, records "The Laughing Song" on an Edison cylinder. Because the cylinders cannot be duplicated in mass amounts, Johnson has to sing his song 40,000 times to make 40,000 recordings.

1900-10

Berliner's disks are marketed successfully by Victor (today the RCA division of German giant BMG) and Columbia (today part of the Sony empire). Berliner also sets up the Gramophone Co. (today EMI) in Britain and helps with Germany's Deutsche Grammophon Gesellschaft (today part of PolyGram). Both Berliner's disk and Edison's cylinder continue to battle for market dominance.

1913

Sensing that the future of recorded music might not be the cylinder after all, Edison introduces the Edison Diamond Disk player. The cylinder eventually fades away. However, there are still inconsistencies in the size of disks. Some are as small as seven inches while others are 14 inches or more in diameter.

1920s
The ten-inch 78 RPM disk gains wide acceptance. It can store between three and five minutes of material on each side. (By the 30s, engineers will extend playing time even further but remain unable to break the magic ten-minute barrier.)

1925
Up until the 20s, all sound recordings were made acoustically, i.e. sounds were funneled through a large recording horn where they moved a diaphragm connected to a needle. Now scientists at Western Electric demonstrate how recordings can be made using electrical principles. Microphone, loudspeaker and amplifier technology improves.

1926
Since the technology of the day limits things to one (or two) songs per record, artists who want to release more than one song at the same time have to bundle them together in paper and cardboard binders called "albums." Although Edison introduces a 12-inch disk capable of storing 40 minutes of music, acceptance of the long-playing record is more than 20 years away.

1927
The German division of RCA introduces the first automatic record changer.

1930
Hollywood phases out the silent movie. Radio stations begin to rely more heavily on recorded music, finding it cheaper to play recordings than to constantly hire live performers. The 78 RPM record rules, although Western Electric introduces a 16-inch 33 1/3 disk for professional use by radio stations, film studios and the American Armed Forces Radio Network.

1931
The first three-way speaker systems (with woofers, mids and tweeters) are introduced by Western Electric. Alan Blumlein makes improvements to record cutter technology, laying the foundations for stereo records.

1946
Captured German "magnetophones" show how sound (and other data) can be stored on thin cellulose tape coated with a magnetic material, a huge improvement on the wire recorders of the 30s. Magnecord, Brush and Ampex start marketing

machines to radio networks and record companies. Bing Crosby, tired of broadcasting live every week, hastens the adoption of the new technology when he decides to finance the purchase of Ampex recorders so he can pre-record and edit his shows for ABC radio. Reel-to-reel recorders for home use appear by 1950.

June 1948

Columbia sets off the "battle of the speeds" by introducing the 12-inch 33 1/3 RPM long playing record. For the first time in history, long pieces of classical music can be enjoyed in one sitting, while other artists are free to include more than one performance/song per disk. Record companies enjoy a brief boom, as consumers change their collections over from brittle 78 RPM records to the new, more durable "microgroove" long-players.

February 1, 1949

To combat Columbia's LP, RCA introduces the seven inch 45 RPM single. To help ensure market acceptance, the company also markets a 45-only record player for less than $15. "Gaie Parisienne" by the Boston Pops Orchestra is the first 45 single ever pressed.

1950

Consumers are further confused by the introduction of 16 RPM records, an ultra long-playing format designed for stage plays, operas and book readings. Record sales slump as a bitter format war rages. Columbia and other labels begin manufacturing 45s while other companies (including RCA) adopt Columbia's LP.

1954

Record companies begin to send radio stations 45 RPM singles instead of the old bulky shellac 78 RPM records. The seven-inch slowly becomes the format of a new music called "rock 'n' roll."

1956

Born out of dictating machine technology and used by radio stations, pre-recorded four-track continuous loop tape cartridges begin to be sold by several companies interested in developing a recorded music medium for the car. Each cartridge is about the size of a paperback book.

1957

With the format wars under control (although 78 RPM records will be sold until the early 1960s), stereo records are introduced using a universally-accepted technical standard.

1963

Dutch manufacturer Philips introduces the compact cassette. Essentially a reel-to-reel design in a plastic case running at 1 7/8 inches per second, Philips encourages other manufacturers to license the technology, and by 1968 there are close to a hundred different companies making cassette players. The first pre-recorded cassettes appear in 1964. Dr. Ray Dolby turns the cassette into a high-fidelity medium with the introduction of Dolby Noise Reduction for recording studios in 1966. By 1971, home units with Dolby begin to appear.

1964

The Lear Company (the jet manufacturer) approaches Ford with a new continuous loop tape cartridge design that uses eight tracks instead of four at 3 3/4 inches per second. Ford accepts the proposal and Motorola builds Lear 8-track players for Ford automobiles starting in 1966. RCA becomes involved, offering hundreds of pre-recorded 8-track tapes alongside cassettes and vinyl formats.

1970

The first four-channel (or quad) systems are introduced. Although the concept fails, the spin-off technologies help with the development of surround decoders.

1972

The oil crisis forces record manufacturers to change the formulations of their vinyl. Quality suffers.

October 1976

PolyGram introduces the 12-inch single to the pop music market in Britain.

1977

Sales of cassettes begin to challenge the sales of vinyl.

1979

After years of pressing for its development, Masuru Ibuka and Akio Morita convince Sony to invest in an ultra-personal cassette stereo that uses tiny headphones instead of external speakers. After a poor initial attempt with the Soundabout, the Walkman is introduced. Sales of cassettes soar as more than 50 million Walkmans are sold in the next ten years. By 1981, all of Sony's competitors market something similar.

1980

The 12-inch single and the EP (a three to six track mini-album) gain in popularity.

February 3, 1982

Sony and Philips announce the arrival of the compact disk (CD). Universal standards are established and the technology is licensed to companies around the world. By the early 1990s, the 33 1/3 album has almost completely died out. The 7-inch single remains popular as a low-cost format for indie bands while the 12-inch single continues to dominate the dance and techno scenes.

1987

Digital audio tape (DAT) is introduced. The format fails to catch on after the recording industry, fearing an explosion of perfect digital copies, decides not to pursue the consumer market. Most DAT machines end up being used by professionals in recording studios and radio stations.

1992

Philips introduces the digital compact cassette (DCC). It also fails in the marketplace. Sony's minidisc fares somewhat better.

March 1997

DVD (digital video disk or digital versatile disk) is introduced.

The Big Six Labels

All it takes is a quick walk through a record store or a glance at the album reviews section of any music magazine to come away with the impression that there are hundreds, if not thousands, of different record companies out there. Actually, the opposite is true. While there is an abundance of record *labels*, the truth is that anywhere from 80 to 90 percent of all the recorded music on the planet is released by just *six* multinational entertainment conglomerates, the so-called "major labels."

These companies generate billions of dollars in revenue every year and, to a large extent, they determine what we hear and even in what *form* we hear it. That's because these companies are so big and powerful that they can dictate what kind of stereo equipment we buy—equipment that they manufacture. In other words, these companies control a lot of the software and the hardware of music. Cynics will say that's what happened with the compact disk; they believe that it was a new format developed by two of these companies (Sony and Philips) and introduced at a time when both the record industry and the consumer electronics industry were suffering in a recession. We, the consumers, bought into the new technology, abandoned our record collections for CDs (with their higher profit margin) and replaced our turntables with new compact disk players. The result was that the "Big Six" enjoyed consistently high profits for more than a decade.

The six major labels are actually a tangle of subsidiaries. If you go through your record collection, you'll find all kinds of imprints: American Recordings, Dedicated, SpinArt, Virgin, Hut, Maverick, DGC, Island, Fiction, Bong Load—but most of them can be traced back to one of six parent companies. If a band is signed to any one of these labels, they're considered to be signed to a "major label."

1. Sony Corporation

Sony did not start out as a major label. The Japanese electronics giant bought their way in at the top. Up until 1987, Sony was known for their music hardware: TVs, stereos, the Sony Walkman, radios and, of course, the compact disk. Sony, however, wanted more. They knew that if they were to continue to grow (something that shareholders insist upon), they also needed to control the creation and distribution of software. They wanted to have a say in supplying material that consumers watched on their Sony TVs and listened to on their Sony Walkmans. And the quickest way to do that was to buy a movie studio and a record label.

In mid-1988, Sony, armed with $2 billion in cash, outbid EMI and purchased the recorded music division of CBS, a company which had been in the music business since 1938. At the time, it was the largest purchase of an American firm by a Japanese company. The $2 billion price tag also included all the subsidiary labels controlled by CBS and all the artists signed to those labels.

These days the Sony family is responsible for somewhere around 10 percent of all the recorded music sold worldwide. Columbia, Epic and Creation are just a few of the imprints under the company's direct control. Sony also has licensing and distribution agreements with a variety of indie labels—not to mention a major Hollywood studio.

2. BMG

Like Columbia, the Germany-based Bertelsmann Music Group can trace its roots all the way back to the first years of the 1900s, when Emile Berliner was marketing his gramophone around the world. Along with owning some two dozen different record labels, BMG owns newspapers, cable companies, magazines and several very large book publishers. And like the rest of the Big Six, BMG got big by buying up the competition.

BMG was born in 1987 when a German company called Ariola went on a spending spree, its board of directors having decided they wanted a bigger market share of the very lucrative recorded music industry. One of their big purchases was the music division of RCA, which was promptly added to a stable that included Arista. Today, BMG properties include Zoo and American Recordings—it holds about a 5 percent share of the market.

3. Universal Music Group

Holders of a market share similar to that of BMG, Universal (then called MCA) was purchased in 1995 from Japan's Matsushita Corporation (the parent of Panasonic, Technics and others) by Seagram, a Montreal-based company which made its fortune selling liquor. By purchasing Universal, Seagram also picked up Universal Pictures and a bunch of cable companies, in addition to all the record labels under the MCA umbrella, including Geffen and DGC. The company later picked up the very profitable, but controversial, Interscope (along with its subsidiaries Trauma and Nothing) from Time-Warner.

An aside: it seems that Seagram head Edgar Bronfman treasures his music division above everything else. A closet songwriter, he has written several songs under pseudonyms and at least one of them was recorded by Celine Dion.

4. Time-Warner Inc.

In 1988, Time-Warner was born out of a $13 billion corporate merger, one of the largest of such transactions of the decade. The new company controlled everything from movie studios, to cable systems, to magazine concerns like *Time* and *Sports Illustrated*—plus there was the sizable recorded music division. The company was already the largest entertainment conglomerate in the world when they merged with Ted Turner's empire (CNN, TBS, the Cartoon Network, etc.) in 1996.

At the core of the music division is WEA, which itself was the result of a merger between Warner Brothers Records, Elektra and Atlantic. Circling WEA are literally dozens of small subsidiaries, many of them former indies (such as Sub Pop, Sire and Reprise) that were gobbled up over the years. WEA also leads the way in the area of "vanity labels," special labels set up for the exclusive use of some of the company's more valuable artists. For example, Maverick is run by Madonna, while Igloo is the domain of Tori Amos. WEA also has distribution agreements with several important indie labels (such as Depeche Mode's Mute) which increases their overall market share even further. Put all these properties and arrangements together and you'll find that Time-Warner issues anywhere from 12 to 15 percent of all the records sold in a given year.

5. EMI Music

As is the case with the previous four conglomerates, music is just one division of Britain's huge multinational Thorn-EMI. In 1979, Thorn was a defense contractor for the British government with money to burn. On the advice of their financial people, Thorn invested some of that cash in the music industry, buying a company called EMI, formerly Electrical Music Instruments, Ltd., a company with roots all the way back to the 1870s.

More than a quarter of the records sold in the world are in some way connected to Thorn-EMI. They own Capitol (home of Apple and the Beatles), Virgin, Food and many others. And as an added bonus, they sell a lot of those records out of HMV, their healthy chain of record stores. The American division of EMI records was shut down in a major restructuring in July 1997.

6. Philips

Netherlands-based Philips is massive. With roots extending back to Emile Berliner, Philips makes everything from CD players, to washing machines, to movies. And they sell records—*lots* of records.

Philips owns a 75 percent stake in PolyGram NV, which owns a piece of Mercury, A&M, Motown, Island, London, and dozens of other smaller labels. As the result of a series of aggressive mergers, smart purchases and shrewd deals with some key indie labels, almost one in every three records sold on the planet can be traced back to Philips. Key artists include everyone from U2 to Andrew Lloyd Webber.

Cool Indie Labels

Even though the Big Six control up to 90 percent of the recorded music market, enough records are sold each year to make it worthwhile to chase that remaining 10 percent. And, in the view of many people, it's this last 10 percent that's vital to the continued well-being of alt-rock.

Indie labels are small and nimble, able to either specialize in a specific genre/ sound or to respond to a change in trends with little or no trouble at all. Costs are kept low, allowing the label to work with new exciting acts, often the type of performers who are on the leading edge of musical evolution. On the other hand, smallness and specializing in a particular musical niche means cash flow is almost always an issue. This is why many indies work out distribution and/or licensing deals with one of the Big Six. As distasteful as this may be from a philosophical point of view, it's often the only way to get records into stores across the country and around the world.

Here are thumbnail sketches of some of alt-rock's better known indie labels, both past and present.

Alternative Tentacles

Back in the late 70s, a couple of different labels were interested in signing San Francisco's Dead Kennedys—but if and only if the group would change its name. Finding that option unacceptable, singer Jello Biafra and the rest of the band created Alternative Tentacles (AT) as a way of distributing their own records. What began as a one-act roster has since experienced exponential growth, signing not only punk bands, but everything from experimental acts to spoken word performers.

AT has a history of thumbing its nose at established conventions. In addition to his ongoing battle against Tipper Gore's PMRC (Parents' Music Resource Committee), Biafra ran for mayor of San Francisco in 1979, finishing fourth in a field of ten. In the mid-80s, AT survived a long and bitter legal struggle. At the center of the controversy was a poster by Swiss surrealist artist H.R. Giger (the designer of the scum-dripping monster in the *Alien* movies) called *Landscape No. XX* that was included free with the band's *Frankenchrist* album. After enduring a raid on his home by police and a trial that lasted almost 18 months, Biafra and AT were acquitted of trafficking in harmful matter in June 1988. (For Jello's side of the story, check out his spoken word release entitled *High Priest of Harmful Matter*.)

On April 4, 1997, a federal judge in Philadelphia awarded $2.2 million to policeman James Whalen and his union in a lawsuit involving the unauthorized use of his photo on the cover of *Our Will Be Done*, a 1992 compilation by AT act the Crucifucks. At issue was the alleged anti-police sentiments of both the label and the band.

Amphetamine Reptile

Founded by ex-Marine Corps lance corporal and Halo of Flies guitarist Tom Hazelmeyer in 1987, the label has been home to some of the best and most uncompromising underground bands to come out of Minneapolis and elsewhere. Established because no other company would touch Halo of Flies material, Hazelmeyer ("Haze" to his friends) used some of the experience he gained working with Husker Du's Reflex Records to start the company.

At first, everything except the actual pressing of the records was done by hand at a marine barracks just north of Seattle. Other bands joined up, such as the Throw-Ups, featuring future Mudhoney members Steve and Mark Arm. After

Hazelmeyer received his honorable discharge, he moved to Minneapolis to work on AmRep during his spare time. In 1989, the company joined forces with Twin/Tone-Rough Trade in a manufacturing and distribution deal, increasing its sales by more than 100 percent. Roster acts soon included Boss Hog (featuring Jon Spencer), Lubricated Goat and Helmet.

The company maintains its operation on First Avenue South in Minneapolis in an old basement dental office. The offices also feature a recording studio, used by many acts on the label's roster.

Beggar's Banquet

Martin Mills's label was a spin-off of his chain of British record stores. During the height of the punk explosion, Mills was amazed at the number of customers who were asking for records by some of the new acts of the day. Recognizing that there was obviously a hole in the market, but frustrated by the lack of available product, Mills decided to take matters into his own bands by starting a label dedicated to releasing material from some of these new groups. Unlike Stiff, Rough Trade, Factory and other upstart indies, distribution wasn't a problem because, of course, Mills had his chain of record shops. The company thrived, signing successful acts ranging from Bauhaus to the Cult to the Charlatans.

Creation

Formed in 1983 by Alan McGee, a former British Rail clerk, night club entrepreneur and member of a Scottish group called Biff Bang Pow, Creation first grabbed attention when they sold 50,000 copies of "Upside Down," the debut single from the Jesus and Mary Chain. The Creation roster grew and achieved considerable notoriety for big failures (like Momus and Baby Amphetamine), major crises (nearly being bankrupted by the recording costs incurred by My Bloody Valentine and their *Loveless* album) and huge successes (such as Oasis and, on a lesser scale, Ride, Adorable and the Boo Radleys). Facing a mortal financial crunch, McGee sold 49 percent of the label to Sony in the early 90s.

Dischord

Co-founded in 1981 by Ian McKaye, a longtime member of the Washington, D.C. underground scene, Dischord was designed as a home to some of the community's most important bands—Eggplant, Teen Idols, Minor Threat, Embrace and Fugazi—all groups featuring Ian McKaye. Along with documenting the region's punk scene (known locally as "harDCore"), the label maintains a policy of offering their product at the lowest price possible. The company has since moved from its original offices in McKaye's house to a cottage in Arlington, Virginia.

Epitaph

Fed up with not being able to find a label to distribute its records, southern California punk legend Bad Religion decided to form its own label in 1981. By 1988, the Orange County company was strong enough to offer support to other groups like L7, NOFX and a new group called Offspring, eventually selling upwards of a million punk records a year. Epitaph's biggest coup came when it spent $5,000 to make a video for "Come Out and Play," a single from the Offspring album *S*M*A*S*H** that had enjoyed some success on local radio. Once MTV picked up the clip, the album started selling like crazy and ended up becoming the best-selling indie release of all time with more than 9 million copies sold. Despite many offers to sell (and despite losing Offspring to Sony after a bitter court battle), Epitaph label head Brett Gurewitz is determined to keep the company independent.

Factory

Tony Wilson was a TV reporter based in Manchester who was also a big fan of the local music scene. Striking up a partnership with Alan Erasmus, manager of the Duritti Column, they created a label named after The Factory, their Manchester nightclub. Most of the company's roster featured some of the more promising groups that appeared during Wilson's new music showcases at the club. Joy Division soon became Factory's most important asset, especially after the release of the excellent *Unknown Pleasures* album in 1979. Other important signings included OMD, Cabaret Voltaire, James and, of course, New Order. Factory was hit with an unmanageable financial crisis in 1992 and was forced to close down. The old Factory building on Princess Street in Manchester is now, ironically, a night club. Meanwhile, Tony Wilson is trying to make a go of another label which he calls Factory Too.

4AD

One of the most influential indie labels of all time, 4AD has not only introduced the world to the Pixies, the Cocteau Twins, Lush, the Breeders, Dead Can Dance, This Mortal Coil and many others, it has also set new standards for artwork and packaging. Ivo Watts-Russell and Peter Kent were given £2,000 by their employers (Beggar's Banquet) to start a spin-off label called Axis. After changing the company's name to 4AD (there was already a label named Axis), they struck it big by first signing Modern English, which ended up with a major hit single called "I Melt With You." Since then, 4AD has prospered and continues to be one of the most respected indies.

Matador

Featuring one of the most user-friendly of all web sites, Matador was created in the fall of 1989 by Johan Kugelberg (now with Swedish-American Records) and has been home to some very big names from the American underground. Pavement, Liz Phair, Guided By Voices and Jon Spencer are just some of the acts who have released records with Matador. The label had a deal with Atlantic, but that fell apart in 1995. In February 1997, Matador gave up its independent status when it entered a partnership with Capitol Records. It was a difficult decision, but it was the only route to go without having to cut costs by dropping a large number of acts from the roster.

Mute

When Daniel Miller released the single "Warm Leatherette" under the name the Normal in 1978, he did it independently on his own label, which he called Mute. Although he made a fair amount of money from that single, he soon realized that he would fare much better as a businessman than as a musician. That's when Mute began to sign other acts, beginning with Fad Gadget, DAF and an unknown act from Basildon, England, called Depeche Mode. At first, the label had a policy of signing mainly synthesizer-based bands, a policy which was of great benefit to acts such as Depeche Mode, Yazoo, Erasure, Nitzer Ebb, and Throbbing Gristle. Depeche Mode remains the company's most valuable asset. Mute also issues material from a variety of techno acts as well as from performance artist Diamanda Galas.

Nettwerk

Like Creation, Rough Trade, Factory and others, Nettwerk is an indie that doesn't have a specific sound. Instead, the company's roster has featured a wide variety of performers since its inception in 1984, ranging from intensely industrial (Consolidated) to delicate (Sarah McLachlan). Originally created as the home of a Canadian electronic band called Moev, Nettwerk soon branched out, striking distribution deals with several international distribution companies, thus ensuring that their products reached the maximum number of record stores. In a reciprocal move with those same companies, Nettwerk became a North American outlet for other indie bands and indie labels from around the world who were more or less in the same boat.

At first, the entire Nettwerk operation was run out of founder Terry McBride's apartment. One of their first signings was Skinny Puppy, which soon become one of industrial music's most influential pioneers. But their biggest break came in the fall of 1985 when Moev played a show in Halifax, Nova Scotia. On the bill that night was October Game, featuring 17-year-old Sarah McLachlan. After some projected negotiations with both Sarah and her parents, she signed with Nettwerk on October 2, 1987. She is now the label's most valuable property, having sold millions of records.

Not only does Nettwerk have a sterling reputation for signing new and innovative talent, but this Vancouver-based label is also recognized as being one of the first companies to embrace new technologies such as web sites and enhanced CDs. Sarah McLachlan's *Freedom Sessions* became the first enhanced CD to make the *Billboard* Top 200 charts on April 15, 1995, debuting at number 78.

Rough Trade

Rather than take a job as a teacher at a girls' school, Geoff Travis opted for a trip across America, on which he bought a huge number of records for as little as 25 cents each. When he finally returned home, he realized that he didn't have enough room for all of them and began to sell them off at a slight profit. That back room enterprise grew into a Kensington record store called Rough Trade by mid-1976, just as the whole punk scene began to explode. Dealing in the latest U.K. releases, as well as a wide variety of imports, business was good enough for Travis to create a formal distribution system for all these records. Forming a label was the next logical step.

Rough Trade's first signing was a French group called Metal Urbain, followed in short order by releases from Stiff Little Fingers, the Fall and the Slits. The label's golden years began in 1983 when Travis agreed to take on a Manchester band called the Smiths, who eventually sold millions of records. Unfortunately, Rough Trade couldn't replace the Smiths when they broke up in 1987 and the company was soon reduced to a shell of its former self.

SST

After the label that had agreed to release their records decided that punk was dead, Southern California pioneers Black Flag formed their own company in 1977. They took their name from an old electronics company, Solid State Tuners. Managed entirely by guitarist Greg Ginn, bassist Chuck Dukowski, and two roadies, the first SST release was a four-track 7-inch in 1978. After weathering a difficult legal battle with giant MCA, SST went on to release a series of important and influential underground records from groups such Husker Du, Sonic Youth and Dinosaur Jr. Other SST signings have included the Meat Puppets, Soundgarden and Bad Brains. SST maintains their head office in Lawndale, California.

Stiff

Born in the basement of the Hope and Anchor pub in the Islington area of London, Stiff was one of the first British indie labels dedicated to the exciting indie music scene of the mid-70s. Starting by investing £45 in "So It Goes," the first Nick Lowe single, Stiff became one of the most important labels of the era. The first true British punk release, "New Rose" from the Damned, came out on Stiff. Other signings included Elvis Costello, Ian Dury and the Blockheads, Richard Hell, Lene Lovich, Devo, Kirsty MacColl, Madness and even the Pogues. One of the label's most endearing qualities was its cheeky slogans ("If It Ain't Stiff, It Ain't Worth a Fuck") and the company's strange singles, such as the special 7-inch entitled "The Wit and Wisdom of Ronald Reagan." Both sides of the record were completely blank.

The company began to fall apart in 1983 after an ill-conceived merger with Island Records. Stiff has since faded away.

Sub Pop

In 1986, Bruce Pavitt was supposed to be working as a shipper/receiver in the warehouse of Muzak Corporation (the elevator music people) in Seattle. Instead, he was plotting a way to document the city's growing local music scene. He managed to scrape together $20,000 in start-up capital with his partner, a one-time college radio DJ named Jonathan Poneman, to create Sub Pop (from *Subterranean Pop*, Poneman's indie music 'zine and later a column in a local magazine called *The Rocket*). They began with a compilation album of local acts called *The Sub Pop 100*, one of the landmark releases in the genre that became known as "grunge," a term allegedly coined by Pavitt's buddy Mark Arm, of the Seattle band Mudhoney. One of the company's more interesting inventions was the Sub Pop Singles Club. From November 1983 until December 1993, subscribers would get a brand new limited edition single from a new band through the mail every month.

Sub Pop was on the brink of financial disaster for years. Things got so bad at one point that the company issued a T-shirt that read "Sub Plop: What part of 'we don't have any money' don't you understand?" Staff were laid off, bills piled up and the label eked out a meager existence until DGC came along, offering a $75,000 buyout for Nirvana's contract, plus a share of the royalties in the unlikely event that the group's next album sold more than 200,000 copies. *Nevermind* went on to sell more than 10 million copies. Having dug themselves out of a very deep hole and grossing more than $200 million in revenues, Pavitt and Poneman decided to sell a majority stake in the company to WEA for $20 million in 1994. Pavitt formally resigned from the company for an early semi-retirement on April 14, 1996.

2 Tone

Jerry Dammers was an unemployed suedehead from Coventry, England, who was fascinated by punk as well as by the reggae and bluebeat music imported from Jamaica. Forming a band called the Specials, he couldn't find any mainstream label in England willing to take a chance on their new, updated ska sound. That's when he decided to take matters into his own hands, forming his own label and calling it "2 Tone" after the black and white suits worn by mods and skinheads back in the 60s. Armed with £700 borrowed from family and friends, the Specials went into the studio in March 1979 and emerged with a single called "Gangsters." The screeching brakes at the beginning were sampled directly from a song done originally by ska master Prince Buster.

Even though that single sold quite well for an indie, the costs of recording were just too high. In an effort to share the burden, the next 2 Tone record was a split single with a hastily-assembled band named the Selecter. The double A-side from March 1979 is generally considered to be the record that marked the beginning of the post-punk ska revival.

The 2 Tone look caught on amongst ska fans: the tonic and mohair suits with suspenders, porkpie hats, and loafers, brogues or Doc Martens for shoes. Many of them adopted the black-and-white checkerboard logo that Dammers (a former graphic artist) created for 2 Tone record jackets. The most popular icon of the era was "Walt Jabsco," the rudeboy drawing that appeared on every 2 Tone record. It was a sound and look that promoted cooperation and racial harmony.

Ska ran into trouble in the early 80s, in large part due to the increase in racial violence that kept plaguing shows. The Specials broke up and 2 Tone was later absorbed into the giant Thorn-EMI record empire.

Wax Trax

In 1973, Denver natives Jim Nash and Dannie Flesher started a record store called Wax Trax that relied on their personal record collections and was augmented by the occasional "ten records for a penny" deal offered by the music clubs. After a series of trips to England to observe the growing punk scene, Nash and Flesher decided that their store should get into the business of releasing some of this weird punk stuff. Selling the Denver store and relocating to Chicago in 1978, they set up a new Wax Trax on Lincoln Avenue. The store soon became a meeting place for many fans of the underground music scene.

When a group called Strike Under (featuring some regular customers) pressed up a thousand copies of their debut EP, *Immediate Action*, Wax Trax became a record label almost by default, since the only place anyone could buy this record was at that store. Because the Strike Under EP sold so well, Nash and Flesher decided to release a record by Divine (the transvestite star of *Pink Flamingos* and other underground films) after they saw her perform at the Alternative Miss World pageant. From then on, the store also doubled as the headquarters for the Wax Trax record label.

Although the company suffered many financial scares during its lifetime, including a $15 million lawsuit brought forth by Divine (who appeared in court in full drag. The suit was eventually dismissed), it also enjoyed many successes. Known primarily as an industrial label, featuring Ministry, Revolting Cocks, 1000 Homo DJs, and Front Line Assembly, the company also served as a distributor for some of the harder sounds coming out of Europe (such as Front 242, Laibach and KMFDM, etc). Despite being driven into bankruptcy in 1992, Wax Trax survives as part of TVT Records. Jim Nash died of AIDS-related illnesses on October 10, 1995, at age 47.

The Most Important Indie Releases

Independent labels are a treasure. Because they don't have the baggage and the not-seeing-the-forest-for-the-trees attitudes of the majors, they take chances on new artists and thus are often the source for some of the world's most important and influential releases. Here are a few examples of indie records that changed the world.

"Hey Joe" b/w "Piss Factory"—Patti Smith (1974)
Released on a tiny New York label called Mer on June 5, 1974, this is considered by some to be the first-ever punk record. Mer was owned by Patti's friend, artist Robert Mapplethorpe, and although "Hey Joe" (a tribute to Patty Hearst) was technically the A-side, it was the flip side that attracted all the attention. The recording was an afterthought. "Hey Joe" was recorded in less time than anticipated and rather than give up the studio time, Smith, guitarist Lenny Kaye, keyboardist Richard Sohl and Tom Verlaine (of Television) decided to vamp along while Smith recited a poem inspired by the time she was fired from her factory job because she spent too much time writing poetry instead of working. Even though the 7-inch was sold through various record shops and bookstores in Greenwich Village, the thousand copies that

were pressed up sold out quickly and the new music scene of New York's Bowery began to acquire some serious momentum. Within a year, people were talking about a new thing called "punk" and flocking to clubs like CBGBs to see bands such as the Ramones, Blondie, Television and the Talking Heads.

The Modern Lovers—Jonathan Richman (1972)

Jonathan Richman started the Modern Lovers in 1971, partly in reaction to the hippie culture he saw all around him in Boston. Rather than having long hair and an interest in free love, Richman liked to point out that he had short hair and was against drugs. Being a big Velvet Underground and Iggy Pop fan, he wanted to emulate his heroes by making music that was truly different. In 1972, he recorded some demos, most of which were produced by John Cale, for a tiny indie label called Berserkley. It wasn't quite punk but its stark, stripped-down sound caught the attention of people who were bored with the state of music. Fans included the Sex Pistols, who would later cover the Modern Lovers classic "Roadrunner." The Modern Lovers was so far ahead of its time that even today it doesn't sound out-of-date.

Spiral Scratch—The Buzzcocks (1977)

The Buzzcocks were probably the first punk band in the world to form their own label in order to release their own records. With a £250 loan from singer Pete Shelley's father, the group formed the label, paid for a five-hour recording session, pressed up a thousand copies of the record and arranged for distribution. To save money, the cover art was nothing more than a Polaroid photo of the group taken by their manager. When it was finished on January 29, 1977, it was a 7-inch four-track EP entitled Spiral Scratch. It became the DIY blueprint for not only hundreds of U.K. bands, but for ambitious indie groups around the world.

Unknown Pleasures—Joy Division (1979)

Factory Records was owned by former TV reporter Tony Wilson who also ran a Manchester nightclub called The Factory. On June 8, 1978, a new group called Joy Division played a short set that captured Wilson's attention. Exactly one year later, Joy Division was one of the first bands to release an album on Wilson's new Factory label. Produced by Martin Hannett, the album was so different from what was going on in music at the time that no one really knew what to make of it. It was stark, gloomy, minor-key music—but at the same time, the material had an undeniable accessibility about it. Along with the sounds of breaking glass, the atmosphere of the music was enhanced by the way the drums and bass were recorded. Wilson gambled his last £8,500 on pressing up 10,000 copies of the album, and *Unknown Pleasures* became a huge hit, directly influencing the direction of several branches of post-punk music. Today, the album is considered a classic.

The Smiths—The Smiths (1984)

Smiths guitarist Johnny Marr had always been a big fan of Rough Trade Records and vowed that if he should ever have a band, he wanted to be signed to Rough Trade. In April 1983, he had his chance. Marr hunted down label head Geoff Travis and cornered him in the kitchen of the Rough Trade offices in London. After giving in to Marr's demand that he listen to the Smiths' demo tape over the weekend, Travis was impressed and agreed to offer the band a deal. A month later, Rough Trade issued the single "Hand in Glove," a basic guitars/drums/bass song in a world that was awash in synthesizers. Even more notable were Morrissey's eloquent lyrics and his ability to express his angst on various levels. *The Smiths* was released to great acclaim in February 1984, and went on to become one of the most influential English pop records of the decade. Even today, more than a decade after the Smiths broke up, their influence is still felt.

Daydream Nation—Sonic Youth (1988)

Sonic Youth was *the* indie American alt-rock band of the 80s. Their outlook on music was so radical that, in a world filled with Van Halen and Huey Lewis and the News clones, no major label would even think of touching them. Only indie labels such as SST were interested. As their reputation grew through the 80s, they became underground icons. Some of their albums were complete misses, cacophonous swirls of self-indulgent noise—but when Sonic Youth was on, they were awesome. Their finest moment came in 1988 with the release of the inventive and unrestrained *Daydream Nation*, a lifeline for indie fans who loved their guitars loud, fuzzy and distorted. The album took six weeks and just $30,000 to record. It was so good that at least one major label decided it was time to take a serious look at Sonic Youth. Several years later, a new group from Aberdeen, Washington, looked to Sonic Youth's signing with DGC for guidance. Seeing that Sonic Youth had been able to retain creative control, Nirvana agreed to a contract—the deal that resulted in *Nevermind*.

"Touch Me I'm Sick"—Mudhoney (1988)

For some people, the "Touch Me I'm Sick" single marks the beginning of the whole grunge era—and why not? Mudhoney's Mark Arm is generally credited with being the first to describe his group's heavy, sludgy sound as "grunge."

After this recording became the first record to be released by the new Sub Pop Records (run by Arm's friend and coworker, Bruce Pavitt), the term just kind of stuck. Part of the credit must also go to Jack Endino, owner of Seattle's Reciprocal Recording, and producer of many local bands. Even though he worked with a band who loved using the cheapest, cheesiest sounding distortion pedals for their guitars, Endino was somehow able to capture the band at its best.

Surfer Rosa—The Pixies (1988)

The Pixies really should get more credit for having an influence on the new music of the 90s. Maybe it's not widely known that Kurt Cobain admitted he was trying to come up with a "good Pixies record" when he wrote the songs for Nevermind, or that Billy Corgan intentionally incorporated Pixies-like dynamics into the sound of the Smashing Pumpkins. But then again, not everyone knew what to make of the Pixies, especially when they started out playing the bars around Boston. They couldn't even find one American label interested in them—instead they signed with 4AD, the adventurous British company. Oddly enough, the strange frat-rock attitude and the noisy chords recorded by Steve Albini blended nicely with 4AD's artsy elements, creating an image and sound that became a blueprint for guitar-based alternative rock in the 90s.

The Stone Roses—The Stone Roses (1989)

The Stone Roses started making records as far back as 1985, but it wasn't until 1989 that conditions were absolutely perfect for them. In the late 80s, Manchester had one of the hottest music scenes in England. Young people had embraced the new rave culture complete with baggy trousers, flowery T-shirts and "E," the new drug of choice. Part of that culture was a semi-psychedelic, 60s-ish sounding dance music practiced by three local bands: the Happy Mondays, the Inspiral Carpets and the Stone Roses. To everyone who thought that punk was too negative, the "Madchester" sound was perfect: uplifting, inspiring, anthemic. After building a solid local following, the Stone Roses issued their self-titled debut album on an indie called Silvertone (with whom the band would later have serious legal disputes). Not only did the album bring "Madchester" to a boil, it also set the stage for much of the Britpop (Oasis, Blur, Elastica) of the 90s.

S*M*A*S*H*—The Offspring (1994)

By the time they got around to issuing S*M*A*S*H* in 1994, the Offspring had already released two other albums, neither of which sold very well beyond the confines of Orange County. The third record was a different story. Artistically, it was very representative of what was happening in the California hardcore scene:

loud, fast and melodic songs with lyrics featuring basic concerns. Commercially, however, *S*M*A*S*H* became unlike anything the indie world had ever seen. After "Come Out and Play" received some local radio airplay, Epitaph's $5,000 gamble on making a video paid off when the clip was picked up by MTV. From there, sales increased exponentially, eventually reaching somewhere close to 10 million copies, making *S*M*A*S*H* the biggest-selling independent album of all time. That alone makes it one of the most important indie records in history.

The History of Bootleg Recordings

Coveted by collectors and reviled by the music industry, the manufacture and distribution of bootleg recordings is a multibillion-dollar venture that extends around the world. Sold on CD, cassette and vinyl (and now often over the Internet), bootlegs feature unreleased material recorded at concerts, studio outtakes, radio broadcasts and TV shows. The U.S. record industry maintains that bootleg recordings cost them $300 million a year, while Canadian officials complain about an annual loss of another $10 million.

First, a little clarification. Bootlegs are just one of three types of illegal recordings that the music industry would like to see stamped out. A *counterfeit* album is a knock-off of a legitimately released album. It looks like the real thing, but just like a counterfeited $20 bill made with a high-end laser copier, it's a fake. A *pirate* album is similar to a counterfeit, except that whoever made it didn't even bother to make it look like the real thing. Save for the person or organization operating these rackets, no one makes money from these CDs and tapes—not the artist, the record label or the music publisher.

Unfortunately for the legitimate music industry, most counterfeits and pirates originate in parts of the world where it's almost impossible to win a conviction. Bulgaria, the former Yugoslavia and Poland (where up to 90 percent of the cassettes sold are pirated) are home to many counterfeiters and pirates, some of whom find ways to export their product. Despite pressure from the United States and other western governments, factories in China continue to churn out CDs and cassettes that feature not only stolen music, but also very expensive computer software. The problem is complicated further by the fact that there are elements of organized crime involved in manufacturing and distributing this blatantly illegal material. There was even a British newspaper report in the summer of 1994 that alleged profits from the sales of bootleg and pirate records were being used to buy weapons for the Irish Republican Army.

Bootlegs are another matter. These are recordings (or collections of recordings) that were never authorized or intended to be released to the general public. Most bootleg releases come out of western European countries like Italy, Germany, Belgium and Luxembourg, while a lesser number originate in Australia and Japan. Unlike counterfeits and pirates, some gray areas on the fringe of international copyright law give some bootleg labels some legal room to maneuver. This means that while an Italian CD featuring an unreleased live performance by Nirvana may be illegal in the U.S. or Canada, it may be sold legally in Rome because of the peculiarities of Italian copyright law.

Bootleg labels come in a variety of sizes. Some have been around for years while others last no more than a few weeks. Other companies have to keep moving in order to stay ahead of the law, popping up now and then under different names. Bootleg titles can be pressed in runs of as little as several hundred or as many as several thousand, depending on the material and the company; however, most CD titles are manufactured in runs of 500 or a thousand. While there's no doubt that 99 percent of these companies do not pay any royalties to the artists or to the performer's record label, some do pay fees to music publishers.

The word *bootleg* comes from the late nineteenth century. In order to smuggle illegal home brew from place to place, moonshiners would often stick a bottle in the leg of their boot. But bootlegging was a problem long before the days of temperance unions and prohibition. Back in Shakespeare's day, unscrupulous printers would distribute pamphlets featuring his plays without first receiving the bard's permission. In 1619, a printer named Thomas Pavier leaked some early drafts of *King Lear* and *Richard III*—the seventeenth century equivalent of issuing an unreleased demo recording of a song by the Smashing Pumpkins. Antics like this forced the English parliament to pass the first copyright laws in 1719. With more and more printing presses coming on line every day and with more people learning to read, writers lobbied for some kind of law that regulated the "right to copy" their work.

Copyright protection for sound recordings was a different story. Although a 1906 British act covered material that had been committed to disk or cylinder, the United States Congress had a hard time getting its act together. And while there were many attempts at copyright reform, the U.S. spent decades trying to work things out.

The father of the musical bootleg recording was probably Lionel Mapleson, the librarian at the Metropolitan Opera in New York. Thomas Edison gave him one of his "talking machine recorders" somewhere around the turn of the century and, between 1901 and 1903, Mapleson surreptitiously made hundreds of wax cylinder recordings from his perch in the loft above the stage. His recordings soon became immensely important from a historical point of view, because they featured some of the last performances of the legendary tenor Enrico Caruso (who, by the way, had a legitimate recording deal with the Victor Talking Machine label, a company owned by Edison's rival Emile Berliner). Mapleson's cylinders, and those made by other music fans, quickly became highly-prized collectibles among classical music fans.

Through the 30s, 40s and 50s, jazz fans started making their own recordings. Using primitive acetate recorders, ancient wire recordings and early reel-to-reel tape machines, fans, club owners and music journalists set up their equipment in clubs to capture performances from such legends as Louis Armstrong. Ironically, if it hadn't been for these bootlegs, some of these important jazz performances would have been lost forever. And, as the use of sound equipment spread and the popularity of the home hi-fi grew, hardcore music fans began to trade copies of radio broadcasts, movie soundtracks and even the odd TV performance.

As for rock 'n' roll, no one seemed to be interested. The big market was in underground jazz and classical recordings. But that all changed on September 11, 1969, when a Bob Dylan double album called *Great White Wonder* began to turn up in Los Angeles. Two enterprising hippies had somehow acquired some unreleased Dylan tapes from 1961 and 1967 and found someone willing to press them onto vinyl. The era of the modern bootleg had begun.

Bootlegs have come a long way since then. The cheap white sleeves and photocopied liner notes have been replaced by full-color artwork. The first bootleg on compact disk appeared in 1987, and these days the CD is the bootlegger's format of choice. By the mid-90s, demand often outstripped supply for bootlegs featuring Tori Amos, Nine Inch Nails, the Cure, Smashing Pumpkins and Oasis. Some artists vehemently oppose bootlegs of their work, while others tolerate it to a degree, realizing that being bootlegged is a form of flattery. Some artists actually encourage it, setting up "taping sections" at their concerts.

Bootlegs can be broken down into several categories. The most common of all is the *audience recording*. Someone sneaks a tape recorder (quite often a high-end portable DAT machine) into a concert, finds a good spot in front of the PA and hits the "record" button. Because of the way they're made, the quality of audience recordings can vary sharply. Sometimes the final product is loud and clear and maybe even in stereo. On other occasions, the recording is muffled and thin with the crowd noise often drowning out the music.

Soundboard recordings are tapes made at the PA mixing console in the back of the venue. Many groups record each of their performances by arranging for the PA technician to pop in a cassette or a DAT at the start of every show. Again, the quality may vary but usually the result is a clear, well-balanced stereo recording featuring a minimum of crowd noise. Eddie Vedder (who once confessed to making his own bootleg by smuggling a tape machine into a 1993 Pete Townsend show) insists that all Pearl Jam performances be taped at the soundboard. Is there any wonder that there are close to 200 Pearl Jam boots out there? Soundboard recordings may also come from good-quality TV and FM radio broadcasts, such as the widely-traded 1977 Elvis Costello performance at the El Mocambo in Toronto, now available as a legitimate release as part of the *2 1/2 Years* boxed set.

The third type of bootleg is the *studio outtake*. These are studio recordings that have never been formally released by a band or their label. Bootlegs made from outtakes can consist of demo versions of well-known songs, alternate mixes and songs that were for some reason declared junk and not worthy of release. This is the material most coveted by collectors, since it can give additional insight into their favorite performers. Artists, on the other hand, often hate for anyone to hear what they may consider substandard and occasionally embarrassing material. Some studio outtake boots also feature bonus tracks that were only released in selected parts of the world, and limited edition singles, intended only for members of a group's official fan club.

The routes this material takes in getting to the bootlegger are almost as varied as the material itself. Audience tapes are copied and traded until a good quality copy reaches someone willing to mass produce it on cassette or CD. Roadies give soundboard tapes to their families and friends. There have been cases where people have found raw tapes in the glove compartment of a car in for service at the garage; copies were made before the owner returned. There are stories about recording studios going out of business, throwing away reels and reels of old master tapes from their vaults and allowing anyone to dumpster-dive for treasure. A five-disk bootleg set called *The New U2: Rehearsal and Full Versions* turned up in Germany in 1991, long before the *Achtung Baby* album was released. Those disks were allegedly made from cassettes that the band left behind in the garbage can of their Berlin hotel room. U2 was stung again in late 1996 and early 1997 when material from the *Pop* album leaked all over the Internet. Other tapes are just plain stolen. They disappear from recording studios, from personal collections, and from the archives of major networks.

Governments have always been slow to plug the loopholes that make bootleg records possible. The United States didn't declare bootlegs to be illegal until February 15, 1972, almost three years after that first Dylan bootleg hit the streets. However, the U.S., Canada and Britain have gradually taken a tougher stance on illegal sound recordings, amending their laws to make it more difficult for bootleggers to conduct business. For example, an anti-bootleg amendment to the Canadian Copyright Act came into effect on January 1, 1996, making it illegal for any person to make an unauthorized domestic or imported recording of a performance, or to distribute or sell copies of bootleg recordings. Anyone caught breaking this law can be sued by the owner of the copyright and criminally prosecuted, with a maximum penalty of $1 million or five years in jail— or both. On July 26, 1995, U.S. Customs seized $100,000 worth of illegal CDs in New York; a second raid in August 1995 uncovered a stash worth more than a million dollars. On March 27, 1997, a sting operation by U.S. federal agents in Orlando resulted in the seizure of more than 800,000 boots and the arrest of 13 employees of well-established overseas bootleg operations, including the San Marino-based Kiss the Stone, one of the largest and most sophisticated bootleg labels. If convicted on a variety of copyright infringement charges, the punishment could be up to 35 years in prison.

Meanwhile, individuals continue to purchase bootlegs—or "live imports" as they are sometimes euphemistically called—through the mail or from stores who dare to keep a supply under the counter for special customers. Fans also trade tapes and CDs through fan clubs and over the Internet. However, as governments around the world continue to crack down on bootleg operations and illegal pressing plants in countries like China, supplies of actual CDs and tapes will continue to tighten, forcing more collectors to turn to the Internet. Sites featuring decent quality recordings pop up and disappear almost daily. As more band width and speed become available, the Internet will no doubt become a haven for bootleggers.

Judging a Record by its Cover: Album Artwork

Album artwork is almost as old as sound recordings themselves. The first commercially available disks and cylinders were wrapped in sleeves to identify their contents. As the market for pre-recorded music grew through the first decades of the twentieth century, album artwork evolved into a bona fide art form as more and more records had to compete for attention in the stores.

The first color record jackets appeared during World War II. By the late 50s and early 60s, the plain brown wrapper had given way to portraits and mug shots of the artists. As the 60s progressed, artwork concepts became more ambitious and more concerned with reflecting (and in some cases, creating) a specific image for the performer, a trend perhaps best exemplified by the famous Beatles' *Sgt. Pepper's Lonely Hearts Club Band* album and the anti-image of the *White* album.

From that point on, album art exploded, spawning specialists such as Roger Dean and Hipgnosis. When punk came along in the mid-70s, the new musical aesthetic extended to the artwork which adorned 7-inch sleeves and album jackets. These days, artwork continues to be an important part of virtually every CD and cassette that's sold.

Here are some unknown, under-reported stories that go along with some well-known album covers.

The Ramones (1976)—The Ramones
The most famous Ramones picture of all time is the one that appeared on the cover of the group's debut album. Photographer Roberta Bayley, the person who took the cover charge at the door of CBGB, had learned to use a camera by taking shots at Ramones gigs. One day, she begged the band to go outside so she could get them to pose leaning up against a brick wall in a nearby vacant lot. So, under duress (they hated having their pictures taken), the group trudged outside and she took the picture.

When it came time for Sire to release the Ramones album, they asked to see all of Bayley's pictures and they loved the "brick wall shot." When the album came out, the cover became a classic and was even chosen by *Rolling Stone* as one of the best 100 album covers of all time. Bayley's net earnings? A very modest $125.

U2:3 (1979), *Boy* (1980) and *War* (1983)—U2
All three releases (along with the video for "Two Hearts Beat As One") featured a young boy named Peter Rowen, the ninth of ten children in a family that lived down the street from Bono. No money exchanged hands for any of those cover shots. Peter was paid with a box of chocolates each time. He's now a photographer's assistant in Dublin and says that he's never owned a copy of any of those records.

Unknown Pleasures (1979)—Joy Division

Chances are that the only people to recognize the graph-like illustration on the cover of Joy Division's debut album were into advanced radio astronomy. The figure is actually 100 consecutive pulses from Pulsar CP1919, otherwise known as the radio source at the center of the Dumb Bell Nebula in the constellation Vulpecula.

Factory Records was determined to take great care with their album artwork, believing that the group's image should extend across all facets of their material. Tony Wilson wanted his label's releases to look and feel better than anything the majors were putting out. Wilson's chief artist was Peter Saville, a young graduate from the Manchester Art College. He believed that album packages should be designed as opposed to decorated, especially when it came to typography and how information was presented—or, in the case of Joy Division, omitted.

The Smiths (1984)—The Smiths

Morrissey has always been very particular about album artwork even when the Smiths were just starting out. He wants every picture to reflect some of his personal concerns, desires and even obsessions.

The first Smiths album featured a shot from an underground Andy Warhol movie called *Flesh*. The actor in the picture is Joe Dallessadro who played the role of a male homosexual prostitute. Another Smiths release was withdrawn because the artwork featured actor Terrance Stamp who objected to the use of his image. The sleeve for the "What Difference Does It Make" release consisted of a still from the actor's 1965 movie *The Collector*. The single was eventually reissued with Morrissey striking a similar pose.

Nothing's Shocking (1988), *Ritual de lo Habitual* (1990) and *Porno for Pyros* (1993)—Perry Farrell

Like Morrissey, Perry Farrell demands complete control over the artwork that adorns any of his projects. In fact, one of the reasons Jane's Addiction signed with Warner Brothers in the first place was because they guaranteed that Farrell would be in charge of what was on the cover.

"Good taste," Farrell once said, "stifles creativity." This determination to push the edge of the envelope when it came to album artwork was first demonstrated in 1985, when his pre-Jane's group, Psi-Com, issued an EP with a cover featuring an emaciated African woman. Her dead body was superimposed over a sunny background to make it look as though she were dancing. The band referred to the photo as the "dancing anorexic."

The cover of *Nothing's Shocking* was another Perry Farrell original. It featured the sculptured naked double image of Casey Niccoli, Perry's girlfriend, as Siamese twins with heads on fire. Perry says the image came to him in a dream.

Ritual de lo Habitual featured the sculpture that Farrell had hanging on the wall of his apartment (his landlady hated it so much that she had him evicted). It was the intertwined nude images of Farrell, Casey and a mutual friend named Xiola Blue. Not only were the executives at Warner Brothers offended, but a record store in Michigan was charged with obscenity for displaying a poster for the album in the window. Once incidents like that started piling up (and when giants like Wal-Mart refused to stock the album), a compromise was worked out. Warner Brothers continued to issue the album with the original artwork, but they also provided a version featuring a plain white cover with nothing more than a "parental advisory" sticker and the First Amendment of the U.S. Constitution, the section dealing with free speech.

The cover of the first Porno for Pyros album also threatened to create some serious controversy. Before the record was released, Farrell announced that the artwork would feature a *yantra*, an ancient Indian symbol that looks very much as if it combines the Jowish Star of David with a swastika. To avoid the inevitable firestorm, Farrell was talked out of the concept and the symbol never appeared. The substitute cover featured another sculpture of a devil riding a rocket ship. The sculpture was later destroyed when Farrell affixed it to a real rocket and launched it out of his back yard. It didn't go very far; it came down on his house, setting it on fire.

Pretty Hate Machine (1989) and The Downward Spiral (1994)—Nine Inch Nails
The cover of *Pretty Hate Machine* was created by a company called Föhn Design. Photographer Gary Talpas, looking for something appropriately menacing, took some shots of a turbine blade and then stretched out the photo to look like bones of a ribcage.

Having admired the work he had done for albums by Brian Eno and David Sylvian, Trent Reznor hired Russell Miles to create something for the cover of his second album. Reznor commissioned a total of four abstract paintings, asking him to capture the decaying, organic concepts of *The Downward Spiral*. He was so pleased with the results that he retained Miles to come up with several new treatments of the Nine Inch Nails logo.

Nevermind—Nirvana (1991)

During the sessions that resulted in *Nevermind*, Kurt Cobain and Dave Grohl saw a TV documentary on babies that were born under water. Kurt mentioned the show to the art director assigned to Nirvana and they began to discuss how to incorporate some of those ideas into the artwork for the album. After some searching, they found a stock photo of a swimming baby—but when the photographer demanded $7,500 a year for every year the album was in print, the decision was made to stage their own photo shoot.

A photographer was hired, five different babies were rounded up and everyone headed for the pool. Five month-old Spencer Eldon of Eagle Rock, California emerged the winner. The fishhook baited with the dollar bill was added later at Kurt Cobain's insistence. Although Geffen wanted to airbrush out Eldon's penis, Cobain demanded that it should stay. For his trouble, Eldon was paid $200.

Everybody Is Doing It, So Why Can't We? (1993) and *No Need to Argue* (1994)—The Cranberries

The first two Cranberries albums featured a simple brown sofa that was rented by the Island Records art department from a local record store for less than £100. The group wanted to carry the theme through to *...to the Faithful Departed*, but the store, realizing that the Cranberries were selling millions of records, wanted more money. Unable to buy the couch outright, that particular visual hook was abandoned.

A Boy Named Goo—The Goo Goo Dolls (1995)

The cover shot, which featured young Carl Gellert covered in goo (blackberry juice), originally appeared in a book of photographs taken by his father, Vance. In the summer of 1996, Wal-Mart announced that they would no longer stock copies of the album (after already selling some 51,000 copies), because some customers had interpreted the blackberry juice as blood (or excrement), connecting the photo with the glorification of child abuse.

Johnny Rzeznick of the Goo Goo Dolls was outraged, calling the photo "no more offensive than a bearskin rug photo of a baby." He asserts that the people who look at the picture and see something obscene are the ones with the problem.

Several other groups have incurred the wrath of Wal-Mart over their artwork. The model on the cover of White Zombie's *Supersexy Swingin' Sounds* was airbrushed with a bikini before Wal-Mart would agree to stock it. Albums from Nirvana, Catherine Wheel, 311, Primitive Radio Gods, Beck and many others have been altered (in terms of artwork and/or content) to suit Wal-Mart's policies.

Electriclarryland—Butthole Surfers (1996)

Having already agreed to change the album's title from *Oklahoma!* (copyright problems), the group ran into further trouble when several American record store chains objected to the cartoon of a pencil being jammed into a guy's ear. In order to get those important chains to take the album, the band's label quickly whipped up an alternate cover featuring an inoffensive prairie dog under the name "B-H Surfers."

Everything ever released by Oasis

There's a story behind every single Oasis cover, thanks to art director Brian Cannon and photographer Michael Spencer Jones. Cannon runs a company called Microdot and Noel Gallagher has been a fan of his work for years.

The shot that appears on the cover of the first album was taken in Bonehead's living room. The Burt Bacharach photo is there because Noel insisted upon it; likewise the picture of Rodney Marsh dressed in the uniform of Oasis' favorite team, Manchester City. And if you look at the TV, you'll see a frame from *The Good, The Bad and The Ugly*, simply because the photographer wanted something on the screen and Bonehead just happened to have a copy of the movie in the house.

Some other explanations:

• *The shot of the "Some Might Say" single features a train station in Cromford, England. The woman with the pots and pans is a local barmaid—and the dog has appeared in movies with Kevin Costner.*

• *The cover of the "Live Forever" single is a picture of John Lennon's house on Menlove Venue in Woolton.*

• *The conventional wisdom is that the woman on the cover of the "Wonderwall" single is Noel Gallagher's wife, Meg Matthews. It is not. The woman's name is Anita Heryet, an employee at Creation Records. The arm holding the frame belongs to Brian Cannon, the man responsible for all Oasis artwork.*

A Basic Guide to Record Collecting

Although less than 1 percent of all new music is sold on vinyl these days, there is still a huge demand for *old* vinyl. This is the domain of the collector, the person who gladly spends hours combing for treasure in used record stores, at garage sales, flea markets and record fairs. Sometimes this patient prospecting can pay off with a find worth hundreds, if not thousands, of dollars.

The basic principles of record collecting are as follows.

1. The value of a rare record is determined by the marketplace.

The obvious tenet here is that the smaller the supply of a given release, the higher the price. However, a rare record is only valuable when someone else is interested in owning it. A one-of-a-kind 12-inch picture disk acetate with a hand-painted color sleeve may be rare, but if it involves an act that no one cares about, it's worthless on the open market.

Promo copies (special editions of records issued to record stores, label reps, radio stations and journalists, but not the general public), DJ copies (special 12-inch singles distributed only to dance club DJs), hard-to-find imports, records released only to members of official fan clubs, records with limited edition runs on colored vinyl and releases with special or ornate packaging are just some of the types of things for which collectors look.

Bootlegs are another matter. Despite the fact that most individual titles are released in very limited numbers, most of the big publications will refuse ads featuring bootlegs due to their general illegal nature and their often 'iffy' quality. Most bootlegs are priced by the seller who will charge as much as much as possible.

2. Prices are sometimes tough to fix.

If a seller can find someone willing to pay $500 for an obscure 12-inch in a private sale, fine. If that same 12-inch is put up for sale on the open collectibles market, the price may be significantly different. This is why serious collectors will consult international price guides published by such magazines as *Goldmine* or *Record Collector*. While not necessarily the last word in prices, these guides give the collector an idea of what an individual record should be worth.

3. The condition of any collectible record is affected by the condition of the record and its packaging.

Collectors and dealers are constantly looking for "near mint" copies of rare records. This means that both the vinyl and the sleeve are in pristine condition. Other records may be graded as "very good," "good," "fair" and "poor." The quality of each individual record obviously affects the price. Contrary to what many people think, it doesn't help if the rare record is still in the original shrink-wrap. It's important that the vinyl be examined for authenticity, because there are many counterfeits on the market passing as the real thing.

4. There is a growing market for collectible compact disks.

Realizing that the supply of new vinyl collectibles is finite, collectors are also looking for rare CDs. The rules for vinyl also apply to CDs.

Ten Collectible Alternative Records

All prices are in U.S. dollars or British pounds as of mid-1997.

1. "This Charming Man" 12-inch (1983)—The Smiths

Rough Trade, determined to break the second Smiths single in the dance clubs, issued four different remixes and distributed them to various DJs across the U.K.: the "New York," the "London," the "Manchester" and an instrumental mix. The 12-inch was a huge hit in the clubs and soon Smiths fans were demanding that they be allowed to buy copies. The label, recognizing a chance to make some money, hastily pressed up some singles and sent them off to the record stores.

In each case, however, they had neglected to consult the Smiths. Morrissey was furious, accusing Rough Trade of corrupting the band's work for the sake of selling a few records. The 12-inch was withdrawn from the stores and the master tapes remained locked up in a vault somewhere. Naturally, anyone who owned one of those withdrawn records found themselves being envied by other Smiths fans. The price of the "This Charming Man" 12-inch went way up before stabilizing at between $20 and $50, following the limited edition release of all the remixes on CD in the early 90s.

2. *Screaming Life* (1987)—Soundgarden

Back in the days when Soundgarden was signed to Sub Pop, the label was into gimmicks such as releasing records on colored vinyl. The company released the first 500 copies of their *Screaming Life* EP on gaudy orange vinyl. A near mint copy has been valued at $150. Other colors of the EP are worth substantially less.

3. "Radio Free Europe" (1981)—REM

On April 15, 1981, one year and one week after REM played their first gig at that old church in Athens, Georgia, they recorded three songs at the Drive-In Studio in Winston-Salem, North Carolina. Four hundred copies (featuring "Radio Free Europe" b/w "Sitting Still") were pressed up on the band's own Hib-Tone label and sent off to various labels and college radio stations. In July, a new edition of the single was pressed up and released to the general public. Sharp-eyed REM were able to tell the two apart by looking for the address of Hib-Tone on the label. If it's missing, it's a copy of the original batch of 400. One of those 7-inch singles are worth around $150. This original version of "Radio Free Europe" was made available on CD with the release of REM's 1988 album *Eponymous*.

4. "Love Buzz" (1988)—Nirvana

Nirvana's cover of an old Shocking Blue song (b/w the Kurt Cobain original "Big Cheese") was the first single issued by the Sub Pop Singles Club. When it was released on October 10, 1988, there were just 1,000 hand-numbered copies available exclusively to people on the club's mailing list. Once Nirvana hit it big, the value of this debut single went way up. In fact, demand increased to the point where it also became one of the most counterfeited alternative singles in history, with at least one European and two American fakes surfacing over the years.

An authentic copy of the "Love Buzz" single can be recognized by the following characteristics:
- *The names ALICE WHEELER and SUZANNE SASIC must be on the picture sleeve.*
- *All covers are hand-numbered with a narrow red felt pen with all the numbers leaning slightly to the left (Kurt Cobain was left-handed).*
- *The run-off groove reads "SP-23-A Why Don't You Trade Those Guitars For Shovels? L-31540" in letters that are 2mm high. Side B features the numbers "SP-23-B L-31540X"*
- *The word "Kdisc" is stamped very lightly into the run-off grooves on both sides.*

Prices for an authentic copy of "Love Buzz" range from $150 to $700. The song can be found on Nirvana's *Bleach* album.

5. "Final Solution" (1976)—Pere Ubu
Underground pioneers Pere Ubu released 600 copies of their second single ("Final Solution" b/w "Cloud 149") with a special picture sleeve. Collectors have been known to pay up to $175 for a copy in near mint condition.

6. "Touch Me I'm Sick" (1988)—Mudhoney
Mudhoney received a colored vinyl treatment from Sub Pop similar to that given to Soundgarden for their *Screaming Life* EP—except this time it was an accident. Collectors are interested in the red, yellow, purple or blue pressings manufactured in very small quantities. A near mint of one of these ultra-rare versions (perhaps 200 copies exist) of "Touch Me I'm Sick" b/w "Sweet Young Thing" may fetch up to $200 on the open market.

7. "Baltimore" (1980)—Tori Amos
Back in the fall of 1980, diehard Baltimore Orioles fan Tori Amos recorded a tribute to her favorite team with her brother Michael. She sang and played keyboards while Michael handled some of the other instrumentation. Booking a few hours of studio time, they recorded "Baltimore" and "Walking With You" and released it (perhaps a thousand copies) on Tori's MEA Records (after Tori's real name: Myra Ellen Amos). It was a 7-inch single with an orange label giving writing credit to Ellen Amos and co-writing credit to Michael Amos.

The single made the rounds through Baltimore and attracted a fair amount of local attention before it faded away. A dozen years later, hardcore Tori Amos fans were frantically searching for one of those long-lost copies of "Baltimore." Although it has turned up on several CD bootlegs over the past few years, a pristine copy of the original 7-inch is still worth a minimum of $500.

8. "God Save the Queen" (1977)—Sex Pistols

After the Sex Pistols were jettisoned by EMI in early 1977, A&M thought that they were interested in England's most notorious punk band. Despite a high-profile signing ceremony at the gates of Buckingham Palace and a promise to release "God Save the Queen," the band's next single, the Sex Pistols' relationship with A&M lasted only six days. A fiery backlash from both A&M stockholders and other acts on the label forced the company to exercise a clause in the contract that released the Pistols from all obligations in return for £75,000.

Meanwhile, an order had already been sent to the pressing plant for 25,000 copies of "God Save the Queen." But once the contract was canceled, another call went out ordering the destruction of all the 7-inch singles that had been pressed to that point. The normal procedure in a case like this is to immediately melt down all the records, since the label no longer had any legal right to the single. They were morally, ethically and legally obligated to got rid of all 25,000 copies.

Apparently, someone realized that they might have potential collector's items on their hands. An undetermined number of copies (perhaps a few hundred) were spirited out of the warehouse by persons unknown. Today, a copy of "God Save the Queen" on the A&M label is worth a minimum of £1000.

9. *Diamond Dogs* (1974)—David Bowie

David Bowie is probably the alt-rock performer with the greatest number of collectible records. Prices range from $2 or less for a mint copy of the 1984 "Blue Jean" 7-inch on blue vinyl to the $500 plus often quoted for the unusual 7-inch sampler that came out just before the *Scary Monsters* album in 1980. But the Holy Grail of Bowie collectibles is a copy of *Diamond Dogs* that features the original—and very controversial—artwork.

When the cover was commissioned, Dutch artist Neil Peelaert came up with a painting portraying Bowie as half-man (the front of the jacket) and half-dog (on the back). What concerned the executives at RCA was that the dog half was anatomically correct, complete with the requisite doggy genitalia. Having already been stung by the *Man Who Sold the World* cover (featuring—gasp!—Bowie in a dress), RCA demanded that the offending naughty bits be airbrushed out and that any existing copies of the still-unreleased album featuring the artwork be destroyed.

However, Bowie was already a huge star by 1974 and somehow, an unknown number of albums (certainly *very* few) featuring the un-airbrushed painting survived. Connoisseurs have been known to pay $4,000 or more for an authentic copy. In 1990, RykoDisc re-issued *Diamond Dogs* on CD, complete with the original Peelaert painting (naughty bits restored).

10. "All Tomorrow's Parties" (1966)—The Velvet Underground

In 1966, the Velvet Underground was part of Andy Warhol's crowd, providing music for his parties, art showings and experimental films. Warhol also acted as the band's producer for their debut album, *The Velvet Underground and Nico*, which came out on the Verve label. Verve released "All Tomorrow's Parties" in several forms in very limited runs and a copy in excellent condition may fetch up to $500 on the open market.

There is, however, one extraordinarily special copy. The record itself isn't such a big deal—but the picture sleeve features a hand-painted Andy Warhol original of all four members of the band. Only one such sleeve exists and has a *minimum* value of $5,000. The person who bought it in 1992 has been offered many, many, *many* times that amount since then.

A Brief History of Music Videos

For centuries, humankind has sought to add visual elements to music through such mediums as dance, opera and musical theater. The invention of film in the late 1800s brought a new dimension to this marriage when musical scores were composed to complement the action on the screen. In the 1920s, Oskar Fischinger produced short experimental films featuring abstract shapes and images dancing to jazz and classical music. These films eventually led to his work on that landmark of animation and music, *Fantasia*, produced by Disney in 1940.

In the late 1940s, the coin-operated Panoram Soundie, a type of video jukebox, was introduced. Weighing up to two tons each, the machines displayed a short black-and-white film on a 20-inch screen that was synched up with a popular song of the day, for the price of a nickel. More than 2,000 Soundie films were produced, featuring everything from clips of Hollywood musicals to performances from jazz greats like Louis Armstrong and Cab Calloway. Unfortunately, each Soundie machine was capable of holding just one film. This meant that if the owner of a club or lounge wanted to offer his customers a series of Soundie films, he had to have a series of machines.

By the late 50s and early 60s, a French company introduced the Scopitone, a 1,500 pound video jukebox capable of storing up to 36 different 16mm films and playing them back on a 20-inch screen. Although hundreds of artists shot Scopitone clips (including Nancy Sinatra and Procol Harum), each film cost the operator more than $100 each and the machines were expensive to repair. By 1967, the Scopitone had all but completely disappeared.

Meanwhile, television had become an important part of the equation as a growing TV audience became more and more accustomed to having musical performances delivered directly to their homes. It also didn't take long for managers and record companies to realize that programs such as *The Ed Sullivan Show, American Bandstand* and *Top of the Pops* could be exploited as powerful promotional tools. By the mid-60s, the Beatles (along with the made-for-TV group *The Monkees*) were proving that film and music could be combined in interesting and profitable ways with full-length features like *A Hard Day's Night, Help!* and *Yellow Submarine*, and experimental clips and short films for "Strawberry Fields" and *Magical Mystery Tour*.

In the early 70s, Warner Brothers records had adopted the practice of creating short promotional films, designed to showcase the label's new releases, for retailers. Other short films were commissioned so that various branches of the company could become familiar with all of the label's current products. Directors were given up to half a million dollars to produce clips, featuring up to 60 artists, which were then compiled on 90-minute reels for screening at sales meetings around the world. When shooting schedules didn't allow for the artists to be included in their clips, a quick conceptual piece would be substituted. In rare cases, the artists themselves would be consulted.

Meanwhile, some artists had begun to make promotional videos for themselves. Captain Beefheart created an unreleased one-minute piece for *Lick My Decals Off, Baby* in 1971. The Residents experimented with film and video as early as 1972, while Devo was investing money in video by 1975.

In the mid-70s, some directors made a good living at directing music videos. Bruce Gowers was one of the first, creating videos for Rod Stewart and Genesis before achieving a huge commercial breakthrough with Queen. His $7,000 1975 promo clip for "Bohemian Rhapsody" was so successful in introducing the group to the marketplace that, suddenly, everyone wanted to make videos.

Although dozens of videos were shot (usually with a budget of $10,000 or less), outside of a few TV shows and the odd club or bar willing to invest in expensive video equipment, there were few places where the public could view these clips. It wasn't until cable TV came along that videos found a permanent home. To anxious cable systems in cities like New York and San Francisco, music videos became an inexpensive way to fill airtime on some of the new channels.

The music video hit the big time at exactly 12:01 a.m. EDT, on August 1, 1981, when MTV (a co-project of Warner Brothers and American Express) debuted on cable systems and satellite dishes across North America. Starting with "Video Killed the Radio Star" by the Buggles (an appropriate choice), the network flogged their library of 250 videos until all record labels realized the promotional value of the medium and began to produce clips on a regular basis.

By the early 90s, not only had MTV's reach extended across the world, spreading music and North American culture to all corners of the globe, but other video channels such as MuchMusic and The Box had signed on. These days, outside of a few anti-video acts like the Replacements and Pearl Jam, the music video is considered to be an essential marketing tool, no matter what the music.

Eleven Acclaimed Music Video Directors

With the explosion in music video production that began in the early 80s, dozens of directors specializing in this particular form of filmed entertainment have emerged as stars. Here are just a few of them.

1. Sam Bayer
Although he's worked with a number of clients, Bayer will always be remembered for three very popular clips. The first was his visual interpretation of Nirvana's "Smells Like Teen Spirit," the clip that landed grunge on MTV. Filmed in Culver City, California, on a soundstage designed to look like a high school gym (and featuring the real janitor from Bayer's apartment building), the video was shot for $33,000. Bayer fought with Kurt Cobain over direction and had trouble controlling the unruly audience for the entire shoot. There was also the matter of bassist Krist Novoselic, who allegedly passed out drunk about halfway through the day. In the end, the final edit was supervised by Cobain. Bayer's two other big clips were Hole's "Doll Parts" and Blind Melon's "No Rain," featuring the infamous "Bee Girl."

2. Peter Christopherson

As Trent Reznor's director of choice for three songs from the *Broken* EP ("Pinion," "Wish" and "March of the Pigs"), Christopherson's quick cuts, elaborate sets and shocking images helped establish Nine Inch Nails as one of the most intense acts in the world. Christopherson also worked with Reznor on the infamous *Broken* movie which features a hostage being forced to watch NIN videos, while being tortured and ultimately killed by a masked captor. Designed to look like a genuine snuff film, the final cut was considered to be too intense and was never released. Some bootleg copies exist.

3. Anton Corbijn

Since leaving his job as a freelance photographer for the *NME*, this Dutch-born artist's work has made him the still photographer of choice for some of the biggest names in music. Along with shooting album cover photos for U2's *The Joshua Tree*, creating portraits for REM and designing stage sets for Depeche Mode, Corbijn has directed a number of impressive music videos since the mid-80s, including "Barrel of a Gun" and "It's No Good" for Depeche Mode, and the surreal "Heart-Shaped Box," Nirvana's last clip.

4. Steve Hanft

Aquainted with this independent filmmaker for years, Beck asked Hanft to take time out from working on his indie film, *Kill the Moonlight*, to direct the clip for Beck's breakthrough single "Loser." Few people realize that the line in "Loser" that goes "I'm a driver/I'm a winner/Things are gonna change/I can feel it" was sampled directly from this movie. (*Kill the Moonlight* was finally realized in the summer of 1997). Hanft was also enlisted to direct the "Where It's At" video.

5. Spike Jonze

Born Adam Spiegel (the same family that founded the famous Spiegel catalogue), Spike spent his early years riding his skateboards and BMX bikes. Venturing into publishing with an advance on his sizable inheritance, he co-founded a BMX racing magazine called *Freestylin'* and later *Dirt*, a teen boy's equivalent of *Sassy*.

Although Spike was mainly a still photographer, a well-connected friend asked him to shoot some skateboard footage for Sonic Youth's "100%" video, directed by Tamra Davis, the wife of Mike D of the Beastie Boys. Mike was so impressed by his work that he asked Spike to direct the video for the next Beastie Boys single. After sitting down with the band to watch a lot of cop shows from the 70s, they shot the clip for "Sabotage" in just two days. The success of that clip instantly established Spike as a superstar director in the world of alternative music. Next came the Happy Days-theme "Buddy Holly" video for Weezer which—although it came in thousands of dollars over budget—proved to be so popular that it practically doubled the sales of the band's debut album. Other bands to benefit from Spike's touch (and the $100,000 budgets he often receives) include Bjork ("It's So Quiet"), the Breeders, Dinosaur Jr. and REM (he directed the Japanese karaoke kids in "Crush with Eyeliner"). Meanwhile, Spike and his company, Satellite Productions, have also shot high-profile TV commercials for clients such as Coors, Nike, Nintendo and the much-talked about "Tainted Love" operating room ad for Levi's.

6. Russell Mulcahy
Mulcahy was behind the camera for a series of videos from Duran Duran's *Rio* album in 1982. Armed with a budget of $200,000 (an outlandish sum at the time), everyone flew to Sri Lanka to shoot footage that would portray the band as sexy playboys, an image their label thought would help sales. In terms of cinematography and general production values, no one had ever seen music videos as polished or as professional as "Hungry Like the Wolf" and "Rio." They caused a sensation, not only in the offices of MTV, but with audiences as well. Some record stores were selling out of Duran Duran records on the basis of MTV's screening of the videos alone. Mulcahy's *Rio* videos set a new standard for the art form and, from the summer of 1982 on, music video budgets increased and the overall quality improved.

7. Mark Pellington
Mark Pellington has gone down in history as one of the few people to ever direct a video for Pearl Jam. When it came time to release the third single from *Ten*, Pellington decided to go the conceptual route rather than shoot another straightforward performance clip. The final product for the song "Jeremy" featured a head shot of a sinister-looking Eddie Vedder between images of a young man being bullied at school and fighting with this parents. When the band saw the final cut, they dismissed it as too artsy and too expensive. The final nail in the coffin was when Mark Eitzel of American Music Club (someone Vedder held in high esteem) offered the opinion that the video was terrible and that it ruined his vision of the song. At the same time, MTV loved the clip, placing it into high rotation and giving it several awards. Despite the commercial success attributable to the clip (it helped push *Ten* into multi-platinum territory) Pearl Jam would film just one more video (for "Ocean") before declaring a personal boycott of the medium.

8. Jesse Peretz
Son of *New Republic* magazine owner Martin Peretz, Jesse Peretz started in the music industry alongside Evan Dando, playing bass in the Lemonheads. Putting his film studies work at Harvard to use, Peretz directed his first video in 1989 when he was put in charge of the Lemonheads' "Mallo Cup" clip. He left the band in 1991 to

pursue a career as a filmmaker, but continued to work with the group, directing five more videos. That led to directing jobs for Helmet, the Breeders, Nada Surf and the very funny "Big Me" clip for the Foo Fighters. Peretz was also responsible for the Jimmy McBride cab driver promos for MTV. Like Spike Jonze, Peretz received offers from several studios to direct full-length feature films.

9. Mark Romanek
When he was looking for someone to direct the videos for *The Downward Spiral,* Trent Reznor asked Mark Romanek to come up with something appropriately intense and disturbing. Using some vintage film stock from the 1920s, Romanek created a clip that paid homage to the work of photographer Joel-Peter Witkin and featured strange shots of monkeys and crucifixes. MTV cut out several scenes before they would air it. (An uncensored video also exists.) Romanek was also behind the camera for Michael Jackson's $7 million video for "Scream."

10. Floria Sigismondi
Italian-born and the daughter of two opera singers, Sigismondi grew up in Hamilton, Ontario, and graduated from the Ontario College of Art with a degree in photography. She soon found work shooting photos for various Canadian advertisers and magazines, winning several awards along the way. At the suggestion of a friend, Sigismondi began to dabble in video, beginning with a clip for Catherine's "Four Leaf Clover." Another video for a Canadian band called Harem Scarem attracted the attention of Marilyn Manson who hired her to direct the clips for "Beautiful People" and "Tourniquet." The Harem Scarem video also led to a meeting with David Bowie who picked Sigismondi to direct the Ziggy Stardust-esque "Little Wonder" clip.

11. Tarsem
Tarsem Dhandwar Singh was the Indian director, and Harvard MBA dropout, hired by REM to come up with a visual interpretation of "Losing My Religion." The result was a dreamy, semi-religious clip based on such highly intellectual items as the works of Italian painter Caravaggio and director Andrei Tarkovsky. The video was a big part of REM's commercial breakthrough and earned Tarsem six Video Music Awards from MTV. Along with the odd music video, Tarsem has also created commercials for Lee jeans, Levis, Smirnoff Vodka and Anne Klein.

Eleven Examples of Videos That Were Altered or Censored

Video-making is now a fact of life for most performers. But making a video is one thing; getting it played on the network video shows and cable video channels is another.

The biggest player in this equation is MTV, simply because the network's world-wide reach (60 plus countries) gives it such enormous influence and power in the areas of music, fashion and attitude. In other words, if you want to make it big on a global scale, it's almost essential that your video be shown on MTV. And if you want MTV to show your clip, it had better conform to their standards—or else.

Other networks around the world (for example MuchMusic in Canada, MCM in France, Viva in Germany, Z-TV in Sweden, ATV and the BBC in Britain) have similar policies. Here are just a few examples of videos that had to be altered or which have been banned outright.

1. "Da Da Da"—Trio
Some video channels and programs refused this video because the clip features a woman getting stabbed in the back.

2. "Two Tribes"—Frankie Goes to Hollywood
Although BBC radio played the song, the video (directed by Kevin Godley and Lol Creme and featuring a brawl between Ronald Reagan and Konstantin Chernenko look-alikes in a cockfighting ring) was banned by BBC-TV, due to its violent nature.

3. "Closer"—Nine Inch Nails
The monkeys and the crucifixes were too much for the sensibilities of MTV and other video channels around the world. Many channels chose to show an altered version of the clip that featured "scene missing" title cards in place of the offending shots.

4. "Scooby Snacks"—Fun Lovin' Criminals
Because MTV has a policy about refusing to air videos that have anything to do with guns and gun imagery, the word "whacked" had to be edited out of the chorus of "Scooby Snacks" before the network agreed to add the clip to its rotation.

5. "That's When I Reach For My Revolver"—Moby
Moby ran into a similar problem when he presented MTV with the clip featuring his cover of this Mission of Burma classic. The chorus was re-recorded as "That's when I realize it's over." Mission of Burma granted Moby permission to change the lyrics for an appearance on a British TV show but apparently had no idea the edit would be made for an official video.

6. "Love Spreads"—The Stone Roses
The Stone Roses filmed two versions for the first single from their long awaited second album. The first was a concept by the band featuring a collage of images with

one of the members dressed up as the devil. This didn't wash with Geffen (the Roses' American record company which pumped millions into the group during the years it took to record *Second Coming*), because no one could see the band. The video was re-shot so that the audience actually *see* the group for their big introduction into America.

7. "The Ledge"—The Replacements

MTV passed on this clip featuring a young man contemplating suicide on a ledge. The network was worried that some viewers might take the video's sentiments too seriously. Soured by this experience, a series of subsequent videos from the group (directed by Bill Pope and Randy Skinner) featured nothing more than a static shot of a throbbing speaker.

8. "Happiness in Slavery"—Nine Inch Nails

Few people can make it through this video featuring performance artist and S&M aficionado Bill Flanagan. In the video, Flanagan climbs into some kind of torture device that slowly and graphically grinds him into hamburger. Almost no network will touch it.

9. "One"—U2

The more Bono worked on the song, the more he realized that the lyrics could be interpreted as a young man with AIDS speaking with his estranged father. Together with video director Anton Corbijn, U2 came up with a visual concept that featured Bono dressed in drag (a long black gown) addressing his real father. Once the clip was completed, everyone had second thoughts. Due to concerns that some people would take the video to suggest that only gay people can contract the disease, all shots of Bono in the dress were excised from the video.

10. "Pretty Noose"—Soundgarden

Directed by Frank Kozik, the famous concert poster artist, the ending was too heavy for MTV. The original features the camera panning from a shot of a dead woman sprawled under the sheets of a bed to the face of the killer—singer Chris Cornell.

11. "He Liked to Feel It"—Crash Test Dummies

Several video channels were uncomfortable with the clip's premise which featured a kid finding new and interesting ways to pull out his own teeth.

Part 4

Sex, Drugs & R 'n' R: The Artists

Astrological Signs of the Stars

Aries (March 20–April 20)

If you want energy to burn, call an Aries. They are born leaders who love to inspire and motivate others. While they lack subtlety, they are straight shooters who never take no for an answer. Arians can be self-centered and egocentric, while at the same time they can be courageous and competitive.

Damon Albarn (Blur)	March 23	1968
Poe	March 23	1969
Perry Farrell (Porno for Pyros)	March 29	1959
Mike Ness (Social Distortion)	April 3	1962
Stuart Adamson (Big Country)	April 11	1958
Art Alexakis (Everclear)	April 12	1962
Nick Hexum (311)	April 12	1970
Ed O'Brian (Radiohead)	April 15	1968
David Pirner (Soul Asylum)	April 16	1964
Pete Shelley (Buzzcocks)	April 17	1955
Liz Phair	April 17	1967
Maynard John Keenan (Tool)	April 17	1964

Taurus (April 21–May 20)

People born under this star sign are romantics. They are the most sensual of all, which makes sense since the ruling planet is Venus. Besides love, Taureans care about money and often put their creative powers toward making lots of it, frequently in the arts. On the down side, Taureans can be overly materialistic. They don't like change and can be hedonistic and stubborn. Since the Bull is the ruling sign of the throat and vocal chords, it makes sense that Taurus people can be singers and actors.

Robert Smith (The Cure)	April 21	1959
Iggy Pop	April 21	1947
Daniel Johns (Silverchair)	April 22	1976
Kim Gordon (Sonic Youth)	April 28	1953
Dave Gahan (Depeche Mode)	May 9	1962
Bono (U2)	May 10	1960
Sid Vicious (Sex Pistols)	May 10	1957
Richard Patrick (Filter)	May10	1968
Greg Dulli (Afghan Whigs)	May 11	1965
Andrew Eldritch (Sisters Of Mercy)	May 15	1959
Trent Reznor (Nine Inch Nails)	May 17	1965
Joey Ramone (Ramones)	May 19	1951

Gemini (May 21–June 20)

Don't try to pin down a Gemini. They are constantly on the move, if only mentally, analyzing life and their place in it. They are highly intelligent and can't ingest enough information. Gemini people are very vital and curious and always ask "why." They have a short attention span and surround themselves with interesting people and places. If you can pin Geminis down, you will find them witty, intelligent and verbal, as well as unfocused, fickle and nervous. People born under this sign are attracted to work with words.

Kevin Shields (My Bloody Valentine)	May 21	1963
Morrissey	May 22	1959
Jerry Dammers (The Specials)	May 22	1954
Paul Weller (The Jam)	May 25	1958
Lenny Kravitz	May 26	1964
Siouxsie Sioux	May 27	1958
Tim Burgess (Charlatans UK)	May 30	1967
Bill Janovitz (Buffalo Tom)	June 3	1966
Gordon Gano (Violent Femmes)	June 7	1963
Dave Navarro (Red Hot Chili Peppers)	June 7	1967

Cancer (June 21–July 22)

Cancer is the sign of homebodies. People born under this sign have strong roots and often take refuge in memories of childhood. They can be nostalgic and sentimental and because of that, often sensitive and nurturing. But Cancers can also be moody and clinging, overbearing and dependent.

Bobby Gillespie (Primal Scream)	June 22	1961
Mick Jones (Clash/Big Audio Dynamite)	June 26	1955
Tom Drummond (Better Than Ezra)	June 30	1969
Chris Cornell (Soundgarden)	July 7	1964
Beck	July 8	1970
Courtney Love (Hole)	July 9	1964
Kim Deal (Pixies/Breeders/Amps)	July 10	1961
Peter Murphy (Bauhaus)	July 11	1957
Tanya Donelly (Belly)	July 14	1966
Ian Curtis (Joy Division)	July 15	1956
Edward Kowalcyk (Live)	July 16	1971

Leo (July 23—August 23)

Just as the lion is king of the jungle, Leos believe themselves to be rulers; they can be very egocentric and self-important. However, mature Leos can also be powerful and generous. As friends, you will find them warm and affectionate, but they can also get on your nerves with their vain posturing and arrogance. As they are incredibly creative, Leos gravitate toward jobs in the arts.

Martin Gore (Depeche Mode)	July 23	1961
Thurston Moore (Sonic Youth)	July 25	1958
Kate Bush	July 30	1958
Bill Berry (REM)	July 31	1958
Suzy Garner (L7)	August 1	1960
Ed Roland (Collective Soul)	August 3	1963
Adam Yauch (Beastie Boys)	August 5	1964
Jennifer Finch (L7)	August 5	1966
Kristen Hersh (Throwing Muses)	August 7	1966
The Edge (U2)	August 7	1961
Layne Staley (Alice In Chains)	August 22	1967
Tori Amos	August 22	1963

Virgo (August 24—September 22)

You rarely meet a lazy Virgo. They believe that success comes from hard work and are willing to do what is necessary to be financially secure. Sometimes, that makes Virgos a little job obsessed. Other times they can be preoccupied with material wealth. People born under this star sign are organized, dependable and meticulous. They can also be prudish and opinionated. Virgos tend to gravitate toward jobs where they can use their minds, like accounting, medicine, and science.

Elvis Costello	August 25	1954
Doug McCarthy (Nitzer Ebb)	September 1	1966
Grant Lee Phillips (Grant Lee Buffalo)	September 1	1963
Dolores O'Riordan (Cranberries)	September 7	1971
Chrissie Hynde (Pretenders)	September 7	1951
Moby	September 11	1965
Daniel Lanois	September 19	1951
Nick Cave	September 22	1957
Matt Sharp (Weezer/Rentals)	September 22	1968

Libra (September 23—October 23)

Librans crave harmony above all else. They love peace in their surroundings and their relationships, and often compromise to get it. Because they abhor conflict, Librans can appear indecisive and flighty. People born under this star sign are born communicators and romantics. They can get sidetracked by trying to avoid conflict and looking for the perfect love. This is the sign of marriage. It is also the sign of law and Librans care deeply about justice and human rights. They make very good diplomats and judges. Their love of beauty often leads them into professions in music and the arts.

Bryan Ferry (Roxy Music)	September 26	1945
Shannon Hoon (Blind Melon)	September 29	1967
Brett Anderson (Suede)	September 29	1967
Bob Geldof (Boomtown Rats)	October 5	1954
Dave Dederer (Presidents Of The USA)	October 5	1966
Matthew Sweet	October 6	1964
Johnny Ramone (Ramones)	October 8	1951
Al Jourgensen (Ministry)	October 9	1958
Bob Mould (Husker Du/Sugar)	October 12	1960
Flea (Red Hot Chili Peppers)	October 16	1962
Nico (Velvet Underground)	October 16	1938
Cris Kirkwood (Meat Puppets)	October 22	1960

Scorpio (October 24—November 22)

Scorpios are great at keeping secrets. Considered the most intense sign of the zodiac, they have an air of mystery about them. Sex and death are both big influences on people born under this sign. They resist change until there is no choice, and then embrace it and start fresh. Scorpios are great at transformations and that means they are incredibly creative. Their less admirable qualities include being manipulative, controlling, domineering and fearful.

Simon LeBon (Duran Duran)	October 27	1958
Scott Weiland (Stone Temple Pilots)	October 27	1960
Gavin Rossdale (Bush)	October 30	1967
Adam Horowitz (Beastie Boys)	October 31	1967
Johnny Marr (Smiths)	October 31	1967
Anthony Kiedis (Red Hot Chili Peppers)	November 1	1962
Jean-Luc DeMeyer (Front 242)	November 18	1957
Mike D (Beastie Boys)	November 20	1966
Bjork Gudmundsdottir (Sugarcubes)	November 21	1965

Sagittarius (November 22—December 21)

This is the sign of adventure and travel. Sagittarians don't like to sit still. They are logical people who pursue their goals single-mindedly. They also tend to be idealistic and sometimes would rather talk about their dreams than actually take action. These are "people people," happy and cheerful by nature. Sagittarians have a lot of friends who are often enchanted by their dreams and visions about what can be. On the down side, people born under this sign can be sarcastic, obnoxious and fanatical. Sagittarians would do well as promoters.

Mark Lanegan (Screaming Trees)	November 25	1964
Billy Idol (Generation X)	November 30	1955
Nivek Ogre (Skinny Puppy)	December 5	1962
Peter Buck (REM)	December 6	1956
Sinead O'Connor	December 8	1966
Kat Bjelland (Babes In Toyland)	December 9	1963
J. Mascis (Dinosaur Jr.)	December 10	1965
Mike Scott (Waterboys)	December 14	1958
Billy Bragg	December 20	1957
Mike Watt (Minutemen/Firehose)	December 20	1957

Capricorn (December 22—January 20)

This is the sign of the goat and it fits, since Capricorns often achieve lofty heights of success and then must be careful not to fall off. They can be chronic worriers but despite that, or because of it, they climb to the top of corporations and governments. They live for promotions, advancement and new responsibilities. Capricorns are very ambitious and that can translate into them being very materialistic. However, some people born under this sign put aside monetary gains for the greater good. Because they are so organized and industrious, Capricorns do very well in politics and banking.

Eddie Vedder (Pearl Jam)	December 23	1966
Shane MacGowan (Pogues)	December 25	1957
Nash Kato (Urge Overkill)	December 31	1965
Paul Westerberg (Replacements)	December 31	1960
Patti Smith	December 31	1946
Michael Stipe (REM)	January 4	1960
Bernard Sumner (New Order)	January 4	1956
Kate Schellenbach (Luscious Jackson)	January 5	1966
David Bowie	January 8	1947
Zack De La Rocha (Rage Against The Machine)	January 12	1970
Rob Zombie (White Zombie)	January 12	1966
Dave Grohl (Nirvana/Foo Fighters)	January 14	1969

Aquarius (January 20—February 18)

Change is the only constant for people born under this star sign. Aquarians are pioneers. They like unusual places and people, and they don't like rules, unless they themselves make the rules. People born under this sign are rebels, unpredictable and eccentric. They tend to be idealistic and prefer to surround themselves with people who share their beliefs. They are also very creative and egotistical. When it comes to work, Aquarians tend to be inventors, explorers and musicians.

Joe Strummer (The Clash)	January 25	1955
Mike Patton (Faith No More)	January 27	1968
Sarah McLachlan	January 28	1968
Johnny Rotten aka John Lydon	January 31	1956
Tim Booth (James)	February 4	c.1964
Sheryl Crow	February 11	1962
Henry Rollins	February 13	1961
Peter Hook (New Order)	February 13	1956
Peter Gabriel	February 13	1950
Billie Joe Armstrong (Green Day)	February 17	1972

Pisces (February 19—March 20)

People born under this sign are compassionate, selfless individuals. They tend to be imaginative and have a tendency toward martyrdom. Pisceans are spiritual, often in touch with their special muse, but they can also be paranoid, powerless and pretty good liars. Pisceans are attracted to work in the arts and are often actors, poets, philosophers or writers.

Dave Wakeling (English Beat/General Public)	February 19	1956
Kurt Cobain (Nirvana)	February 20	1967
Ian Brown (Stone Roses)	February 20	1963
Mark Arm (Mudhoney)	February 21	1962
Lou Reed (Velvet Underground)	March 2	1942
Evan Dando (Lemonheads)	March 3	1967
Billy Corgan (Smashing Pumpkins)	March 17	1967
Jerry Cantrell (Alice In Chains)	March 18	1966
Miki Berenyi (Lush)	March 18	1967
Terry Hall (Specials/Fun Boy 3/The Colourfield)	March 19	1959

Eight Artists Who Made Good Career Moves

1. Krist Novoselic

Late in 1987, Kurt Cobain was desperately trying to get someone—anyone—to pay attention to his band. Nirvana had some demos that Kurt thought were pretty good and he sent copies out to some of his favorite indie labels: SST in Los Angeles, Touch and Go in Chicago and Alternative Tentacles in San Francisco. Because Kurt knew that indie labels get dozens of tapes in the mail every day, he decided to include little "presents" (a condom full of confetti, a used Kleenex) with each package he sent out. Maybe that's why Nirvana never heard from any of those labels.

Sub Pop didn't get a tape because even though the company was in Seattle, Kurt didn't know they existed. Fortunately for Nirvana, the person who ran the studio where the demos were recorded slipped a tape to Bruce Pavitt and Jonathan Poneman at the label. They liked Nirvana and arranged for the group to release a single. Those early Nirvana singles helped establish the group as a solid underground act. But, because of their never-ending financial problems, Sub Pop and weren't really prepared to offer any group a proper contract and did virtually everything on a record-by-record basis.

This really annoyed bassist Krist Novoselic. After an entire evening of drinking cheap wine and getting wound up about Sub Pop's reluctance to give his band a contract, Novoselic stomped off to Pavitt's house to demand that something be done. Seeing Pavitt, the frustrated bassist turned to leave, but the two men ended up talking about the situation and agreed to go inside to type something up. A few days later, Nirvana became the first group to sign a long-term deal with the label. Had Novoselic not gotten drunk, and had Pavitt not returned home just as Novoselic was about to leave, the story of Nirvana (and of all alternative music) might have been very different.

2. Melissa Auf der Maur

Melissa Auf der Maur grew up in Montreal, the daughter of well-known city councillor, newspaper columnist and Olympic Games advisor Nick Auf der Maur. Melissa, however, was much more interested in music than in politics and played bass for a local outfit called Tinker. On nights when the group didn't have a gig, she would often check out the new bands that came through the city.

One night at a club called Les Foufounes Electriques, Melissa was appalled at how the crowd treated a new group from Chicago. Even though only about 20 people were in the audience, they made it tough for the band—especially after a drunk threw a beer bottle which hit the singer in the head. That set off a brawl and the group was forced to make a quick escape.

Melissa had really liked the group and was embarrassed at how they had been abused in her city. Determined to apologize on behalf of Montreal, she stuck around until the band left the building. They were really touched by this gesture and promised to keep in touch.

In 1994, Melissa and Tinker found themselves opening a gig for this same Chicago band—and to her surprise, the lead singer remembered her kindness. Later in the night, the singer thanked her again and also complimented Melissa on her bass playing. That singer was Billy Corgan and the Chicago group, of course, was the Smashing Pumpkins.

Here's where the good karma comes in. When Courtney Love was looking for a new bass player for Hole, she asked Billy if he knew of anyone who might be interested in the job. Billy immediately thought of Melissa. She auditioned and got the gig, making her debut appearance with Hole at the Reading Festival on August 28, 1994.

3. Flea

Even before the career of the Red Hot Chili Peppers took off, Flea was considered to be one of the finest bass players in all of Los Angeles. Before forming the Chili Peppers, he played with L.A. punk legends Fear, who just happened to have a fan in ex-Sex Pistol and leader of Public Image, Ltd. (PiL), Johnny Lydon. PiL was busy preparing for a Japanese tour, but was stymied in the search for an adequate bassist.

The audition with Flea went very well and he was offered the job. As flattering as it was to be offered the gig, Flea asked for a couple of weeks to decide and in the end said no. Even though he really needed the cash at the time, Flea wasn't interested in being a sideman or back-up musician; if he was going to be in a new band, then it would have to be as an equal partner—something Lydon would never allow. In the end, it was the right move because today the Chili Peppers have sold approximately ten times as many records as PiL.

4. Dave Navarro

Guitarist Dave Navarro has never had a real job. In fact, he's never even had to make up a résumé because he's made his living playing in various groups since he was 15. His first paying gig was playing the Sunset Strip clubs in a speed-metal band called Dizastre. He made his first good career move when he set up his friend Steve Perkins with his ex-girlfriend from junior high. Perkins then met the girl's brother, Eric Avery, who had a friend named Perry Farrell who was in the middle of forming a new group called Jane's Addiction. Perkins met with Farrell and got the drummer's job—and when the original guitarist quit, Perkins got Farrell to call Navarro, completing the group's lineup.

By the time Jane's Addiction broke up, Navarro had a solid reputation as an innovative and exciting guitar player. One of the many job offers he received was from Axl Rose of Guns 'n' Roses. That would have been a very lucrative gig since the group was still selling millions of records each year at the time.

Navarro took some time to think about it but in the end decided not to take the job, mainly because his instincts told him that the Guns 'n' Roses organization was too big and because the style of music just wasn't right for him.

It was a good move because the Red Hot Chili Peppers had been calling, hoping that he would be the solution to their guitarist woes. After refusing several offers, he finally gave in, making his first official appearance as a Pepper at the 1994 Woodstock festival.

5. Robert Smith

As unbelievable as this may seem to many, Robert Smith is not the only singer the Cure has ever had. When the group first started rehearsing in the mid-70s, Smith was the shy, withdrawn guitar player who preferred to stay in the background. No one even remembers the name of the first singer because he was fired after just a few rehearsals. His replacement was a journalist known only as "Martin"—but he lasted exactly one gig before he quit. The third Cure singer was Peter O'Toole, who joined in April 1977 and quit the following September so he could move to a kibbutz in Israel. Desperate for a singer (especially since they had just won a talent contest and had some recording studio time booked), the group convinced Smith to step up to the mike. He's been there ever since.

6. Paul Hewson

At about the same time the Cure was wrestling with the problem of finding an adequate lead singer, a young group in Dublin was going through the same thing. It began when Larry Mullen put a note up on the bulletin board at school, asking for anyone interested in forming a group to show up for a meeting in his parents' kitchen. One of the guys that showed up was Paul Hewson, who bragged that he could play guitar like a pro. The truth was he was awful and, after a while, he was told to put the thing down or leave.

But that's when things started going well. Paul instinctively took over the rehearsals, directing and inspiring the guys who could play. He also started to sing, bumping and grinding like some kind of Irish Elvis and surprising everyone with his voice and commanding presence. When it was all over, a vote was taken and it was determined that Paul could stay if he promised to leave his guitar at home. Paul (whose nickname was Bono) agreed—and he's the only singer U2 has ever had.

7. Kate Schellenbach

Confrontations are often a fact of life when it comes to being in a group, something that Kate Schellenbach knows all too well. Back in the mid-80s, she was in a group called the Young Aborigines before she joined as the drummer for a new group that made their debut at Adam Yauch's seventeenth birthday party on August 5, 1981. Called the Beastie Boys, the band recorded a number of songs with this lineup (documented on the *Some Old Bullshit* album) before there was a showdown between Schellenbach and manager/DJ Rick Rubin. Rubin wanted an all-white rap group and she did not figure into his plans. Tensions escalated and a meeting was called. An ultimatum was delivered: the group had to make a choice; it was either Rubin or Schellenbach. Whether she quit or was fired is unknown, but Kate was definitely out of the band.

The Beastie Boys went on to great success while Schellenbach was forced to start her career all over again. The good news is that she eventually hooked up with Jill Cunniff and Gabby Glaister to form Luscious Jackson. Any hard feelings were set aside when Schellenbach met the Beasties at the funeral of a mutual friend and Luscious Jackson now records for Grand Royal, the Beastie Boys' label.

8. New Order

From the earliest days of their existence, New Order hated doing encores. Everyone in the group thought that encores were pretentious and were an aggravating delay when it came to the post-show party.

Things took a strange turn at one gig when they decided just to turn on Stephen Morris's drum machine and let it go while everyone walked off stage. That way, they could get backstage for a drink before anyone in the audience knew they were gone. Then, for a little spice, they got a sequencer to trigger a basic keyboard loop followed by a simple bass line. As things came together element by element, it dawned on New Order that they were creating a brand new computer-driven dance track unlike anything anyone had ever heard before.

Taking the idea into the studio (and allegedly very buzzed on LSD at the time), layer upon layer were added to the basic anti-encore tracks until they had an eight-minute 12-inch single that they called "Blue Monday." The song sold more than three million copies worldwide and changed the very nature of alternative dance music.

Nine Bad Career Moves

1. Five ex-Nirvana drummers who didn't stick it out

• *Aaron Bruckhard (1987)*
Before Dave Grohl joined the group in 1990, Nirvana had trouble finding the right drummer. The first recruit was Aaron Bruckhard, a Burger King employee and local stoner who had once driven a car through the front door of a convenience store and had been in another accident in which someone was killed. He was fired after he was stopped for drunk driving—in Kurt Cobain's car. While Nirvana later went on to sell millions of albums, Bruckhard had a job laying insulation while playing in a thrash-metal band called Attica.

• *Dale Crover (1988 and 1990)*
Crover, a member of the Melvins, could always be depended on to help out in a pinch. He briefly took over from Bruckhard and played on Nirvana's first demo tape. When Chad Channing was fired (see below), Crover was asked to fill in during a short tour.

• *Dave Foster (1988)*
A friend of the guys in the Melvins, Foster was part of Nirvana for a couple of months before he was jailed for assault.

• *Chad Channing (1988-90)*
Hired just before the *Bleach* sessions, Channing stayed with the group through several major tours. Although he lasted long enough to play on the demos for the *Nevermind* album, he and Cobain couldn't get along and he was fired. Dave Grohl later duplicated Channing's parts for the *Nevermind* sessions.

• *Dave Foster (1990)*
Foster came on loan from Mudhoney for one gig after Channing was fired and before Grohl signed on.

2. Simon Wolstencraft

A native of Manchester, Wolstencraft made two big career errors in the early 80s. In 1981, he hooked up with a local group called the Patrol, who played a few gigs before changing their name to English Rose. Wolstencraft, however, didn't like the guitarist much—so he quit. In a few years, English Rose became the Stone Roses.

Wolstencraft made another mistake less than two years later, when he decided that his next group Freaky Party wasn't going anywhere. Soon after he quit, the group found a singer named Morrissey and changed their name to the Smiths. Fortunately, Wolstencraft eventually found steady work with Mark E. Smith and the Fall.

3. Andy Cousens

Simon Wolstencraft wasn't the only person who missed a chance to be in the Stone Roses. Back in 1981, Andy Cousens sang for the Patrol. When they became English Rose, he moved to guitar with John Squire and continued on with the group when they finally became the Stone Roses in late 1984. Cousens was still with the band when they recorded a series of demos with producer Martin Hannett and can be heard on the first Stone Roses single "So Young." Unhappy working with Squire, Cousens soon quit to form a new group called the High, eventually attracting some success in the U.K.

4. The Happy Mondays

In May 1993, the Happy Mondays should have been grateful that they were being offered a new record contract. Having spent a huge sum of money recording the critically and commercially disastrous *Yes Please* (not to mention wrecking a couple of cars and bragging to the world about their crack habits), their label still believed that the group had potential and was worth re-signing.

In a meeting with label executives and with the new contract on the table awaiting signatures, singer Shaun Ryder suddenly decided to step out of the room. He never came back. Realizing that the group may be a bad risk after all, the contract offer was rescinded and the band broke up.

5. Oasis

Superstars at home, but considered just another pompous English band by most Americans, Oasis was invited to appear on the MTV Music Video Awards in September 1996. Liam Gallagher conducted himself badly in front of a large TV audience, many of whom were seeing Oasis for the first time. He swore, spit on the stage and basically behaved like a boor. The backlash from both the media and the public was so strong that this one performance almost ruined the group's chances of becoming the first Britpop band to make serious inroads in America.

6. Negativland

The worst career move this San Francisco group ever made was to release a single entitled "U2," featuring two unauthorized samples of the U2 song, "I Still Haven't Found What I'm Looking For." Island Records and U2 launched a lawsuit, forcing SST (Negativland's label) to withdraw the single. In 1992, the group released a 96 page magazine documenting the whole case called *The Letter U and the Numeral 2*. This time, Negativland was not only sued by Island Records, but by their own label and a lawyer representing Casey Kasem (who was also the subject of an unauthorized sample). The whole affair has cost the group thousands of dollars in legal fees.

7. Hollywood Records

This Disney-owned label failed to have one hit release between 1989 and 1995. Although they signed Queen (who, by that time, hadn't had a hit record in years), they decided to pass on a promising Chicago band called the Smashing Pumpkins. They almost signed Bush, but when the executive who had been negotiating with them died in a helicopter crash, his successor decided that the group didn't have any potential and passed up an opportunity to release *Sixteen Stone*.

8. Everyone except DGC

Alternative Tentacles, Touch and Go and SST were all indie labels that received demos from Nirvana. None replied. By 1990, Capitol, Columbia, MCA , Slash and several others were bidding for the group.

9. The Sex Pistols

Thinking that America was going to be as easy a conquest as Britain, Sex Pistols manager Malcolm McLaren decided that the best way to proceed was to stay away from major centers like New York, Chicago and Los Angeles and concentrate on the U.S. South. Starting with a show in Atlanta on January 5, 1978, the tour wound westward, hitting such unlikely cities as Memphis, Tulsa and Dallas. They encountered hostile crowds everywhere and were completely unable to control Sid Vicious's voracious appetite for drugs and groupies. By the time the group made it to San Francisco on January 14, the tour was in complete chaos. Following one last show at the Wintergarden, Johnny Lydon decided he'd had enough and he quit.

Former Day Jobs of Twenty-Five Famous Performers

1. Damon Albarn (Blur): tea boy at a recording studio
2. Tori Amos: piano lounge singer

3. Bjork: actress
4. Bono (U2): gas station attendant in Dublin
5. Billy Bragg: tank driver in the British army
6. Peter Buck (REM): record store clerk
7. Kurt Cobain (Nirvana): school janitor
8. Elvis Costello: computer programmer at Elizabeth Arden
9. Rivers Cuomo (Weezer): pizza delivery driver
10. Evan Dando (The Lemonheads): child actor in a JELL-O TV commercial
11. Jonathan Davis (Korn): assistant to the state coroner in Bakersfield, California
12. Perry Farrell (Jane's Addiction/Porno for Pyros): liquor salesman
13. Noel Gallagher (Oasis): roadie, installer and parts department employee for British Gas
14. Martin Gore (Depeche Mode): bank teller
15. Gibby Haynes (Butthole Surfers): accountant
16. Adam Jones (Tool): special effects technician for *Terminator 2*
17. Courtney Love (Hole): stripper, bit actress, maid for actor Dennis Hopper
18. Morrissey: cleaner of surgeon's robes at a hospital laundry
19. Trent Reznor: salesman in a music store
20. Henry Rollins: manager of a 7-11
21. Gavin Rossdale (Bush): house painter, music video production assistant
22. Ed Simons (Chemical Brothers): worker in a law office that dealt with child abuse cases
23. John Squire (Stone Roses/Seahorses): television set designer
24. Eddie Vedder (Pearl Jam): gas station attendant in San Diego
25. Rob Zombie (White Zombie): layout designer for *Celebrity Skin* magazine

Twenty-Three Groups Whose Music Has Been Used in TV Commercials

1. Babylon Zoo, "Spaceman," for Levi Jeans
2. Buffalo Tom, Nike
3. Buzzcocks, "What Do I Get," for Arthur's cat food (France)
4. Clash, "Should I Stay or Should I Go," for Levi Jeans
5. Elastica, "Connection," for Budweiser
6. James, "Born of Frustration," for Westin Hotels
7. Luna, "California (All the Way)," for CK 1
8. Lush, "Sweetness and Light," for Volkswagen
9. Ashley MacIsaac, for Eaton's

10. Ministry, "N.W.O.," for Molson beer
11. Nine Inch Nails, "The Art of Self Destruction, Part 1," for Levi Jeans
12. Papas Fritas, "TV Movies," for Luxotica Sunglasses
13. Pizzicato Five, for Elizabeth Arden
14. Pop, Iggy, "Lust for Life," for Labatt's beer (among others)
15. Pretenders, "Brass in Pocket," for Land Rover
16. Psychic TV, for Volkswagen
17. Ramones, "Blitzkrieg Bop," for Bud Light
18. Smiths, "How Soon Is Now," for Levi Jeans
19. Soft Cell, "Tainted Love," for Levi Jeans
20. Superchunk, for British Knights
21. Trio, "Da Da Da," for Volkswagen
22. Velocity Girl, "Sorry Again," for Volkswagen
23. Velvet Underground, "Venus in Furs," for Dunlop Tires

Plus
- *Matthew Sweet and Mary Me Jane performed jingles for Coca Cola*
- *Kate Bush appeared in a Seiko commercial in Japan. (She was also hired by Coca-Cola to write the music for a series of Fruitopia fruit drink commercials.)*
- *Johnny Lydon can be heard in a Mountain Dew commercial*

Five Bands Who Have Recorded TV Theme Songs

1. Danny Elfman, (ex-Oingo Boingo), for *The Simpsons* (Fox), *Tales from the Crypt* (HBO)
2. Nerf Herder, for *Buffy the Vampire Slayer* (syndicated)
3. Refreshments, for *King of the Hill* (Fox)
4. U2 (a cover of the Beatles' "Happiness is a Warm Gun"), for *Gun* (ABC)
5. Waitresses, for *Square Pegs* (ABC)

Plus Alt-Rock bands who have appeared on *The Simpsons*:
- *The Ramones*
- *Red Hot Chili Peppers*
- *Smashing Pumpkins*
- *Sonic Youth*

Real Names of 100 Famous Performers

1. **G.G. Allin:** Kevin Allin
2. **Tori Amos:** Myra Ellen Amos
3. **Adam Ant:** Stuart Leslie Goddard
4. **Ian Astbury** (Cult): Ian Lindsay
5. **Stiv Bators** (Dead Boys/Lords of the New Church): Stivin Bators
6. **Beck:** Beck Hanson
7. **Adrian Belew:** Robert Steven Belew
8. **Jello Biafra** (Dead Kennedys): Eric Boucher
9. **Bilinda** (My Bloody Valentine): Bilinda Jayne Butcher
10. **Bjork:** Bjork Gudmundsdottir
11. **Frank Black/Black Francis:** Charles Michael Kittridge Thompson IV
12. **Jet Black** (Stranglers): Brian Duffy
13. **Bono Vox O'Connell Street** (U2): Paul Hewson
14. **David Bowie:** David Robert Hayward-Jones
15. **Billy Bragg:** Steven William Bragg
16. **Timmy C** (Rage Against the Machine): Tim Commerford
17. **Captain Sensible** (Damned): Raymond Burns
18. **Nick Cave:** Nicholas Edward Cave
19. **Exene Cervenka** (X): Christine Cervenka
20. **Tre Cool** (Green Day): Frank Edwin Wright III
21. **Gaz Coombes** (Supergrass): Gary Coombes
22. **Elvis Costello:** Declan Patrick MacManus
23. **Howard Devoto** (Buzzcocks/Magazine): Howard Trafford
24. **Thomas Dolby:** Thomas Morgan Robertson
25. **M Doughty** (Soul Coughing): Michael Doughty
26. **E** (Eels): Mickey Einstein OR Mark Everett OR Mark Edwards OR ?
27. **Edge** (U2): Dave Evans
28. **Brian Eno:** Brian Peter George St. John le Baptiste de la Salle Eno
29. **Perry Farrell:** Simon Bernstein
30. **Nik Fiend** (Alien Sex Fiend): Nik Wade
31. **Flea** (Red Hot Chili Peppers): Michael Balzary
32. **Flood:** Mark Price
33. **Foetus:** Jim Thirlwell
34. **Fruitbat** (Carter USM): Les Carter
35. **Nina Hagen:** Katerina Hagen
36. **PJ Harvey:** Polly Jean Harvey
37. **Hayden:** Paul Desser

38. **Gibby Haynes** (Butthole Surfers): Gibson Haynes
39. **Richard Hell** (Television): Richard Meyer
40. **Dexter Holland** (Offspring): Brian Holland
41. **H.R.** (Bad Brains): Paul D. Hudson
42. **Ice-T:** Tracy Marrow
43. **Billy Idol:** William Michael Albert Broad
44. **Lux Interior** (Cramps): Erick Lee Purkhiser
45. **Poison Ivy** (Cramps): Kirsty Marlana Wallace
46. **David J** (Bauhaus/Love and Rockets): David J. Haskins
47. **Brian James** (Damned): Brian Robertson
48. **Jewel:** Jewel Kilcher
49. **Jim Bob** (Carter USM): Jim Morrison
50. **Mick Jones** (Clash): Michael Jones
51. **Holly Johnson** (Frankie Goes to Hollywood): William Johnson
52. **Mick Karn** (Japan): Anthony Michaelides
53. **cEVIN Key** (Skinny Puppy): Kevin Crompton
54. **King Ad-Rock** (Beastie Boys): Adam Horowitz
55. **Lenny Kravitz:** Leonard Albert Kravitz
56. **Paul Leary** (Butthole Surfers): Paul Leary Walthal
57. **Courtney Love:** Love Michelle Harrison
58. **Lene Lovich:** Lili Marlene Premilovich
59. **Annabella Lwin** (Bow Wow Wow): Myant Myant Aye
60. **Marilyn Manson:** Brian Warner
61. **Johnny Marr** (Smiths): John Maher
62. **J Mascis** (Dinosaur Jr.): Joseph Donald Mascis
63. **MCA** (Beastie Boys): Adam Yauch
64. **Mike D** (Beastie Boys): Michael Diamond
65. **Moby:** Richard Melville Hall
66. **Momus:** Nike Currie
67. **Morrissey:** Stephen Patrick Morrissey
68. **Nico:** Christa Paffgen
69. **Krist Novoselic** (Nirvana): Chris Anthony Novoselic
70. **Gary Numan:** Gary Webb
71. **Ric Ocasek:** Richard Otcasek
72. **Nivek Ogre** (Skinny Puppy): Kevin Ogilvie
73. **Blackie Onassis** (Urge Overkill): John Rowan
74. **Poe:** Anne Danielewski
75. **Iggy Pop:** James Jewel Osterberg
76. **Joey Ramone:** Jeff Hyman
77. **Ranking Roger** (English Beat/General Public): Roger Charlery
78. **Lou Reed:** Louis Firbank

79. **Nick Rhodes** (Duran Duran): Nicholas Bates
80. **Henry Rollins:** Henry Garfield
81. **Pete Shelley** (Buzzcocks): Peter McNeish
82. **Rat Scabies** (Damned): Chris Miller
83. **Siouxsie Sioux** (Siouxsie and the Banshees): Susan Dallion
84. **Sonic Boom** (Spaceman 3): Pete Kembler
85. **Joe Strummer** (Clash): Joe Mellors
86. **Polly Styrene** (X-Ray Spex): Marion Elliot
87. **Bernard Sumner** (New Order/Electronic): Bernard Dicken
88. **David Sylvian:** David Batt
89. **Johnny Thunders** (Heartbreakers): John Anthony Genzale
90. **Richard 23** (Front 242): Richard Jonkheere
91. **Tricky:** Adrian Thaws
92. **Eddie Vedder** (Pearl Jam): Edward Louis Severson, later Edward Mueller
93. **Tom Verlaine** (Television): Tom Miller
94. **Sid Vicious:** John Simon Ritchie
95. **Butch Vig:** Brian Vigorson
96. **Jah Wobble:** John Wardle
97. **Dean Ween:** Mickey Melchiondo
98. **Gene Ween:** Aaron Freeman
99. **Youth** (Killing Joke): Martin Glover
100. **Rob Zombie** (White Zombie): Rob Slaker

Origins of 101 Band Names

1. **Alice in Chains**: Created when singer Layne Staley was thinking about forming a glam S&M metal band (plus it sounded better than the group's original name, Diamond Lie).
2. **Bauhaus:** Taken from the German art and architectural movement of the early twentieth century. Group once known as Bauhaus 1919.
3. **Beastie Boys:** Originally an anagram for Boys Entering Anarchistic States Toward Internal Excellence.
4. **Ben Folds Five:** Trio founded by pianist and singer Ben Folds who thought that the alliteration of "Ben Folds Five" sounded more fun than "Ben Folds Three."
5. **Better Than Ezra:** Originally billed as Ezra, the band wanted to prove that they were still in great shape after a line-up change. That's when they started calling themselves Better Than Ezra.
6. **Bettie Serveert:** Literally, "service to Betty," a phrase from a Dutch tennis instruction book by a 1977 Wimbledon finalist.

7. **Blur:** Originally formed as Seymour. Blur was one of several names presented to them by their record company. Other choices included Shining Path, Sub and Whirlpool.
8. **Boo Radleys:** Character from the book *To Kill a Mockingbird*.
9. **Bush:** Three explanations: (1) The group is from the Shepherd's Bush area of London; (2) Bush is slang for marijuana; (3) the pubic connotations.
10. **Butthole Surfers:** Name of an early song by the group.
11. **Catherine Wheel:** A fourth century torture device named after the martyr St. Catherine.
12. **Cibo Matto:** The name literally means "food crazy" and was inspired by an Italian B-movie from the 70s entitled *Seso Matta (Sex Madness)*.
13. **Clash:** Taken from a newspaper headline that described a "clash with police."
14. **Collective Soul:** Phrase from Ayn Rand's *The Fountainhead*.
15. **Concrete Blonde:** Suggested off the top of his head by Michael Stipe of REM.
16. **Cocteau Twins:** Two stories: (1) The title of an early Simple Minds song; or (2) taken as a tribute to French artist Jean Cocteau.
17. **Cranberries:** Contraction of their original name, The Cranberry Saw Us.
18. **Cure:** Shortened from the Easy Cure, which was the name of an early Lol Tolhurst composition.
19. **Depeche Mode:** Name of a French fashion magazine.
20. **Echo and the Bunnymen:** Echo was the group's drum machine.
21. **Einsturzende Neubauten:** Literally translated from German, it means "collapsing new buildings."
22. **Elastica:** Evolved out of Spastica.
23. **Faith No More:** Name of a racing greyhound that brought the group good luck.
24. **Fountains of Wayne:** The name of a store that sells fountains in Wayne, New Jersey.
25. **Foo Fighters:** Name given to French fighter pilots who scrambled to investigate UFO sightings over the Rhine Valley in the 40s.
26. **Gene:** Named after a friend of singer Martin Rossiter who died in 1992.
27. **Goo Goo Dolls:** According to the Johnny Rzeznik, it's a bad name resulting from a drinking binge.
28. **Green Day:** Taken from the band's term for a day spent smoking pot.
29. **Happy Mondays:** A response to New Order's "Blue Monday."
30. **Hole:** Supposedly from a line spoken by Medea, a character in an ancient Greek play.
31. **Husker Du:** The name of a Swedish memory-based board game, literally "Do You Remember?"
32. **INXS:** Finding the name "XTC" to be very clever, the group chose something similar.

33. **James:** No official explanation although it's suspected that the group was named after founding member and bassist, Jim Glennie.

34. **Jamiroquai:** Pseudonym of frontman Jason Kay, who took it from the name of a Native American tribe.

35. **Jane's Addiction:** Two possibilities: (1) The group is named in honor of a prostitute that bankrolled the band in their early days; (2) possibly inspired by Jane (actually "Jenny") in the Velvet Underground song, "Rock 'n' Roll."

36. **Jesus and Mary Chain:** Taken from a line in an old Bing Crosby movie.

37. **Joy Division:** In his novel *House of Dolls*, author Karol Cetinsky describes a "joy division" as an area of a Nazi concentration camp where women were forced into prostitution for the benefit of Nazi officers.

38. **Killing Joke:** Inspired by a Monty Python skit about a lethally funny joke.

39. **KMFDM:** Allegedly from the German phrase, "Kein mehrheit für die mitleid" ("No pity for the majority.")

40. **Kraftwerk:** German for "power plant."

41. **Kula Shaker:** Variation of Kula Sekhara, the Indian guru who advised singer Crispin Mills that his band would have more success if they dumped their original name, the Kays.

42. **Longpigs:** The band alleges that this is the term used by cannibals to describe human flesh, which they say has a pork-like flavor.

43. **Marion:** The first name of singer Jaime Harding's grandmother.

44. **Laibach:** The old German name for Ljubljana, Slovenia, the group's home town.

45. **Laika:** Named after the first Soviet dog in space.

46. **Laika and the Cosmonauts:** Same as above, but involving a different group.

47. **Love and Rockets:** The name of a popular underground comic.

48. **Luscious Jackson:** Adopted after the group saw the name of 70s Philadelphia 76ers' star Lucious Jackson misspelled in a sports record book.

49. **L7:** Sign language for "square" in the 50s (denoted by forming an "L" with the thumb and forefinger of each hand and bringing them together to create a square).

50. **Mighty Mighty Bosstones:** Originally just the "Bosstones." The "mighty mighty" was adopted after someone used the term to describe the band on a flyer.

51. **Ministry:** From an old Ray Milland horror film, *Ministry of Fear*.

52. **My Bloody Valentine:** Allegedly from a 1981 slasher film of the same name. Leader Kevin Shields claims not to have known about the movie when the group chose its name.

53. **Nerf Herder:** Taken from an insult hurled at Han Solo by Princess Leia in *The Empire Strikes Back*.

54. **New Order:** Adopted from a newspaper story describing the "new order," a division of soldiers in the Cambodian army. One story had the band considering the name Witch Doctors of Zimbabwe before finally deciding on New Order.

55. **Nine Inch Nails:** Lots of rumors, none of which are true. "Nine Inch Nails" just sounded better than anything else Trent Reznor was considering.

56. **Nirvana:** Kurt Cobain liked the literal dictionary definition of the term.

57. **No Doubt:** A favorite phrase used by founding member John Spence, who committed suicide just before Christmas 1987.

58. **Oasis:** Several possibilities: (1) After a chain of ladies' clothing stores in England; (2) after a Manchester cab company; (3) after a local nightclub; (4) after a nearby Indian restaurant.

59. **Offspring:** Probably taken from a 1986 movie starring Vincent Price.

60. **Our Lady Peace:** Taken from a poem written by Mark Van Doren, the father of Charles Van Doren, who was at the center of the quiz show scandal of the 50s.

61. **Pearl Jam:** The hallucinogenic peyote jam once made by Pearl, Eddie Vedder's grandmother. The group was originally known as Mookie Blaylock after the NBA star.

62. **Pixies:** Chosen from the dictionary by guitarist Joey Santiago. He thought it would be funny if someone as large as Black Francis fronted a band named after some tiny, delicate fairy creatures.

63. **Pogues:** From "pogue mahone," Gaelic for "kiss my ass."

64. **Pop Will Eat Itself:** Borrowed from a newspaper article entitled "Will Pop Eat Itself?"

65. **Porno for Pyros:** Inspired by a fireworks company flyer that fell out of an S&M porno magazine.

66. **Portishead:** The name of the group's home town near Bristol, England.

67. **Primal Scream:** The name of the psychotherapy created by Arthur Janov in his book *Prisoners of Pain*.

68. **Psychedelic Furs:** Inspired by the Velvet Underground song "Venus in Furs."

69. **Pulp:** Originally Aribicus Pulp, a coffee bean consortium that Jarvis Cocker discovered while browsing through the business section of the newspaper.

70. **Radiohead:** Title of a Talking Heads song from the *True Stories* album.

71. **Rage Against the Machine:** Title of a song by Inside Out, one of singer Zack de la Rocha's pre-Rage bands.

72. **Redd Kross:** Allegedly inspired by a particularly intense scene involving a crucifix in *The Exorcist*.

73. **Red Hot Chili Peppers:** The group wanted something that reflected their spicy, funky sound.

74. **REM:** Taken at random from a dictionary several hours before their very first gig on April 5, 1980.

75. **Screaming Trees:** Adapted from the model name of a guitar effects pedal made by Electro-Harmonix.

76. **Seven Mary Three:** Named after the call numbers of Larry Wilcox's unit on the TV show *CHiPs*.

77. **Sex Pistols:** Named after "Sex," manager Malcolm McLaren's fetish gear shop in London.

78. **Shonen Knife:** A brand of Japanese knife.

79. **Silverchair:** There has never been an adequate explanation for the name—but it's certainly better than their first choices: the Innocent Criminals and Short Elvis.

80. **Sleater-Kinney:** The name of a street in Lacey, Washington.

81. **Sleeper:** Borrowed from the Woody Allen film of the same name.

82. **Smashing Pumpkins:** A nonsensical phrase overheard by Billy Corgan at a party.

83. **Sneaker Pimps:** Inspired by the nickname of a Beastie Boys associate who hunts down rare and collectible running shoes for the group.

84. **Sonic Youth:** A combination of Thurston Moore's two favorite bands in the early 80s: Sonic's Rendezvous Band and Big Youth.

85. **Soundgarden:** The name of a wind sculpture on Lake Washington in Seattle.

86. **Squirrel Nut Zippers:** Originally, the name of a candy manufactured by Squirrel Brand, a candy company in Cambridge, Massachusetts. The company found their name in an old newspaper that described a man who got drunk on Nut Zipper (an old alcoholic drink) and began climbing through the trees of downtown Boston. The paper described him as the "squirrel nut zipper."

87. **Stone Roses:** "Stone" from the Rolling Stones and "Roses" from English Rose, the name of the group immediately preceding the Stone Roses and originally the name of a song by the Jam.

88. **Stone Temple Pilots:** Allegedly inspired by an STP Oil Treatment decal. The group was originally known as Mighty Joe Young.

89. **Suede:** Inspired by the soft feel of singer Brett Anderson's new coat.

90. **Talking Heads:** Two possibilities: (1) Suggested by a friend who saw this term for TV anchors in *TV Guide*; (2) a saying spied on a T-shirt worn by a friend.

91. **Team Dresch:** Named after bassist Donna Dresch, considered to be one of the godmothers of the riot grrl movement.

92. **311:** Omaha police department code for indecent exposure.

93. **They Might Be Giants:** The name of a 1972 film starring George C. Scott.

94. **Toad the Wet Sprocket**: Fictitious band name mentioned in a Monty Python skit called "Rock Notes."

95. **Tool:** Allegedly the group is a "tool" for the lachrymology, the fictitious philosophy created by the equally fictitious Ronald P. Vincent.

96. **Tragically Hip:** Taken from a line in the Mike Nesmith video *Elephant Parts*.

97. **U2:** Suggested by a friend who worked at an ad agency. Originally known as the Hype and Feedback.

98. **Velvet Underground:** The title of an S&M novel about wife-swapping in suburbia by Michael Leigh.

99. **Veruca Salt:** One of the characters in the children's novel *Charlie and the Chocolate Factory* (and also the movie *Willie Wonka and the Chocolate Factory*) by Roald Dahl.

100. **Weezer:** Rivers Cuomo's childhood nickname.

101. **White Zombie:** A 1932 zombie film starring Bela Lugosi.

Twenty Names in Dispute[1]

1. **The Beat:** American New Wave group from San Francisco forced the English ska band to adopt the name English Beat.

2. **David Bowie:** Changed his name from "David Jones," because people kept mistaking him for the Davey Jones in the Monkees.

3. **Bush:** Canadian band led by one-time Guess Who guitarist Dominic Troiano forced the Britsh group to adopt the monicker Bush-X in Canada. The case was settled and the "X" dropped in April 1997 when the British group agreed to donate $40,000 to two charities

4. **Charlatans:** Often referred to as Charlatans UK to avoid confusion with a San Francisco band from the 60s

5. **Chemical Brothers**: Adopted when they realized that there was an American production team also using the name the Dust Brothers.

6. **Dinosaur Jr.**: Originally known as Dinosaur, J Mascis added the "Jr." to appease a San Francisco band.

7. **Elastica**: They were preceded by an English techno-pop group called Hey Elastica which released several singles and one album for Virgin before fading into obscurity.

8. **K's Choice**: Originally known as the Choice in their native Belgium. The "K's" was added when it was discovered that there was already an American group with that name.

---

[1] Trademarks and logos are property that can be protected under law—but disputes involving names almost always involve lawyers and lots of money. To make things even more frustrating, there aren't that many ways of finding out if the name you have selected for your band has already been taken. U.K. law allows for something called "passing off," which basically means that in the event of a dispute over a name, the better-known group usually wins.

One solution for British acts is the National Band Register, a database of over 20,000 names which is available for browsing. The NBR will also help new groups come up with an appropriate name if they're really stuck. The NBR can be called in London at 01734 755396 for more information.

9. **Mission:** Forced to add "UK" to their name in America to differentiate themselves from an American group of the same name.

10. **Nirvana:** Kurt Cobain's group had to pay an out-of-court settlement to Patrick Cambell-Lyons from a 60s group called Nirvana, in exchange for the rights to the name.

11. **Oasis:** Name originally used by a long-forgotten English band from the early 80s that featured Andrew Lloyd Webber's brother on cello. No legal action was taken against the current Oasis. However, there were some discussions with the ladies' clothing chain called Oasis since the company has a patent on all the apparel they sell. An amicable settlement was achieved when the group paid a one-time sum to the company.

12. **Redd Kross:** Originally known as "Red Cross," until they were threatened with legal action by the international humanitarian organization.

13. **REM:** At least five other groups were using the name when the Athens REM was formed. None remain.

14. **Stone Temple Pilots:** Emergency last-minute substitute for their original name, Mighty Joe Young, which (unbeknownst to the band) had already been claimed by another group.

15. **Suede:** Became known as the London Suede in America when a Washington, D.C. singer named Suzanne De Bronkkart complained that she had been working professionally under that name for years. She had registered "Suede" as a trademark because a porn writer had also been using the name. "London Suede" was on a list of suggestions drawn up by her lawyers and offered to the British group.

16. **Superchunk:** Starting as just Chunk, they soon realized that there was a New York jazz outfit already using that name.

17. **Treble Charger:** Forced to adopt the new name when it was discovered that an American band had already laid claim to their first choice, NC-17.

18. **The Verve:** British group forced to change their name to The Verve after complaints of trademark infringement by Verve, the American jazz label.

19. **Warsaw:** When Warsaw found that people were confusing them with a metal band called Warsaw Pakt, they changed their name to Joy Division.

20. **Yazoo:** The Vince Clarke/Alison Moyet project was known as Yaz in the U.S. to avoid being confused with the Yazoo Blues Band.

Explaining All Those Names in Marilyn Manson

With the exception of Zim Zum—who says his name comes from an ancient pagan religious ceremony—everyone who has ever been in Marilyn Manson has taken a pseudonym that combines a cultural icon with a serial killer. Here's a guide to all those names of members, past and present.

Marilyn Manson: Marilyn Monroe (American actress) and Charles Manson (convicted mass murderer). (Note: Mr. Manson's real name is Brian Warner.)

Twiggy Ramirez: Twiggy (famous 60s super model) and Richard Ramirez (the serial killer known as the Night Stalker).

Madonna Wayne Gacy: Madonna (pop singer) plus John Wayne Gacy (a former clown from Chicago who was executed for killing 33 boys and burying them in the crawl space beneath his house).

Ginger Fish: Ginger Rogers (Fred Astaire's dance partner) and Albert Fish (cannibal child killer).

Daisy Berkowitz: Daisy Duke (from *The Dukes of Hazard*) and David Berkowitz (the Son-of-Sam killer).

Zsa Zsa Speck, original keyboardist: Zsa Zsa Gabor (actress) and Richard Speck (killer of student nurses).

Olivia Newton Bundy, original bassist: Olivia Newton-John (Australian pop singer) and Ted Bundy (notorious serial killer).

Gidget Gein, bassist: Gidget (the all-American girl from a series of movies in the 60s) and Ed Gein (cannibal psycho).

Sara Lee Lucas: Sara Lee (the bakery that makes all those frozen pastries) and Henry Lee Lucas (mass murderer).

The Ramones Roll Call

- Joey Ramone (Jeff Hyman), vocals
- Johnny Ramone (John Cummings), guitar
- Marky Ramone (Marc Bell), drums
- Dee Dee Ramone (Douglas Colvin), bass
- Tommy Ramone (Tommy Erdelyi), drums
- CJ Ramone (Christopher Joseph Ward), guitar
- Ritchie Ramone #1, 1974 (unknown)
- Ritchie Ramone #2, 1987 (Richard Beau), drums
- George Ramone (unknown)
- Elvis Ramone (Clem Burke), drums
- Charlotte Ramone (Joey's mom, who sang bits of two Ramones songs on an edition of Geraldo)

Ten Artists Who Have Had to Deal With "Persistent" Fans and Stalkers

1. Brett Anderson (Suede)

Suede seems to attract the kind of fan who will do anything to get close to members of the band. As flattering as this may be, Brett Anderson jealously guards his privacy and tries to keep his home address a secret. One day, though, word got out and Anderson was faced with a group of fans at his front door. After he asked them to go away, the fans decided to exact some kind of revenge for this perceived lack of hospitality. It wasn't long before Anderson realized that the fans had written his address as graffiti all over the neighborhood and the local subway station. Someone even went to the trouble of printing up and distributing flyers that featured a map to his place. Having no choice, Anderson was forced to find somewhere else to live to regain some privacy.

2. Courtney Love and Kurt Cobain

Almost from the moment Kurt Cobain and Courtney Love purchased a huge 1902 mansion in the swanky Lake Washington district of Seattle, Nirvana and Hole fans began to camp out in the park that bordered the property. The situation became worse after Cobain's suicide as fans began to hold vigils on the other side of the fence at all hours of the night. Things improved greatly once Courtney tore down the carriage house where Cobain committed suicide. She finally sold the house in May 1997 for $3 million.

3. Eddie and Beth Vedder

Fanatical Pearl Jam fans have forced Eddie and Beth Vedder to retreat into their large Seattle home that's patrolled 24 hours a day by a security force. Extra precautions were taken in April 1996, when a man threatened to kill Eddie in front of dozens of witnesses. The stalker alleged that his ex-girlfriend was such a huge Pearl Jam fan that it wrecked their relationship; assassinating Vedder was to be his revenge.

4. Trent Reznor

Given the intense nature of his music, it's no surprise that Reznor sees his share of fanatics. There have been a number of occasions where he has received fan letters written in blood.

5. Sarah McLachlan

According to a long and detailed posting he made to the Fumbling Towards Ecstasy Internet mailing list on September 12, 1994, an Ottawa man named Uwe Vandrei discovered Sarah McLachlan's music in 1991. In that message, he described writing a series of increasingly personal fan letters to the singer beginning in the fall of 1991. He never received any reply and apparently met the singer only once, in April 1992.

Given the introspective and confessional nature of McLachlan's music, these types of letters aren't unusual. She has received literally hundreds of letters from obsessed fans over the years, some of whom have been so touched by her music that they believe McLachlan is speaking directly to them. The intensity and frequency of these types of letters led McLachlan to write "Possession," which is sung from the perspective of an obsessed fan. She didn't have any one person in mind; the character in the song is a composite of hundreds of people who have sent her this type of mail. The song was released on September 10, 1993, as the first single from her third album, *Fumbling Towards Ecstasy*.

There were indications that Vandrei suspected the song was about him from the moment he saw McLachlan perform it on TV in March 1993. By late summer 1994, he was convinced. That's when he filed a $250,000 lawsuit against McLachlan, contending that "Possession" was based on his private correspondence with the singer and that using the letters for such a public performance constituted a breach of confidence and moral rights. "I have suffered profound emotional hardships because of the song and subsequent controversy associated with it," he wrote in an Internet posting. "The primary reason of my lawsuit is to establish a legal, public venue where these matters can be finally objectively, candidly examined."

The case never made it to court. On November 3, 1994, Vandrei's decomposing body was found in his truck near Manotick, Ontario, by a group of campers. He had shot himself.

6. Lisa Germano

Germano was stalked for two years by a man from her home town in Indiana. Convinced that God was telling him that Germano was his long-lost girlfriend and that they were destined to be reunited, he wrote her letters, called her on the phone and often followed her around. The man was finally taken into custody when he got into a fight with the neighbor of a friend of Germano. The experience became the basis for the song "A Psychopath" on her 1994 album *Geek the Girl*.

7. Bjork

On September 17, 1996, Scotland Yard intercepted a parcel that had been mailed to Bjork. Inside was a hollowed-out book rigged to spray sulfuric acid in the face of whoever opened it. The parcel was sent by an unemployed 21-year-old ex-pest controller named Ricardo Lopez of Hollywood, Florida. Obsessed with Bjork and angry that she would dare date a black man (Bjork had been going out with trip-hop star Tricky and the British DJ Goldie), Lopez was determined to teach her a lesson. Fortunately for Bjork, he chose to document his obsession on videotape for nine months.

On a tape dated September 12, Lopez explained his plan to the camera. "I'm going to send her a package," he raved, "I'm just going to have to kill her....to send her to hell." After he shaved his head, he painted his nipples red, his lips black and his face with streaks of green and red, turning into a character reminiscent of Marlon Brando's Colonel Kurtz in the film *Apocalypse Now*. Then, sitting completely naked with Bjork's "I Miss You" playing in the background, he pulled out a .38 and shot himself in the mouth.

On the afternoon of September 16, police responded to reports of a strong smell coming from the apartment and broke down the door. Looking for clues, they started going through all the videotapes, until they found the one where Lopez held up the package destined for Bjork. Fortunately, the address was clearly visible to the camera and they were able to alert Scotland Yard to the lethal properties of the parcel. It was safely defused shortly after it arrived at the offices of Bjork's management company in South London. Ironically, Bjork had named her 1995 album *Post*, because she likes to receive things in the mail.

8. Bono

High-profile performers such as Bono receive threats all the time. On one American tour, the FBI received a tip that the singer would be assassinated in the U.S. South if U2 insisted on playing their Martin Luther King tribute, "Pride in the Name of Love." U2 continued to perform the song and nothing happened. On another tour of America, Bono received a fax from someone who said he was going to shoot him; the fax included a copy of the license of the weapon. Once again, nothing happened.

On April 3, 1996, Irish police deported a Toronto man who had been bothering Bono and the other members of the group with threatening letters and phone calls for more than a month. He was arrested on the grounds of Adam Clayton's house after he managed to slip past security.

9. Henry Rollins

Rollins was pestered by a homeless man who continually showed up on his porch, claiming that the big tattoo on Rollins' back was speaking to him. He was physically removed by Rollins himself.

10. Bush

Bush, and especially singer Gavin Rossdale, are constantly shadowed by fans wherever they go in North America. It has become so bad that whenever they go on tour, they make reservations at several different hotels under a variety of pseudonyms. However, there are times when even those precautions are not enough.

Determined Bush fans have been discovered hiding in the toilet stalls of the band's dressing rooms, while others leave messages in lipstick on hotel room doors and elevator doors. Others have sent photos in the mail, including one woman who allegedly inscribed the word "bush" in her pubic hair.

Ten Musical Scandals

1. David Bowie Controversies
Bowie has always had a taste for controversy. The tabloids had a field day in January 1972, when he declared to the British music paper *Melody Maker* that he was gay and always had been. Publicly coming out back then was often tantamount to career suicide, but Bowie managed to endure.

A far more serious incident occurred at Victoria Station in London on May 2, 1976. Bowie had just returned to England following his Station to Station tour and hundreds of screaming fans had turned out to welcome him home. With his hair bleached blonde and dressed in a sharp military outfit, Bowie raised his hand in sort of a stiff-armed wave to the crowd, just as a photographer snapped his picture. When the photo was published, many people believed that it showed Bowie giving the crowd a Nazi salute. This perception was reinforced when the press helpfully pointed out that Bowie had also just visited the site of Hitler's bunker in Berlin and had also recently been detained by Soviet customs agents because his suitcase had been filled with material on Albert Speer and Joseph Goebbels, both high-profile Nazis under Hitler. Stories that Bowie was about to move to Berlin (which were true) didn't help much, either. The controversy was forgotten once Bowie retreated from the spotlight to record his next album.

2. Morrissey and the Moors Murders
Morrissey has been sparring with the press for most of his career. He's been quoted and misquoted many times on everything from British politics to the issue of animal rights. For example, by the time the Smiths issued *Meat is Murder* in February 1985, Morrissey had been supporting some of the more radical forces in the animal rights movement for a couple of years. When asked to comment on the recent bombing of a butcher shop, he replied, "One dead butcher isn't such a great loss."

But the greatest scandal the Smiths had to endure was the outcry surrounding the Smiths song "Suffer Little Children." The song is based on the Moors Murders, a real case of child abduction and murder that gripped Manchester in the mid-60s. When the song appeared on the Smiths' debut album in 1984, few people paid it much attention. It was when it was issued as a B-side that the trouble started. A relative of one of the murder victims was in a pub having a few pints when someone pushed the wrong button on the jukebox. Instead of hearing the new Smiths single, "Heaven Knows I'm Miserable Now," everyone in the place heard "Suffer Little Children." The relative was so outraged and upset that a pop group would turn such a tragedy into a song that he went to the Manchester *Evening News*—which promptly turned it into a front page story. Reaction was swift and fierce. Within a couple of days, two of the biggest chain stores in Britain banned all Smiths records. The group tried to offer some damage control by releasing a statement saying that the song was not an attempt to cash in on such a serious event. There were also frantic phone calls between the band, their label and some of the parents of the murdered children.

In the end, the relative who had heard the song in the pub stepped forward to say that he had misinterpreted the Smiths' intentions and that it was all a big mistake. The Smiths were forgiven and in a gesture of good faith, the group offered to donate some of the song's royalties to charity.

3. The Nine Inch Nails Snuff Film

On a walk through one of his fields one day in 1989, a farmer chanced upon a large balloon tied to a portable video camera. He turned it over to police and they were shocked and frightened by what they saw. The tape from the camera showed a man being thrown off a building, later revealing his broken body on the sidewalk. Convinced that this was a real snuff film, they turned it over to the FBI who promptly launched an investigation.

The probe continued for six months before there was a break in the case. It turned out that it wasn't a snuff film at all. It was raw footage from a Nine Inch Nails video. While trying to get a tricky shot for the "Down In It" video, Trent Reznor had tied a video camera to a balloon—but then a strong gust of wind broke the tether and both the balloon and the camera sailed off into the sky. And the shot of the body on the sidewalk? That was Reznor in full make-up.

4. Courtney Love and *Vanity Fair*

Entire books could be written about the controversies Courtney Love has seen in her life, but few equal the attention she received over an article that appeared in the September 1992 issue of *Vanity Fair*. With Nirvana at the top of the charts and Hole's new album doing well, writer Lynn Hirschberg (someone known for writing brutally frank articles on celebrities) asked if she could do a piece on Love, who agreed, thinking that this kind of exposure could do her career some good. Instead, it turned out to be a public relations nightmare.

The final article was a disaster for Love, portraying her as someone who was possibly using heroin while she was pregnant and strongly hinted that it was she who hooked Kurt Cobain on the drug. Using terms like "train-wreck personality," Hirschberg painted Love as a scheming, reckless person who was a hazard to herself, her husband and her unborn child. It also didn't help that several photos accompanying the article showed a very pregnant Courtney puffing on a cigarette.

The backlash was intense. In the middle of a presidential campaign where the focus was on "family values," Love was assailed by critics from all sides. The firestorm that followed was so strong that word of the article reached the Los Angeles County Department of Children's Services, who promptly launched an investigation into whether Kurt and Courtney were capable parents. It even reached the point where two weeks after Frances Bean was born, the Cobains had to surrender custody to Courtney's sister and, for the next month, they were not allowed to be alone with their new daughter.

The mudslinging continued when two British writers (who were planning to write a Nirvana biography) allegedly received a series of threatening messages from both Kurt and Courtney, demanding that they stop the project. Articles on their drug use appeared everywhere, from the *Los Angeles Times* to all the supermarket tabloids. Things apparently were so bad for Courtney and Kurt that, at one point, there was talk of suicide.

Eventually, the public tired of the stories and the controversy receded into the background. Frances Bean was returned to her parents and remains in the custody of her mother. Courtney even managed to forgive *Vanity Fair*, agreeing to appear on the cover of the magazine for the June 1995 issue.

5. Crispin Mills's Swastika Comment

It's no secret that the lead singer of Kula Shaker is fascinated by ancient eastern culture and language. (Name another western band that sings some lyrics in Sanskrit.) But in the eyes of many, Crispin Mills took things a little too far when he professed admiration for the swastika, an ancient symbol that was forever perverted by the Nazis. In the March 3, 1997 edition of the British music paper *NME*, Mills was quoted as saying, "I love the swastika. It's a brilliant image, it symbolizes peace and the sun and illumination. I'd love to have great big flaming swastikas on stage just for the fuck of it."

To make matters worse, some writers discovered that Objects of Desire, one of Mills's earlier bands, played a gig at a 1993 conference of conspiracy theorists, which included presentations by both right-wing and anti-Semitic speakers. Outraged by his comments, the government of Israel banned Kula Shaker's music, until Mills issued a formal apology. Citing his "long interest in Indian culture," Mills explained that the swastika's original form was "the antithesis of the demonic and monstrous Nazi atrocities." Following this statement, the controversy began to die away—although some members of the Simon Wiesenthal Center remain concerned.

6. Bjork Caught on Tape

In February 1996, Bjork took a trip to Thailand. Before she left London, Julie Kaufman, a reporter from a Thai TV network, arranged for an interview with the singer upon her arrival in Bangkok. Just before Bjork boarded her flight, she suddenly decided to cancel her meeting with the reporter. Undeterred, the reporter and a cameraman went to meet Bjork at the Bangkok airport anyway, as a welcoming gesture. But when Kaufman approached Bjork asking questions about her son Sindri, the singer flew into a rage, knocking the reporter to the ground. Naturally, the camera was rolling and the video was soon being broadcast around the world.

Bjork later apologized for the incident, saying that after constant dealings with paparazzi at home, she just snapped and that, up until that moment, she had never hit anyone in her life. The apology was accepted. Meanwhile, the incident was profitable for Kaufman. As a result of the press coverage she received, she was offered a spot in a hair spray commercial.

7. Jarvis Cocker Rains on Michael Jackson

The lead singer of Pulp had seen enough. Fed up with Michael Jackson's overblown performance of "Earth Song" at the BRIT Awards (the U.K. equivalent of the Grammys) on Monday, February 19, 1996, Jarvis Cocker decided that it was time someone made a statement. After loitering on the side of the stage for a few minutes, Cocker burst onto the stage amongst all the dancing children and wiggled his backside, lifted his shirt and saluted the audience. After a few seconds, someone from Jackson's entourage (dressed in a monk's habit) tried to march Cocker off the stage, almost tackling him in the process. In the confusion, several of the children onstage were knocked over but not hurt. Police were called and Cocker was questioned for two hours in a dressing room before he was arrested, and charged with three counts of "Actual Bodily Harm."

The following morning, Jackson released a statement saying that he was "sickened, saddened, shocked, upset, cheated and angry" and called Cocker's behavior "disgusting and cowardly." (In actual fact, Jackson didn't see the skirmish because he was in the middle of being hoisted above the crowd by a giant crane when everything happened.) With nothing to go on but that press release and a statement from police, Cocker was almost universally condemned by the media.

The outrage lasted for less than 48 hours. By Wednesday, opinion began to turn against Jackson when other British pop stars said they were glad Cocker had crashed Jackson's pompous performance. Meanwhile, video footage of the incident clearly shows that Cocker did not assault anyone and that it was Jackson's people who had come in contact with the children. Faced with visual evidence of what really happened, a British tabloid launched the "Justice for Jarvis" campaign, helping to turn public opinion against Jackson.

On March 11, Cocker battled through a crowd of angry Michael Jackson supporters on his way into Kensington Police station to see if he was indeed going to be charged. While Jackson fans and Pulp fans pelted each other with eggs, Cocker was told that after reviewing the video of the event, the police had decided that no charges would be filed. The whole affair ended happily for Pulp, who received an estimated £250,000 of free advertising, resulting in the sales of another 50,000 albums.

8. Dolores Without Her Skivvies?

In July 1995, a British newspaper called *Sport* ran a story alleging that Cranberries singer Dolores O'Riordan performed in Hamburg, Germany, clearly *sans* panties. Outraged at the allegation, O'Riordan proceeded with legal action until she won a public apology from *Sport*. They also agreed to donate $7,500 to WarChild, O'Riordan's favorite charity.

9. REM Fires Their Manager

Jefferson Holt had been with REM from the very beginning. Many people referred to him as the band's fifth member, someone who wielded as much power and influence as Paul McGuinness had with U2. Holt co-managed the group with attorney Bertis Downs (who took the job right out of law school), steering the group through the music industry and helping them sell more than 30 million albums. It all came to an end in May 1996 when REM surprised everyone by suddenly firing Holt. No reasons were given and his quick departure from the group remains a mystery.

10. Morrissey and Marr Lose a Big One

Before the Smiths broke up in 1987, the group had earned millions of dollars, with 40 percent going to Morrissey, another 40 percent going to Johnny Marr, while drummer Mike Joyce and bassist Andy Rourke split the remaining 20 percent. Years later, Joyce and Rourke decided to contest this arrangement. Rourke soon dropped out, settling out of court for about $133,000. Joyce, on the other hand, was prepared to fight. He took his case before a judge, saying that based on his contributions to the Smiths, he deserved a 25 percent share of the group's earnings outside of songwriting royalties. On December 11, 1996, the judge agreed. Describing Morrissey as "devious, truculent and unreliable" and "overly concerned" with his own interests, the judge ruled that Joyce was entitled to an additional 15 percent of the Smiths' earnings, including a retroactive sum totaling $1.7 million. Morrissey and Marr were also ordered to pay $400,000 in court costs.

"I still have the highest regard for Morrissey," Joyce was quoted as saying, "But I knew ten years ago when I started this action that I would win. This was never about money. It will not change my lifestyle, but it will secure the future for my wife and children." So much for that oft-rumored Smiths reunion.

A Baker's Dozen Worth of Scandals Featuring Oasis

1. May 31, 1993

Having hitched a ride up to Glasgow with Sister Lovers, another Manchester group, Oasis demanded that the owner of King Tut's Wah Wah Hut allow them to play, too. Legend has it that Oasis and their friends threatened to tear the place apart unless they were shown the stage. Wanting to avoid trouble with a bunch of drunken louts, the owner relented and Oasis played an uninvited set of four songs in front of nine paying customers. However, one of the people in the club that night was Creation boss Alan McGee. He was so impressed by what he saw that he wanted to immediately sign the group to a contract. After some negotiation, the group agreed and have been with the label ever since.

2. February 7, 1994

Liam and Bonehead began drinking their duty-free champagne very early in a ferry trip across the English Channel and were quite drunk when they decided to challenge a group of Chelsea soccer fans on their way to see their team play on the continent. Soon, the whole group joined in the fight. When the ferry arrived in the Netherlands, Liam was arrested and sent back to England. Oasis is still banned from that ferry line.

3. Mid-1994

Stories of Oasis's notoriety have spread, thanks to the sensationalist British media. One source quoted Liam about how he used to drink shampoo when he was high on cocaine because it smelled good. Meanwhile, Noel bragged about sprinkling cocaine on his corn flakes. One Swedish hotel demanded that Oasis be deported after the group caused £30,000 worth of damage to their rooms (which included Bonehead throwing various pieces of furniture out the window) and stiffed the bar for a £2,000 tab.

4. September 1994

During a tour through California, Oasis came very close to breaking up when Noel bolted from the band (after Liam bashed him in the head with a tambourine), leaving and taking the rest of the group's tour expense money. He had a change of heart and returned to the group three days later. Meanwhile, the band's manager had to confiscate everyone's passport just in case anyone else decided to leave without warning.

5. 1995

In some of her infamous Internet rants, Courtney Love writes "Oasis must die...do not buy Oasis records...They will come to rape and pillage our women and invade America."

6. Spring 1996

As every newspaper, magazine and TV show in Britain clamored for information about Oasis, it became more and more difficult for anyone to find a fresh angle on them, especially with their over-hyped feud with Blur. But one reporter with *The Observer* found a way. Assigned to shadow Oasis on a tour through Scotland, she quoted Noel Gallagher as saying that he wished that the members of Blur would catch AIDS and die. Naturally, this made front page news all across the country and everyone attacked Noel for being incredibly cruel and insensitive.

Noel eventually did apologize for his remarks—but with an explanation. According to him, the reporter kept pestering him with questions relating to the Blur-versus-Oasis war, even after the official backstage interview was over. Meanwhile, everyone had been drinking heavily. Finally, after an hour of constant interrogation, a tipsy Noel turned to the reporter and blurted out the AIDS wish, hoping that she would be outraged and leave. "I was trying to shock her so we could stop talking about it," he later said, "But I knew I was wrong and I said right away, 'Please don't use that.' I knew I had put my foot in it." Instead, the reporter used the quote and the reaction across the world was very ugly.

7. April 21, 1996

The News of the World, a British tabloid, printed a front page story claiming that the Gallagher brothers were locked into a cocaine habit worth £4,000 a week. The information came from Ian Robertson, an ex-road manager for Oasis and the author of an unauthorized biography on the band called *Oasis: What's the Story?* Oasis chose not to sue.

8. August-September 1996

These were some of the toughest months the band has ever endured. The success of a concert at Loch Lomond in Scotland was marred when roadie James Hunter was crushed to death between a truck and a forklift while helping to set up the stage. Noel Gallagher witnessed the accident and spent four hours answering questions at the local police station.

Things began to unravel within the group when Liam, complaining of a sore throat, didn't appear with the group during an MTV *Unplugged* session at the Royal Festival Hall on August 23. Although the show went on with Noel on lead vocals, MTV was not pleased. The very next day, their estranged father Tommy Gallagher was sentenced to one month in jail on a charge of driving without a license. The national press covered the story, especially since there had been recent revelations that Mr. Gallagher allegedly once beat his sons when they were children.

With tensions running high within the group and under tremendous pressure to make a good showing in America, Oasis almost blew apart again. On August 26, Liam refused to board the band's British Airways flight to Chicago just 15 minutes before the group was scheduled to leave on their ninth North American tour. Saying that he was too busy to tour (he said he was moving), he told the group that he wouldn't be joining them. Some tabloids suggest that the outburst occurred after Liam found he had been seated next to Noel on the plane. After one show, Liam relented and joined the group.

The peace didn't last long. Oasis turned in a terrible performance during the MTV Music Video Awards on September 4, with Liam captured spitting on the stage. A week later, following a five-hour meeting in Charlotte, North Carolina, Noel decided he'd had enough and flew back to England. The *Sun* ran a headline that read "Blowoasis: Hotel fist-fight then Noel and Liam axe band" and actually set up a hotline for mourning fans. Another paper, *The News of the World,* alleged that Liam was suicidal during the tour. Eventually, everyone calmed down and the band went into the studio to record the next album.

9. October 1, 1996

The English tabloids reported that Noel Gallagher created a scene when he tried to charge a $5,000 leather coat to his credit card. When the woman behind the counter insisted on calling to verify his card, Noel (insulted at not being recognized), began yelling at the clerk.

10. November 1996

At the beginning of the month, Liam was cleared by police after a weird nose-biting incident at an Ocean Colour Scene show in London. Then on November 9, a very stoned Liam Gallagher was mistaken for a drunken homeless man by police and was picked up early one morning on Oxford Street in London. When they found a quantity of mysterious white powder (later determined to be .035 ounces of cocaine worth about $160), they took him to the police station. When he finally appeared in front of a judge on January 7, 1997, he received a "drug caution," a common practice with first-time offenders.

11. December 1996

Anti-smoking groups in England were outraged after Oasis released a collection of singles in two boxes that looked like packages of cigarettes. Shortly afterwards, evidence of an Oasis backlash surfaced in Manchester when several cars were vandalized with anti-Oasis graffiti.

12. March 1997

There was considerable panic in the Oasis camp when stories began to circulate that someone had stolen some master tapes from their studio and were threatening to sell the tapes to an unidentified newspaper tabloid. The group immediately issued a statement condemning the threat and warning the paper not to publicize anything that may be contained on the tapes. It turns out that no one had anything to worry about because it was all a hoax orchestrated by two brothers. Deciding to play a joke, one brother told the other that he had stolen tapes from Oasis' studio and played a tape to prove it. The second brother, not all that familiar with the group, didn't realize that he was actually listening to a series of B-sides that had already been released. Thinking he had a scoop, the second brother contacted the tabloid, reported the theft and offered to sell the tapes to the paper.

13. May 1997

Complaining that far too many web sites were violating copyright laws by posting Oasis lyrics, pictures and videos without permission, the band announced that they would begin shutting down all unauthorized Oasis pages.

There have been many more scandals involving the group, but we'll stop here.

Eleven Tragic Deaths

1. Ian Curtis—May 18, 1980

In the beginning, the lead singer of Joy Division was a fairly healthy person. His greatest medical problem was an occasional allergic reaction to sunlight, something which caused his hands to swell up like big red balloons. He also was known to be somewhat moody and people sometimes made fun of his phobia of foam rubber.

Ian may have first realized he was an epileptic when he took a civil service job that required he learn something about the condition. Reflecting on an incident in his mid-teens when a strobe light at a nightclub sent him into a seizure, Ian may have suspected that something was wrong, but if he did, he never pursued the matter. After midnight on December 27, 1978, all four members of Joy Division were on their way home from their first-ever gig in London when Ian suffered a strong seizure. He was taken to the hospital and upon his release was told to visit his family doctor. When he did, the doctor just shrugged and put Ian on a waiting list to see a specialist.

The seizures started to come much more frequently, sometimes as many as four in a week. Finally getting to see a specialist in January 1979, he was prescribed a series of anti-convulsive drugs. When the first didn't work, he tried the second; when that one had no effect, he moved to a third drug, and so on. Although some of the medication helped control the seizures, they were never eliminated and people around Ian began to wonder what was making his life more miserable: the epilepsy or the anti-epileptic drugs. Whatever the case, some of his friends and family noted that Ian's lyrics were getting darker and even more gloomy. "She's Lost Control," one of the songs on the Joy Division's *Unknown Pleasures* album, was allegedly written after Ian witnessed a woman having a seizure.

Ian's mood and outlook continued to deteriorate. As Joy Division's schedule became busier, the frequency of the attacks increased. During one particularly arduous series of shows in May 1979, Ian suffered four *grand mal* seizures in one night. It got to the point where he was afraid to hold his new baby daughter for fear he would lapse into a seizure. Adding an even more surreal touch to the story, Ian's doctor, the one who was supposed to be treating his illness, fell into a deep depression and shot himself.

By October 1979, things were not going well between Ian and his wife Deborah. Ian had become withdrawn and difficult, sometimes faking a seizure to get out of a tense situation or to manipulate people. He was also mixing his prescriptions with illegal drugs and lots of alcohol, resulting in wild mood swings and subtle but serious physical damage. Although Joy Division was slowly becoming more popular, money was so tight that the couple could no longer afford to keep the family dog. Then there was the matter of the secret affair he was having with a Belgian woman named Annik Honore.

Once Joy Division finished recording the *Closer* album, the group embarked on a gruelling series of gigs. During the first week of April, the band sometimes had to play two shows in two different venues on the same day. The pressures of the album, the tour, the prospect of an upcoming North American tour, his affair with Annik, his failing marriage with Deborah, his role as a new father, the epilepsy, the anti-epileptic drugs, the illegal drugs and the alcohol all combined to make things truly miserable for Ian.

On April 4, Ian suffered three attacks during the first five songs of a show in London before collapsing completely. The band would have stopped long before Ian passed out, but it had become impossible to tell whether Ian was having a seizure or just dancing in his trademark herky-jerky way. Disaster struck on April 7 when Ian purposely overdosed on his medication. He was rushed to the hospital, where he had his stomach pumped. Incredibly, the psychiatrist who examined Ian after this obvious suicide attempt concluded that he was *not* suicidal and sent him home.

The final Joy Division concert took place on May 2 at Birmingham University. The show was recorded and later released on the *Still* album—and if you listen carefully to the end of "Decades," you'll hear the crowd cheering madly. That's because Ian had just collapsed with another seizure.

On Thursday, May 15, Ian spent some time hanging out with bassist Peter Hook and playing pool at a local club. The next day, Peter dropped Ian off at his parents' house with instructions to start packing because the group was scheduled to leave for a big North American tour on Monday morning. On Saturday, Ian canceled plans to go over to guitarist Bernard Albrecht's house, saying that he wanted to rest up for the trip. That was the last time anyone in the band heard from him.

On the evening of Saturday May 17, Ian went back to his house at 77 Barton Street in Macclesfield, a suburb of Manchester. By this time, Deborah had moved out and was working as a bartender. She and Ian had spoken, agreeing that he needed some time alone and that she would spend the night at her parents' home and wouldn't come back to the house until at least ten the next morning.

Alone with the TV, Ian sat down to watch a 1977 film entitled *Stroszek*, which, ironically, tells the story of a musician and former mental patient who travels to America and is unable to decide between the two women in his life. During the movie, he drank several cups of very strong coffee, chasing it down with a shot of whiskey. Then, with pictures of his wife and daughter in front of him, he wrote a very long note to Deborah. He wrote all night.

It was dawn by the time he finished on the morning of May 18, 1980. He went over to the stereo and put on *The Idiot*, his favorite Iggy Pop album. Then he went out into the garden and got a length of rope from the clothesline. As the sun came up and Iggy Pop sang, Ian hung himself in the kitchen.

2. Ricky Wilson—October 13, 1985
Very little has ever been made public about the death of one of the founding members of the B52s, other than the fact that he died from an AIDS-related illness.

3. Nico—July 18, 1988
Icy cool and mysterious, Nico was a blonde ex-model/actress and an associate of Andy Warhol. Warhol persuaded the rest of the Velvet Underground to let her sing several songs on the group's debut album. After recording a number of solo albums over the years (and becoming somewhat of an icon to some members of the goth music community), she died while on vacation in Ibiza. A fall from her bicycle resulted in a fatal brain hemorrhage.

4. Pete de Freitas—June 14, 1989
De Freitas bolted from Echo and the Bunnymen in 1986, relocating from Liverpool to New Orleans where he formed a group called the Sex Goods. His departure, however, was short-lived and by early 1987, he was back playing drums behind Ian McCulloch, Will Sergeant and Les Pattison. On June 14, while the Bunnymen were auditioning new singers (McCulloch left in mid-1988), de Freitas was killed in a motorcycle accident.

5. Martin Hannett—April 18, 1991
The legendary Manchester producer, who helped make records with everyone from the Buzzcocks to Joy Division to the Stone Roses, died of complications resulting from years of alcohol and drug abuse.

6. Kurt Cobain—April 5th (?), 1994
By the end of 1993, it was very obvious that something was definitely bothering Kurt Cobain. Although he boasted that his drug problems were behind him, he continued

to have serious stomach pains which often had him taking powerful prescription drugs like Percodan and Buprenex for relief. But that's not all that was wrong; Cobain was very unhappy with life in general.

The first real hint that something was wrong came in July 1993 when police were called to settle a domestic dispute between Cobain and Courtney Love at their house in Seattle. At the time, a large quantity of guns and ammunition were seized. Six months later, disturbing news about the imminent breakup of Nirvana began to circulate. Other rumors mentioned that Cobain was very depressed and was back to using heroin again.

The beginning of the end was March 4, 1994, in room 541 of the Excelsior Hotel in Rome. Shortly after midnight, Cobain had one of the staff sent out to an all-night drug store to fill his prescription for Rohypnol, a strong tranquilizer and sleeping aid. Six hours later, Love found Cobain unconscious on the floor after he'd washed down a large amount of Roypnol with a bottle of champagne. A suicide note was found nearby.

By 6:30 a.m., Kurt was at Umberto I Hospital having his stomach pumped and for the next five hours, doctors administered emergency treatment for the overdose. His condition was so serious that CNN carried at least one report saying that he had died. Instead, Cobain was transferred to a private luxury clinic across town and by 3:45 that afternoon, he had regained consciousness. Within several days, an announcement was made that Cobain was "ill" and "suffering from exhaustion and the flu," and that all remaining dates on Nirvana's European tour had been canceled.

On March 18, police responded to another gun crisis at the Cobain house in Seattle. During a fight with Love, Cobain locked himself in a room full of guns and threatened to kill himself before the police arrived and diffused the situation.

That was enough for Love. Two days later, she organized a "tough love" intervention which apparently convinced Cobain to seek some kind professional help, and within a week he checked into nine-by-six Room 206 at the Exodus Recover Center at Daniel Freeman Hospital in Marina del Rey, California, the same rehab facility he had attended two years earlier. This time he lasted less than 48 hours. After a visit from Gibby Haynes of the Butthole Surfers on April 1, he climbed the six-foot security wall and caught Delta flight 788 for Seattle.

Two days earlier, Cobain had his friend Dylan Carlson buy a Remington M11 20-gauge shotgun from Stan Baker Sports in Seattle, paying $308.17 in cash. Carlson, knowing that his friend was a little paranoid, thought Cobain wanted it for protection

(Cobain probably didn't want to buy it himself since he was already on record as having had several guns confiscated by the Seattle police.) After spending the night at the house on Lake Washington Boulevard, he took a cab early the next morning to Seattle Guns and purchased 25 shotgun shells. Several witnesses who encountered him over the next two days recall that he looked wasted and depressed, and that he was acting strangely.

By the afternoon of April 2, Courtney Love was frantic and called a private detective named Tom Grant, ordering him to find Cobain and to make sure that he didn't hurt himself. On April 4, Cobain's mother, who was also very concerned about her son's state of mind, filed a missing persons report with police, indicating that she felt Cobain was definitely suicidal.

Some time on April 5, Cobain returned to his house in Seattle. After moving to the room above the garage in the back yard, he wrote a long letter to his wife and child, laid out his wallet to display his driver's license and then injected a mixture of valium and heroin into his right arm. Taking the gun his friend had purchased the previous week, Cobain put the barrel in his mouth and pulled the trigger. His body was not found until the morning of April 8 when an electrician came to do some work at the house. The autopsy later revealed that the amount of heroin in Cobain's blood (1.52 milligrams per liter), along with the amounts of valium and diazepam, would have been fatal had he not shot himself.

7. Jim Ellison—June 20, 1996

To this day, no one is sure why the Material Issue singer took his own life. Although the band had under-performed in terms of expectations and were without a contract at the time of his death, Ellison's friends and family said that his music career had nothing to do with his death. Ellison was well-respected within the alt-rock community and had plans, not only for a new Material Issue album, but also for a new spin-off group called the Wild Bunch, featuring Smithereens singer Pat DiNizio, former Psychedelic Furs drummer Mars Williams and Blondie drummer Clem Burke. He had also written songs with longtime friend Liz Phair, one of which ended up in the Bertolucci film *Stealing Beauty*. And to top it off, drugs and alcohol were never big in Ellison's life. It's no wonder that many people were shocked when he was found in his closed garage, slumped over the handlebars of his moped, dead of carbon monoxide poisoning. A suicide note was found nearby.

8. Rob Collins—July 23, 1996

Having survived a trip to prison after somehow getting mixed up in the armed robbery of a liquor store in 1992, things were looking up for the Charlatans' keyboardist. The group appeared to be making a comeback, and sessions for their fifth album were going well. Working out of Monnow Valley studios in Monmouth, South Wales, the group decided to take a break by joining the birthday party of a friend at a local pub. After a few drinks, everyone headed back to work—everyone except Rob, whose red BMW had been blocked in the parking lot. When he was finally able to get going, Rob stepped on the gas so he could catch up with the rest of his mates. That's when disaster struck.

Some time just after 11:30, the car caught a bit of the curb, causing Rob to lose control. The BMW swerved violently, hitting several cars before careering through a hedge and into a ditch. Rob, who was not wearing a seatbelt, was thrown from the car. A woman who heard the crash called an ambulance and administered mouth-to-mouth resuscitation before Rob was transferred to Abergavenny Hospital. Shortly after midnight, Rob Collins was declared dead.

A coroner's inquest in October reported that Rob had a blood alcohol level that was twice the legal limit. Gwent coroner David Bowen was quoted as saying, "Mr. Collins should not have been anywhere near the steering wheel of a car, let alone driving it." His passenger, a friend named Robert Peet, was injured but survived.

9. Jason Thirsk—August 5, 1996

Several months after he left his job playing bass for the hardcore punk band Pennywise, Thirsk was found on the floor of his home in Hermosa Beach, California, dead of a fatal gunshot wound to the stomach. Although police treated his death as a suicide, a statement from the band insisted that Thirsk shot himself accidentally.

10. Chris Acland—October 17, 1996

On Friday, October 18, 1996, 4AD Records issued a short press release: "4AD and CEC management are devastated to announce the tragic news that Chris Acland, Lush's drummer, sadly took his own life yesterday."

Chris had spent the last weeks of his life in a rather sudden state of depression. Discouraged by the lack of any major commercial success by Lush and living on less than $1,000 a month after seven hard years in the music business, Acland was unsure whether he wanted to join the band on a string of European dates.

Realizing that he had a problem, Acland went to a doctor who prescribed some common anti-depressants. Then, accepting an invitation to stay with his parents, he moved to their home in Cumbria, England. For reasons that aren't clear, Acland's mood suddenly deteriorated and two weeks later, to the shock of everyone, he hung himself in his parents' garage. His body was discovered by his father Oliver.

11. Jeff Buckley—May 29, 1997

The last anyone saw of Jeff Buckley was late Thursday, May 29. In Memphis to work on pre-production for a new album, he and his friend Keith Foti spent part of the evening on the banks of the Mississippi near a marina at the Mud Island Harbor, playing the guitar, singing some songs and listening to the radio. At around 9:00 p.m., Buckley decided to wade into the chilly river in his jeans and Doc Martens, singing Led Zeppelin's "Whole Lotta Love." Just as he began to swim on his back, a tugboat went by, leaving behind a large wake. Seeing that the resulting wave was coming his way, Foti turned to move the radio so it wouldn't get wet. When he looked back at the water, Buckley was gone. Police believe that the combination of the strong current and wake generated by the boat caused Buckley to lose his footing, and that once he fell under, he was unable to recover. His body was spotted from a passing riverboat the following Wednesday night at the foot of Beale Street. Because no drugs or alcohol were involved, his death was ruled an accident. Buckley's father, folk hero Tim Buckley, died of a drug overdose in 1975.

Twelve More Unfortunate Deaths

1. **Billy Murcia (New York Dolls)—November 6, 1972:** Choked or drowned on coffee force-fed to him by his girlfriend in order to keep him awake following an overdose.
2. **Peter Laughner (Pere Ubu)—June 22, 1977:** Acute pancreatitis.
3. **D. Boon (Minutemen)—December 23, 1985:** Van accident in the Arizona desert.
4. **Jon Spence (founding member of No Doubt)—December 1987**: Committed suicide after bout of depression.
5. **Stiv Bators (Dead Boys, Lords of the New Church)—June 4, 1990:** Although he walked away after being run over by a bus in Paris, he died from his injuries that night.
6. **Rob Tyner (MC5)—September 17, 1991:** Died from a heart attack.
7. **Joe Cole (Black Flag roadie)—December 19, 1991:** Killed during a robbery at the home of his friend, Henry Rollins.
8. **Jerry Nolan (New York Dolls)—January 14, 1992:** Suffered a stroke, brought on by pneumonia, meningitis and years of drug abuse.
9. **Mia Zapata (Gits)—July 7, 1993:** Murdered in the Capitol Hill area of Seattle.
10. **Doug Hopkins (Gin Blossoms)—December 5, 1993:** Depressed over being tossed out of the band and his alcoholism, he shot himself in the head at his home in Tempe, Arizona.

11. **Fred "Sonic" Smith (MC5 and husband of Patti Smith)—November 4, 1994:** Died from a heart attack.
12. **El Duce (Eldon Hoke of the Mentors)—May 20, 1997:** Hit by a train in Riverside, California, while intoxicated.

10 Infamous Drug Deaths

1. Sid Vicious—February 2, 1979

On October 12, 1978, after he was charged with second degree murder in the death of his girlfriend Nancy Spungen, Sid was sent to the detox unit at Ryker's Island Prison in New York. Bail was set at $50,000, which was paid on October 17 by the Sex Pistols' manager Malcolm McLaren. Five days later, Sid attempted suicide and was sent to a hospital psychiatric unit. Shortly after his release, he got into a broken beer bottle fight on December 9 with Patti Smith's brother at Hurrah's, a Manhattan disco. His bail was revoked and Sid was once again thrown in jail. Sid remained in jail until February 1, 1979, when he was finally released to await trial at home.

One of the people waiting for him was his mother Anne Beverly. Affectionately known among Sid's punk friends as "Ma Vicious," she thought she'd surprise her son with a heroin treat. After a quick hit and a spaghetti dinner at the apartment of Michelle Robinson, Sid's new girlfriend, everyone went to bed.

At some point that night, Sid got up and fished the rest of the heroin out of his mother's purse, injected it and went back to bed. Sid's body, uncommonly clean after two months without drugs, couldn't handle the heroin and some time during the early morning hours of February 2, at 63 Bank Street in Manhattan, Sid slipped into a coma and died.

On September 6, 1996, his mother followed. Depressed at the notion that the Sex Pistols would reunite without her son and discouraged at the lack of success with her new band (Road Rage, who often performed Sex Pistols covers), she carefully packed her bags and wrote out a suicide note, before deliberately overdosing on a mixture of drugs and alcohol.

2. Hillel Slovak—June 26, 1988

Slovak tried heroin for the first time in 1984, just as the Red Hot Chili Peppers were really starting to make a name for themselves. Within a year, he was a full-blown addict, often getting his supply from a dangerous drug ring controlled by the mob. When the band went on tour, he managed to develop relationships with dealers in every city. The rest of the band saw what the drug was doing to him, but no matter how much they tried to reason with Slovak, he refused to get help. Things came to a head during a European tour in the spring of 1988, when Slovak walked out on the band in the middle of a show, saying that he simply didn't want to play anymore.

When the group returned to LA, all he could think about was scoring more heroin. On the evening of Saturday, June 25, 1988, Slovak decided that three weeks without shooting up was just too much. Leaving his apartment to buy a stash, he visited an unknown dealer who sold him a quantity of heroin. When he returned home in the early morning hours of June 26, he injected the drug, which hit his body like a bomb. He slipped into a coma and died. His body wasn't discovered until some time on June 27.

3. Andrew Wood—March 19, 1990
Not only was Andrew Wood a big supporter of the Seattle music scene, he also supported the city's heroin trade. Wood had wanted to be a big-time rock star all his life and he believed that doing drugs was part of the scene. By the time he was 18, he was already carelessly injecting heroin using dirty needles, a habit that led to a case of hepatitis in 1986.

In 1988, his band Mother Love Bone was in big demand by several major labels, and the group signed a lucrative contract with Polydor. Promising to make an honest effort to clean up his act, Wood enrolled in a drug treatment program which slowly weaned him off his habit. But on Friday, March 16, 1990, just a few weeks before the group's debut album was scheduled to be released, Wood failed to show up for a band meeting. That night, he was found at his girlfriend's apartment, a syringe still hanging out of his arm containing the remnants of his first fix in 116 days. He was rushed to the hospital, but never regained consciousness. On the following Monday, with Queen's *A Night at the Opera* playing in his room, Wood was declared clinically dead and, with the consent of his parents, was removed from life support. On March 28, the King County medical examiner declared his death to be an accidental overdose of heroin.

4. Johnny Thunders—April 23, 1991
When it was announced that punk guitar icon Johnny Thunders had died, most people weren't surprised that he was dead—they were surprised that he had lived as long as he had.

Thunders was an extremely influential guitarist. He once said, "Rock and roll is simply an attitude. You don't have to play the greatest guitar." He was also a notorious substance abuser. Stories of his excess were legendary among the people who knew him from the mid-70s at CBGB, Max's Kansas City and other New York punk clubs. Still, he managed to hang on for years, supporting his habit in any way he could.

In 1990, he had plans to form a band with Wayne Kramer of the MC5. Sickly, gaunt and obviously past his prime as a musician, he never managed to complete the project. Instead, armed with $20,000 he had earned during a solo tour of Japan, he decided to move to New Orleans, where his plan was to hire some blues musicians to do a solo album. He checked into the St. Peter's Guest House in the French Quarter and started to circulate through the streets, making contacts for drug buys. Several days later, on April 23, 1991, police were called to his room, where his body had been discovered on the floor. He apparently had been given a strong shot of LSD, which he tried to counteract with a massive dose of methadone.

5. Kristin Pfaff—June 15, 1994
Seventy-eight days after Kurt Cobain died, Hole bassist Kristin Pfaff died of a heroin overdose. She had been trying to shake her drug habit for years, but it had gripped her even tighter when she moved to Seattle, a city notorious for its heroin scene. Tragically, she was literally just hours away from moving back to Minneapolis in an honest effort to clean up. But one final dose, as she lay in her bathtub, proved to be enough to kill her. Fearing the worst, friends contacted the police who broke her door and found Pfaff lying on her back with all her drug paraphernalia beside her.

6. Bob Stinson—February 15, 1995
Fired in 1987 by the Replacements for excessive drinking, Bob Stinson was virtually the only original member of the band not to release a solo album. He was found dead of a drug overdose in his Minneapolis apartment, the victim of many years of depression and drug and alcohol abuse.

7. Dwayne Goettel—August 22, 1995
Skinny Puppy was a group that endured a long, slow death. In the last years of the band, there were problems with their record label and with a series of record producers, not to mention major issues between the members of the group. Drummer Dwayne Goettel had a very hard time dealing with all of it. He became erratic and self-destructive, sometimes cutting himself up with strings of barbed wire. He went on drug binges and then kept clean for a few weeks before the cycle started again.

On June 12, 1995, Nivek Ogre finally carried through on his threat to quit the band, which invalidated the contract between Skinny Puppy and their label. The group was officially cast adrift a month later. Goettel was terribly distraught, since music was the only thing he knew how to do. He left the house in Malibu where Puppy had been working and went home to his parents' place in Edmonton, Alberta, to collect his thoughts. On August 22, 1995, he took a large dose of heroin and died.

8. Shannon Hoon—October 21, 1995

The night before he died, Shannon Hoon performed with Blind Melon at a show in Houston. It hadn't been a great gig, mainly because Hoon had dug deep into a new stash of cocaine before the band even went on. After the show, he was angry and irritable, ranting about how Blind Melon didn't seem to be going anywhere—and the more he yelled, the more coke he snorted.

At 7 a.m. the next morning, the band's tour bus pulled into the parking lot outside the Hotel Inter-Continental on Charles Avenue in New Orleans and, some time before 9 a.m., Hoon called his girlfriend, talking to her for about an hour. At around 10 a.m., he slipped out for a newspaper and a bit of breakfast before returning to the bus. Most of the crew were asleep, so Shannon crept past everyone to his area at the back of bus and settled into guitarist Christopher Thorn's bunk. He went to sleep and never woke up. The official coroner's report listed the cause as a cocaine overdose.

"This city got him every time—the minute he got here," guitarist Rogers Stevens later told *Rolling Stone*. "It got him this time."

9. Brad Nowell—May 25, 1996

Sublime had been waging the punk wars from their base in Long Beach, California, since 1988 and were finally on the verge of breaking things wide open. A new album was ready, the European tour had been booked and indications were that 1996 was going to be Sublime's best year ever.

Things were looking good on a personal level; Nowell had just been married a week ago and he was looking forward to his new life with his 11-month-old son. Most of all, Nowell seemed to have his substance abuse problems under control. For the last five years, he had been in and out of rehab centers, battling with an addiction to heroin and cocaine. By the spring of 1996, he had been clean and sober for two months and it looked like he was going to be able to remain clean indefinitely.

But on the evening of May 24, Brad fell off the wagon at his motel in San Francisco. He went on a big drug binge, just hours before a sold-out show, five days before the start of a European tour. The relapse killed him. Having been drug-free for so long, his body couldn't tolerate the shock of what would have been a normal dose in the past.

10. Billy Mackenzie—January 23, 1997

The Associates attracted attention in the middle of the British New Romantic movement of the early 80s. Together with partner Alan Rankine, Billy MacKenzie enjoyed several hits in Britain before the duo split in 1983. After languishing in obscurity for most of the 80s, MacKenzie had just signed a deal with Nude Records, the home label of Suede, when his mood took a turn for the worse.

He was last seen by his father in Auchterhouse, near Dundee, Scotland. Two days later, he was found dead of a deliberate overdose of prescription drugs in the shed where he kept his dogs. A suicide note was left behind, but gave no reason as to why he took his life. Some people believe that MacKenzie was deeply depressed over the death of his mother Lily.

Ten More Heroin Casualties

1. **Darby Crash**, singer, the Germs—December 7, 1980
2. **James Honeyman-Scott**, guitarist, Pretenders—June 16, 1982
3. **Pete Farndon**, bassist, Pretenders—April 14, 1983
4. **Tracy Pew**, bassist, the Birthday Party—1986
5. **Will Shatter**, bassist, Flipper—December 9, 1987
6. **Jeff Ward**, touring drummer, Nine Inch Nails. Date unknown
7. **Stefanie Sargant**, guitarist, Seven Year Bitch—June 28, 1992
8. **G.G. Allin**, extreme performer—June 28, 1993
9. **Jonathan Melvoin**, touring keyboardist, Smashing Pumpkins—July 12, 1996
10. **Craig Scott**, the Dylans and touring keyboardist with Elastica—March 23, 1997

Eleven Musical Prodigies

1. The Jam

Soon after Paul Weller (age 15), Bruce Foxton (age 17) and Rick Buckler (age 17) began meeting to rehearse during lunch at school in Woking, England, they adopted the name the Jam because that's what they did every day. As early as 1973, they were winning awards for "best local group." They got to be so good that they were hired to play at local pubs, strip clubs, community centers and even a prison. It didn't take long for word of this new, young pop band to attract the attention of several major record companies. Acting as their manager and chief negotiator, John Weller (Paul's father) worked out a deal with Polydor for £6,000 and on April 29, 1977, the Jam released their first single "In the City," the first of two dozen hits over the band's career. Paul Weller was one month short of his twentieth birthday.

2. U2

The members of U2 have been playing together since they were all in their mid-teens. By the time most of them had turned 18, they were playing regularly all across Ireland, even winning an important national talent contest. Part of the reason U2 managed to get all this work and exposure so soon was because Adam Clayton was expelled from school and, with nothing else to occupy his time, he began acting as the group's manager. U2's first record, a three-track 7-inch entitled *U2: 3*, was released in October 1979. Bono, Clayton and Larry Mullen were all 19 while the Edge was 18.

3. Tori Amos

In the 60s and 70s, a number of people in the Washington-Baltimore area were convinced that little Myra Ellen Amos was a true musical prodigy. She began banging on the family piano at age two and by the time she was four, she was playing pieces that she picked up by ear. When she was five, Ellen won a full scholarship to the prestigious Peabody Conservatory of Music at Johns Hopkins University in Baltimore. Both her parents and her instructors were convinced that Ellen was on her way to becoming a truly great concert pianist.

But it didn't work out that way. Ellen was more interested in playing the songs she heard on the radio, rather than the works of Mozart and Chopin. Her refusal to learn to sight read music frustrated her instructors, who complained that picking up music by ear was *not* how it was done. Finally, fed up with Ellen's lack of seriousness and discipline, the Peabody expelled her at age ten. So much for being the next great concert pianist.

But Ellen still loved her piano and by the time she was 13 she was playing the piano lounge circuit, along with the occasional gay bar, always chaperoned by her father, a Methodist minister. In 1980 at age 17, Ellen and her brother Michael recorded and released an independent 7-inch single called "Baltimore" on Ellen's own MEA Records label. Several years later, Ellen adopted the name "Tori" (after a type of pine tree) and turned professional.

4. Redd Kross

Steve and Jeff McDonald have been working on Redd Kross for a lot longer than most people realize. They started the group in Los Angeles in 1979. Jeff, age 15, was the singer while Steve, age 11, played bass. Within a year, they were opening punk shows for bands like Black Flag. A few months after that, Redd Kross recorded their debut album *Born Innocent*. Some observers referred to the group as the "punk Partridge family."

5. Live

The members of Live really can't remember being in any other band, having started playing together in York, Pennsylvania when they were just 13 years old. Guitarist Chad Taylor was perhaps the most serious of the bunch. When he was barely 13, he sent a letter to the head of a major record label and told him that the company could save a lot of time and effort if he would sign Live now, before they turned into one of the biggest bands in the world. As conceited as that sounded, Taylor turned out to be correct.

As the members of Live progressed through their teens, they attracted a decent following of fans. By the end of high school things had reached the point where the guys had to make a serious decision: go to college or continue with the group? Although their parents weren't pleased with their choice, it turned out to be the right one. Live was soon discovered and signed by RadioActive Records, after they were spotted playing a club in New York City. At the time of that gig, all the members were still too young to buy a beer at the bar.

6. Ash

Ash is one of the youngest professional groups to ever come out of Northern Ireland. They were formed in 1992 and, by 1994, they were attracting attention from all over the U.K. All of them were just 17 years old. During the day, they went to high school like normal teenagers. But at night, they were either rehearsing or playing clubs and bars.

But school kept getting in the way. Homework forced them to turn down offers of opening slots for Pearl Jam and Soul Asylum. On the day their first single came out, they were too busy to celebrate because they were studying for their final exams. But it was worth the wait—that first single made the group the subject of an international bidding war. Thinking that Ash would be the "next Green Day," the group was flown to America (forcing them to miss an exam or two) to discuss several potential major label contracts.

The youth angle was played up with *Trailer*, the first Ash EP. The original cover featured a woman talking on the phone and saying, "They're still kids—too young to marry, vote or drink in a pub. But tragically, they're not too young to sell themselves for sex."

7. Supergrass

When they were about 14 years old, guitarist Gaz Coombes and drummer Danny Goffey were members of the Jennifers, a group that released at least one single on the Nude label in 1990. When they broke up, they were joined by bassist Mickey Quinn. When their first single "Caught by the Fuzz" was released in 1994, Danny was 18, while Gaz was barely 19.

8. Green Day

Bille Joe Armstrong and Mike Dirnt had been playing in bands together in Oxford, England, since they were 11 years old while drummer Tre Cool started his musical career with a group called the Lookouts when he was about 12. When Green Day officially came together in Oakland, California, in 1989 and recorded an EP called *1000 Hours*, they were all 17.

9. Silverchair

After years of listening to their parents' Black Sabbath and Led Zeppelin records, three school chums from Newcastle, Australia, decided in 1992, at age 13, to form their own band. Two years later, they entered a demo tape into a national talent contest sponsored by one of the country's largest radio stations. Out of more than 800 entries, Silverchair's "Tomorrow" was picked as the winner and within weeks, the group had the number one single in the nation. This success led to a four-track EP (which featured another number one single) and then to a full album entitled *Frogstomp*. Recorded in just nine days, the album went on to sell several million copies around the world and landed the group dozens of gigs at big outdoor festivals, opening slots for bands like the Red Hot Chili Peppers and several sold-out headlining tours—all before any of the members were even old enough to drive.

10. Radish

Led by 15-year-old Greenville, Texas native Ben Kweller, Radish was the subject of a major label bidding war in late 1996 after the group put together a three-song demo tape and sent it off in the mail. Ben started playing the piano when he was five and by the time he was ten, he was also playing the guitar and drums, as well as writing songs. The group's 1997 debut album was entitled *Restraining Bolt*.

11. Stinky Puffs

Simon Fair Timony probably holds the record for being the youngest person to ever release an alt-rock record. Born in 1984, he began writing lyrics when he was nine, and by the time he was ten, the Stinky Puffs had an EP entitled *A Little Tiny Smelly Bit of the Stinky Puffs*. Simon was accompanied by his mother on drums, his stepfather Jad Fair (of the band Half Japanese), indie producer Don Fleming and Cody Ranaldo (son of Sonic Youth's Lee Ranaldo) on guitars.

Part 5

New Adventures in Hi-Fi: In the Studio

True Stories Behind Famous Songs

"Blasphemous Rumours"—Depeche Mode
Some Great Reward, 1984

Martin Gore has been in charge of writing all of Depeche Mode's material since 1981 and, as with all good songwriters, he keeps his eyes open for things that move and inspire him. One of the most controversial songs he ever wrote was "Blasphemous Rumors."

The song has its roots in two events. The first was an unsuccessful suicide attempt by a 16-year-old boy who had pronounced himself "bored with life." Martin had also recently heard of an 18-year-old who had experienced a much needed life-altering religious epiphany. Two days later, he died in a terrible car accident. The irony of the two situations was not lost on Martin and the more he thought about it, the more he felt that God and Christianity didn't make much sense to him anymore. At some point in his discussions on the matter with friends, someone said, "God must have a sick sense of humor"—and that became the foundation for the chorus of "Blasphemous Rumors."

"Panic"—The Smiths
Single, 1986

The hated DJ in the song seems to have been Steven Wright, a BBC Radio 1 announcer who often commented on how much he disliked the Smiths. However, the nuclear accident at Chernobyl also played a role in the lyrics. On the date of the meltdown, April 26, 1986, Morrissey was listening to the radio when the news flash came across. As soon as it was over, the announcer went straight into "I'm Your Man" from Wham! Morrissey thought playing a vacuous pop song immediately following such grave news was terribly insensitive. He remembers his first reaction was "that DJ should be killed."

There was also a third element to the song. Morrissey was very distressed over the general state of pop music and discouraged by the fact that all the attention was going to acts like Wham! and Janet Jackson, instead of the Smiths. His frustration came out in the lyrics to "Panic."

"One Tree Hill"—U2
The Joshua Tree, 1987

Greg Carroll was a U2 fan from New Zealand who signed on as a member of the band's road crew in 1984. When the Unforgettable Fire tour wrapped up, Carroll insisted on staying with the group in Dublin. One rainy night in 1986, he and a friend went for a ride on their motorcycles, deciding at the last minute to have some fun by swapping machines. Carroll wasn't ready for his friend's more powerful machine and had a hard time controlling it. He ran into the back of a car driven by a drunk driver who didn't signal when making a turn. Greg was killed instantly.

The incident shook Bono and Larry Mullen deeply. Both had considered Carroll a friend and insisted on accompanying his body back to New Zealand. Carroll was buried in a traditional three day, three night Maori funeral outside Auckland in a place called One Tree Hill, a place where he had taken Bono on his first trip to the country. Angry and sad at what had happened to his friend, Bono wrote down some of his impressions and feelings, later shaping them into a song for *The Joshua Tree*.

"Smells Like Teen Spirit"—Nirvana
Nevermind, 1991

Centuries from now, musicologists will look back with amazement on how a musical revolution was launched by a brand of deodorant.

When Kurt Cobain was living on North Pear Street in Olympia, Washington, he would occasionally go out with Kathleen Hanna, leader of a local riot girl group called Bikini Kill. After a few drinks, they decided to indulge in their common passion of spraying graffiti everywhere. The spree continued even after they returned to Cobain's apartment; they covered the walls, the furniture and even the floor with various slogans and sayings. One of the lines Kathleen sprayed on the wall was "Kurt Smells Like Teen Spirit." Thinking that she was referring to the "teen revolution" in Olympia he had heard others talking about, he took Kathleen's words as a compliment, later incorporating it into a song he was writing for Nirvana's first major label album. It wasn't until after the song was finished that he realized that Hanna was referring to a fruity-smelling brand of deodorant manufactured by Mennen and marketed to teens.

"Jeremy"—Pearl Jam
Ten, 1991

Jeremy Delle was an unhappy kid from Richardson, Texas, for whom things were not going well at home or at school. On January 8, 1991, Jeremy decided that he had had enough. Shortly after his English teacher yelled at him for missing so many classes, he took out a .357 magnum and shot himself in the head in full view of the rest of the class. The story was covered in media reports around the world and came to the attention of Eddie Vedder, who knew what it was like to grow up with troubles at home. The Pearl Jam song "Jeremy" features Vedder's impressions of the incident.

"Me and a Gun"—Tori Amos
Little Earthquakes, 1991

The song stems from an incident after a show in Los Angeles in the mid 80s. Having agreed to give a member of the audience a ride home, Tori was held hostage and raped. After being silent on the matter for many years, Tori courageously helped found RAINN (the Rape, Abuse and Incest National Network), an organization designed to help victims of sexual assault.

"Spoonman"—Soundgarden
Superunknown, 1994

The man who inspired this song is also featured in the video. Artis is a real-life Seattle performer who began playing the spoons in 1974. Busking was his only source of income for years. Eventually, he became something of a local legend. Since the guys in Soundgarden were big fans, they decided to write a song about him.

"Country House"—Blur
The Great Escape, 1995

The whole song is a shot at Dave Balfe, the former head of Food Records, Blur's label. For the first part of their career, the band had a love-hate relationship with Balfe, who had a reputation for being a very demanding boss. But in April 1994, Balfe sold Food to EMI, making a lot of money in the process. He took some of that money and bought himself a very large and very expensive home in the country.

"Hey Man, Nice Shot"—Filter
Short Bus, 1995

When the song first came out, rumors began to spread that the song was a snide look at Kurt Cobain's suicide. The truth of the matter was that while the song did deal with suicide, it had nothing to do with Cobain.

In the 80s, R. Bud Dwyer, treasurer for the state of Pennsylvania, faced serious allegations of corruption. There were stories of bribes, kickbacks and odd contracts extending back over years. By December 1986, the law had caught up to Dwyer and he was convicted on 11 counts of conspiracy, perjury, mail fraud and racketeering. On January 22, 1987, just one day before he was sentenced, he scheduled a press conference. All the media was there, expecting Dwyer to do the honorable thing and resign from his post. After reading a long statement, Dwyer reached into a yellow manila envelope and withdrew a .357 magnum. Then, with all the TV cameras rolling, he shot himself in the head.

Several TV stations decided to show the unedited tape on the evening news and naturally many people were ready with their VCRs. Someone gave a copy to Richard Patrick, Filter's guitarist who was then moved to write "Hey Man, Nice Shot."

"J.A.R"–Green Day
Angus soundtrack, 1995
"J.A.R." were the initials of Jason Andrew Relva, a fun-loving friend of the band who was killed in a car accident. The abruptness of his death is symbolized by the way Billie Joe Armstrong doesn't finish the last line of the song.

Five Examples of Material That Was Inspired by Books, Literature and High Culture

1. "Killing an Arab"—The Cure
The very first Cure single was based on Albert Camus's novel *L'Etranger*.

2. "Wuthering Heights"—Kate Bush
The song is based on the classic book by Emily Bronte.

3. "Cloudbusting"—Kate Bush
Both the song and the subsequent video co-starring Donald Sutherland were inspired by *A Book of Dreams* by Peter Reich, the story of a scientist who built rain-making machines. In the book, he and his son test the inventions over a stretch of land called Organon.

4. "Scentless Apprentice"—Nirvana
This track was written by Kurt Cobain after he read a 1986 novel entitled *Perfume* by Patrick Süsskind. It tells the story of a perfume maker in revolutionary France who has no sense of smell.

5. *Pinkerton*—Weezer

Much of the album is based upon B.F. Pinkerton, the lead tenor character in the Puccini opera *Madame Butterfly*.

Thirteen Songs Allegedly Inspired by Kurt Cobain's Suicide

1. "About a Boy"—Patti Smith
2. "Mighty K.C."—For Squirrels
3. "You're One"—Imperial Teen
4. "Let Me In"—REM
5. "I Love You Anyway"—Stinky Puffs
6. "Sleeps With Angels"—Neil Young
7. "Queen/Mother"—Julian Cope
8. "Into Yer Shtik"—Mudhoney
9. "Last Exit"—Pearl Jam
10. "My Hero"—Foo Fighters
11. "Don't Wake Daddy"—The Tragically Hip
12. "Saint Cobain"—Vernon Reid
13. "I'm Still Remembering"—The Cranberries

Seven Accusations of Plagiarism

1. In 1992, the manufacturers of a toilet bowl cleaner called Flushco sued the Clash, alleging that the song "Inoculated City" was based on one of the company's advertising jingles.
2. New Order settled a case out of court with American folk singer John Denver, when Denver complained that New Order's "Run" sounded far too similar to his 1969 song "Leaving on a Jet Plane."
3. In 1983, British Airways used an unauthorized snippet of the Beastie Boys' "Beastie Revolution" in a commercial. The airline ended up paying the group $40,000.
4. Oasis was sued by the members of the Monty Python comedy troop when it was pointed out that "Whatever" sounded a little too much like "How Sweet to be an Idiot," a song from a 1973 TV sketch. "Shakermaker" was scrutinized by the Coca-Cola Corporation after it came to their attention that some of the melody was very similar to "I'd Like to Teach the World to Sing," a Coke jingle from the earlier 70s. It also didn't help the Oasis case much when Liam Gallagher insisted

on inserting words from the original Coke jingle into "Shakermaker" whenever the band performed live.

5. The Cranberries were the target of a lawsuit launched by a band called Blink which contended that their 1994 song "It's Not My Fault" was parroted in the Cranberries' "Forever Yellow Skies." One musicologist declared the similarities between the two songs were too close to be a coincidence.

6. In 1995, a judge ordered Elastica to compensate the Stranglers, ruling that their song "Waking Up" bore too many similarities to "No More Heroes." A similar ruling forced Elastica to share the royalties from "Connection" with Wire, because the introduction of the song was almost identical to their song "Three Girl Rhumba."

7. In January 1997, Kevin Rowland of Dexy's Midnight Runners apologized for saying that he wrote the group's 1982 hit "Come On Eileen" by himself. He admitted he stole the idea from guitarist Kevin Archer, who later quit in disgust. In a public statement, Rowland said, "The idea and sound was his. I stole it from him, hurting Kevin Archer deeply in the process. I conned people all over the world, from the people close to me and the people I worked with, to the fans, to the radio and TV programmers, and I made a lot of money. To everybody I conned, I'm sorry."

A Guide to Hidden Tracks on CD

With a capacity of 650 megabytes, a single compact disk can hold approximately 75 minutes of music. But since that's much more than the typical album, most CD releases have many megabytes of unused capacity. Some artists (such as Sarah McLachlan, the Cranberries, Soundgarden and dozens of others) have issued so-called "enhanced" CDs which, along with the expected music, also contain data that can be read by a computer's CD-ROM. This material may include everything from lyric sheets and pictures to complete full-motion videos.

Other artists have used this excess capacity to hide some buried treasures, extra musical surprises that are not listed on the disk or in the liner notes. These unofficial, uncredited, unlisted mystery tracks may be full songs, strange musical snippets or even random bits of studio noise.

This material can be put into three distinct categories. The first is the "unlisted bonus song," full songs that are not listed in the liner notes but nevertheless get a distinct and separate track on the CD. "Mystery songs" are tacked on at the end (and lately, at the beginning) of the disk and are not given a separate track. Finally, there's "mystery audio," strange, unidentifiable, non-songs that are hidden somewhere on the CD.

Why go through all this trouble? Perhaps for shock value. Maybe the artist wants to reward fans who take the time to explore the whole CD. Maybe it's a subtle way to sabotage the "random play" function on the CD player. Or maybe this is a way of making up for the fact that the artwork for CDs is so small, making it difficult to hide messages and other cool things the way it used to be done with full-size vinyl record sleeves.

With all this in mind, here are some examples of hidden material that has appeared over the years. There are many other examples (including albums from KMFDM, Big Audio Dynamite, Bush, Spacehog and more), but this is a good start.

1. *Another Music in a Different Kitchen*—The Buzzcocks (1978)
Watch for a semi-reprise of "Boredom."

2. *London Calling*—The Clash (1979)
When *London Calling* was released as a double vinyl album, fans soon noticed that although the liner notes listed 18 songs, there was a nineteenth song at the end of side four. The fault lay with the Clash, who decided to include the song at the last second, long after the artwork and liner notes had been printed. Since then, "Train in Vain" has never been listed on any version of *London Calling*, even when the album was transferred to CD.

3. *Lifes Rich Pageant*—REM (1986)
REM decided to add more songs to the album after the artwork and liner notes had been finished. To make matters even more confusing, the track listing doesn't match up with the actual running order of the CD. For example, one version of the album lists "Fall on Me" as track nine, when in fact, it comes up as track three. The first extra song appears on track six and is entitled "Underneath the Bunker," a tribute to San Francisco's Camper Van Beethoven. The second extra song "(I Am) Superman" shows up on track 12. This is a cover of a 1969 B-side originally issued by an obscure Texas band called Clique. The sound at the beginning of the song is a string-operated talking Godzilla doll which the band found during a Japan tour.

4. *Green*—REM (1988)

The eleventh song on the album is listed in the liner notes, but without a title. As a result, it became known as "Untitled." When it turned up on the B-side of the "Stand" 12-inch, it was listed as "The Eleventh Untitled Song."

5. *This Is The Day…This Is The Hour…This is This*—Pop Will Eat Itself (1989)

Track 15 features a Youth remix of "Wise Up! Sucker!" which was previously available only as a hard-to-find 12-inch single.

6. *Nevermind*—Nirvana (1991)

Although the original version of *Nevermind* features 12 songs, subsequent editions featured an unlisted song called "Endless, Nameless" that appears out of the silence ten minutes and three seconds after the end of "Something in the Way." Early editions of *Nevermind* don't include the extra track because when the CD was being mastered for the first time, no one knew that there was anything beyond track 12 to master. If you listen closely at the 19:32 mark, Kurt Cobain can be heard smashing his guitar. Weird Al Yankovic parodied "Endless, Nameless" on his album *Off the Deep End*.

7. *Ten*—Pearl Jam (1991)

There's an unlisted reprise of "Once" (track one) that appears about 20 seconds after "Release" fades away.

8. *Broken*—Nine Inch Nails (1992)

There are at least four versions of this release. All four contain six clearly labeled songs, while three also include two unlisted bonus tracks. The first edition of Broken featured the two bonus songs on a separate 3-inch single that was packaged along with the main CD. Another version includes the songs on tracks 98 and 99. A third edition features the two bonus songs on tracks seven and eight. In each case, the two extra tracks are the same: "Suck" (a song by the industrial outfit Pigface) and "Physical" (an Adam Ant cover).

9. *Gish*—Smashing Pumpkins (1992)

Thirty seconds after the end of "Daydream," there's a quick, one minute song that doesn't seem to have a title.

10. *Opiate* EP—Tool (1992)

There's a seventh song on the disk, appearing shortly after the title track fades out.

11. *Undertow*—Tool (1993)

Although "Disgustipated" is listed as track ten, it actually shows up on track 69. Running some 16 minutes, the track begins with six minutes of nighttime sounds. A mysterious narrator appears with just under two minutes remaining.

12. *Come On, Feel the Lemonheads*—Lemonheads (1993)

Evan Dando saw fit to include various bits of studio noise throughout the last half of the disk.

13. *Kerosene Hat*—Cracker (1993)

A CD player will read this disk as having 99 tracks. Tracks one to 12 are clearly listed and contain the promised music. Tracks 13 and 14 are blank, while track 15 features "Hi-Desert Biker Meth Lab." Once it's over, the tracks continue to click by, one every three seconds, until the player reaches a full 8-minute version of "Eurotrash Girl" on track 69. There's another unlisted song on track 88 and an informal jam on track 99.

14. *Saturation*—Urge Overkill (1993)

Most versions of the album feature a song called "Dumb Song, Take Nine" that appears out of the silence about 20 minutes after the final song fades out.

15. *No Alternative*—Various Artists (1993)

The unlisted nineteenth song is "Verse Chorus Verse" from Nirvana. The band demanded that the song not be included in the liner notes, because they felt the hype generated by a new Nirvana song would overshadow the purpose of the CD.

16. *Fumbling Towards Ecstasy*—Sarah McLachlan (1993)

Most versions feature an unlisted acoustic rendition of "Possession" that appears about 20 seconds after track 12 ends. (Note: for an interesting "Easter egg" on McLachlan's *Freedom Sessions* multimedia disk, type "Tyde Music" at the second credit screen when exiting.)

17. *Bang*—World Party (1993)

A very limited number of CDs feature "Kuwait City," a song that shows up 27 minutes after most people figure the CD is over.

18. *Troublegum*—Therapy (1994)

Watch for a very strange version of "You Are My Sunshine."

19. *Mellow Gold*—Beck (1994)

There's some strange noodling with a synthesizer at the end of the album.

20. *Beer Can and More* EP—Beck (1994)

Twenty-three seconds after track five, there's a loose experimental jam that sounds like it could be an extremely early version of "Loser."

21. *Purple*—Stone Temple Pilots (1994)

Although the liner notes list 11 songs, there's a very good reason why the artwork features a picture of a cake with icing that reads "12 Gracious Melodies." Thirty-three seconds after track 12 is "The Second Album," a song written by an eccentric Seattle street musician named Richard Peterson. STP had been playing the original version over the PA when the lights went up at the end of their concerts. Peterson was paid a lump sum for the use of the song and also receives royalties from the sales of *Purple*.

22. *Dookie*—Green Day (1994)

Deep in the end of *Dookie* is an untitled, unlisted track that lasts all of 97 seconds.

23. *S*M*A*S*H**—Offspring (1994)

There's a goodbye message with about 7:46 left on the CD, followed by a short instrumental. With 1:30 left on the disk, there's a mellow version of "Come Out and Play."

24. *Second Coming*—Stone Roses (1994)

Track 90 is entitled "The Fox" and features the group playing some instruments they found in a Welsh pub while they were recording the album in a nearby studio.

25. *Throwing Copper*—Live (1994)

Although it has its own separate track on the disk, the liner notes neglect to mention that the final track on the album is called "Horse."

26. *Everything I Long For*—Hayden (1995)

Chefs will find an interesting recipe for cookies at the end of this CD.

27. *(What's the Story) Morning Glory?*—Oasis (1995)

The two unlisted tracks (numbers 6 and 11) are essentially the same thing: an instrumental known as "The Swamp Song." A complete version of the song (featuring Paul Weller on harmonica) can be found on the CD single for "Wonderwall."

28. *Goosefair*—China Drum (1996)

Fourteen songs are listed, but when the last track fades away, there are still over 30 minutes left on the CD counter—a sure indication that there's something hidden in the silence. With about three and a half minutes remaining, there's a rockin' version of Kate Bush's "Wuthering Heights."

29. *1000 Mona Lisas* EP and *New Disease*—1000 Mona Lisas (1996)

Although the semi-hidden (listed on the disk but not in the liner notes) track six—a frantic punk cover of Alanis Morissette's "You Oughta Know"—brought the band some initial notoriety, few people seem to have discovered their cover of the Wings song "Jet" at the end of the debut album.

30. *All Change*—Cast (1996)

The disk ends with a quiet instrumental hidden deep into track 12. It starts with about 1:24 left on the countdown clock.

31. *Like Cats and Dogs*—Catherine Wheel (1996)

Most later editions of the album feature an extra 11 minutes of material following the end of track 12. There are three songs clustered together on track 13, including a cover of Rush's "Spirit of Radio" which was commissioned by 102.1 The Edge in Toronto, the radio station that inspired Rush to write the original in 1980. The two other bonus tracks are "Angelo Nero" and "Something Strange" and are unavailable on any other Catherine Wheel release.

32. *1977*—Ash (1996)

Few hidden tracks can top the gross-out factor of what appears at the end of this Ash album. About 5:41 after the end of the final song, the disk features the audio portion of a trip to the bathroom. According to drummer Rick McMurray, everyone in the group was quite drunk after a long day in the studio. Feeling unwell, bassist Mark Hamilton announced that was going to be sick and made a beeline for the toilet. The rest of the band followed with a microphone and managed to get the whole thing on tape. Ash has since dubbed the track "Sick Party."

33. *Songs in the Key of X*—Various Artists (1996)

Not all hidden tracks appear at the end of CDs. If the person mastering the disk is very clever, there is a way to hide songs at the *beginning* of the disk. This technique was used for this collection of songs from a TV series that deals with the strange and the unexplained. There are two full songs hidden before track one. To access them, all one needs to do is allow the CD player to cue up to track one, hit "pause" and then hold the "scan back." Once the counter reads minus 9:12, hitting "play" will start a song called "Time Jesus Transeuntum et Non Riverentum" (Latin for "Dread the Passage of Jesus, For He Does Not Return") by Nick Cave and the Dirty Three. It's immediately followed by a Nick Cave remix of the *X-Files* theme.

34. *Music For Pleasure*—Monaco (1997)
Peter Hook's side project offers the final word on hidden tracks. With five seconds remaining on the disk, a voice (Hook?) comes on and says, "Oi! You can take it off now!"

Six Great Guitar Stories

1. The Ramones Begin with Cheap Guitars
John Cummings had been in love with the guitar ever since the night the Beatles appeared on *The Ed Sullivan Show* in 1964. He owned a cheap guitar, but soon grew discouraged when he realized he couldn't learn to play it like John Lennon or George Harrison.

Almost ten years later to the day, Cummings and his new friend Douglas Colvin got together after work for a couple of beers at a nearby strip club. They talked about forming a band to get out of their dead-end jobs. At some point in the evening, they headed over to Manny's Guitar Center on 48th Street in Manhattan to check out a few instruments. By the time they left the store, Cummings had laid out $50 for a blue Mosrite guitar and another $150 for a cheap amp. Colvin spent $50 on a Dan-Electro bass. Four days later, they had their first rehearsal. And almost two years later, Cummings (Johnny) and Colvin (Dee Dee) joined Joey and Tommy as the Ramones and released their debut album.

2. The Origin of Joy Division
When the Sex Pistols played the Lesser Free Trade Hall in Manchester on June 4, 1976, Peter Hook and his friend Bernard Albrecht (formerly Bernard Dicken and later Bernard Sumner) were among the several hundred curious music fans willing to pay 50 pence for a ticket. Neither of them were all that impressed by the band—but they did notice how much fun the Pistols seemed to be having. Forming their own band seemed like a good idea.

The next day, Hook spent £35 on a cheap bass guitar and joined Albrecht in the front room of his grandmother's house. Without a proper guitar amplifier, they wired both guitars through the pickup of the turntable in grandma's stereo and started writing songs. Eighteen months later, Joy Division was born.

3. The Girl in the See-through Plastic Shirt
REM, the prototypical "college rock" band, played their first gig at a birthday party near the University of Georgia in Athens. They gradually moved up through the ranks before signing a contract worth $80 million in 1996.

One of the things that makes REM stand out is their guitar sound. Guitarist Peter Buck has become a better player over the years, but in the beginning, it was the sound of his guitar that not only attracted attention, but also influenced other up-and-coming "college rock" guitarists. And the item responsible for Buck's eventual position among the alt-rock guitar gods was a see-through plastic shirt.

In 1981, very early on in REM's existence, the group was booked to play a show in Nashville. The arrangements were very spartan: the venue was a tent with a low ceiling, while the stage was nothing more than a couple of tables lashed together with duct tape. When REM began their set, Buck noticed an attractive woman wearing a plastic shirt that was virtually transparent—and she appeared to be flirting with him. Loaded on beer and adrenalin, Buck began showing off more and more as the set progressed. Finally, as he leapt into the air with a fancy split-kick move, he hit his head and the neck of his Fender Telecaster on one of the steel supports that held up the roof of the tent. Although his head and his pride would heal, Buck's one-and-only guitar was damaged beyond repair. He threw what remained of it into the crowd.

This was a disaster for the band. With a series of important gigs coming up, Buck had to find a replacement guitar in a hurry. Scraping together $175, he headed over to Chick Pianos, a music store in Athens that carried used guitars, hoping to pick up another Telecaster. He was very disappointed when he found that the store only had one guitar in stock, a unique-sounding model made by a company called Rickenbacker. Buck was familiar with the guitar, having been a fan of George Harrison, Roger McGuinn and Pete Townsend, all well-known Rickenbacker players, but he never thought about playing one himself. With little choice and the immediate future of REM hanging in the balance, he took the guitar.

At the time of the "Nashville Incident," Buck was experimenting with playing more than just straight chords, learning to pick at the strings almost like a banjo. When he tried the same technique with the Rickenbacker, he was astonished to find that REM originals sounded better, taking almost everything the band did to a new level. That used guitar encouraged Buck to go off into a completely different musical direction, which soon became an integral part of REM's overall sound. The group's uniqueness was also underscored by the fact that Buck was one of the few alt-rock guitarists playing a Rickenbacker at the time. Who knows? Had it not been for the girl in the see-through shirt, REM might have ended up as another no-name college band.

4. Kurt Cobain Buys A Guitar

When he was in the third grade and determined to be like Ringo Starr, Kurt Cobain took drum lessons. He eventually lost interest, but soon became a big fan of rock music, and of groups like Kiss, Queen, Led Zeppelin, Black Sabbath, and even the Monkees. On his fourteenth birthday, his Uncle Chuck gave him a cheap used guitar and a ten-watt amp. It wasn't much, but it was a start.

In 1984, his mother got into a big fight with her new husband and, in a rage, grabbed his entire gun collection, throwing it all into the Wishkah River. Cobain paid some local kids to fish out the guns which he then sold. The proceeds went to pay for a proper guitar and amplifier.

5. Billy Corgan Discovers the Guitar

In 1965, Bill Corgan had visions of being a rock star. He auditioned for a spot with a group, called the Amboy Dukes, which was looking to add another guitarist before they moved from Chicago to Detroit. Corgan was offered the job, but ultimately turned it down, realizing that his day job was much better paying and more secure than anything the Dukes could offer. The position of guitarist eventually went to a Detroit man named Ted Nugent.

By the early 80s, Corgan was raising a family in Chicago, sometimes giving one of his younger sons the odd guitar lesson and encouraging him to take up a music career. Corgan's oldest son, Billy Jr., didn't seem all that interested in learning how to play. But one day after school, 14-year-old Billy went over to see a friend who had just bought a Gibson Flying V, the same guitar that Rick Neilson used in local heroes Cheap Trick—and, more importantly, one of the guitars used by Ace Frehley of Kiss. Up until that moment, listening to music had been Billy, Jr.'s escape—but after that evening in his friend's basement, playing music seemed to be even better.

Years later, Billy Corgan decided that it was time that he and his father jammed together. After the *Mellon Collie and the Infinite Sadness* project was completed, Billy went into the studio to record a B-side called "The Last Song." The day he was ready to record the solo, his father just happened to be visiting. He invited Billy Sr. to join in and the result was one of the few father-and-son collaborations in the history of alt-rock.

6. Radiohead's Accidental Big Hit

When singer Thom Yorke first wrote the lyrics to "Creep" while in college, he kept them from the band, thinking that the whole song was lame and too wimpy. Eventually, though, the song was used as a warm-up for rehearsals and recording sessions.

Yorke wasn't alone in his opinion. Guitarist Jonny Greenwood hated "Creep" and was always looking for ways to sabotage the song whenever he was forced to play it. He was trying to be obnoxious during one session of recording the *Pablo Honey* album. The band was warming up with "Creep," as usual, when Jonny turned up all his amps and cranked his effects pedals wide open just before the chorus. Testing everything out, he banged the strings a couple of times, producing a couple of very noisy crunches before he began to play the buzzsaw chords of the chorus. He figured that if he made enough noise, the rest of the group would take the hint and dump the song. At the very least, he could make things rock a bit.

Unbeknownst to the group, the engineer had a tape running in the control room and once the song was over, he played back what he had recorded. Suddenly, everyone agreed that "Creep" did have merit, thanks to Greenwood's scratchy guitar and noisy chords. Opinions of the song changed completely and "Creep" was included on the album after all.

Synthesizers, Samplers and Computers

The introduction of the electronic keyboard changed music forever. The synthesizer allowed musicians to create and control sounds never before heard by the human ear. Even more importantly, the synthesizer could make a single person sound like an entire group—a complete orchestra, if necessary. This made it possible for one person to make a complete album of extremely complex music without any additional help. It also resulted in a shift in power: the synthesizer gave the individual musician as much clout as a full band.

Origins

The roots of electronically-generated music go all the way back to the end of the Russian Revolution when, in 1918, a Bolshevik scientist named Leo Theremin began to demonstrate a device he named after himself. The "theremin" was a box featuring a vertical metal rod sticking out of the top, and a loop of metal protruding from the side. Without even touching it, the theremin player waved his hands about the two strips of metal, controlling pitch with the left hand (the horizontal loop) and volume with the right (the vertical rod). Believe it or not, Soviet leader Lenin was an early theremin fan and promptly sent Theremin on a world tour to promote this new communist technology. Although difficult to play, the theremin found many fans over the years, including Brian Wilson (listen for the theremin in the chorus of "Good Vibrations"), Jimmy Page (there's a theremin solo in "Whole Lotta Love") and Matthew Sweet (the device is used throughout the *Blue Sky on Mars* album).

Leo Theremin was later caught in a Stalinist purge, and after serving time in a labor camp, he invented an electronic bugging device for the KGB.

There were other attempts to tame electronic sounds. Throughout the 20s and 30s, various inventors introduced devices such as the Ondes Martenont, the Trautonium, the Electronde, the Novochord, the Obukov and the giant 200-ton Teleharmonium, which had to be moved from place to place in a railway car. A major break came in 1939 when Rene Bertrand put together a device which gave the operator more control over electronically-generated sounds. He called his invention the oscillator.

Between the 30s and the late 50s, a number of composers with futurist leanings experimented with electronic music. One of them, Karlheinz Stockhausen, began working this into his music in 1953 in an experimental studio built by West German radio. Even though the results were very avant-garde, Stockhausen soon found himself surrounded by disciples, all of whom were eager to push the envelope of music. At about the same time, staff at Columbia University built their own synthesizer. It was a large and unwieldy machine which filled an entire room and required the operator to make hundreds of patch chord connections in order to program and play it.

Another major breakthrough came in 1963 when Don Buchla invented the voltage-controlled synthesizer. It was a little black box that made it much easier to control electronic sounds. His idea was advanced by Dr. Bob Moog, who, in less than two years, found a way to make the device commercially feasible. With help from Columbia, Princeton and the University of Toronto, Dr. Moog refined his invention and in 1967, the Moog synthesizer made its rock music debut in a song by the Monkees called "Star Collector." A year later, Walter Carlos, a well-known classical musician, began working with Dr. Moog on perfecting the new instrument. The result of this collaboration was a totally electronic album of classical music called *Switched On Bach* which sold in the millions. The synthesizer had arrived.

Building on this success, Moog soon introduced the mini-moog, a small, portable, and most importantly, relatively inexpensive electronic keyboard that could do almost everything the giant railway car machines could. On January 24, 1970, his company unveiled another synthesizer that sold for about $2,000—a hefty sum in those days, but still accessible to many musicians, giving them the opportunity to move beyond the realm of the normal selection of guitars, bass, drums, piano and organ. Keith Emerson of Emerson, Lake and Palmer was one of the early adopters, along with a series of German bands, including Can, Tangerine Dream, and most notably, Kraftwerk, the totally electronic ensemble from Dusseldorf, Germany. The title track from their ground-breaking 1974 album *Autobahn* became a worldwide hit. Interest in the synthesizer hit a new high.

The Birth of Techno-Pop

This interest intensified further over the next few years, thanks in large part to Kraftwerk albums like *Radio Activity*, *Trans-Europe Express* and *Man Machine*. After "The Model" (from *Man Machine*) became the highest-charting all-electronic pop song in the history of the U.K. in 1978, the synthesizer was adopted as the instrument of choice by young musicians inspired by the "do-it-yourself" ethic of the punk revolution. Believing in the tenet that everyone should be able to make music regardless of ability, the synthesizer was like manna from heaven. Someone with an electronic keyboard didn't need to know anything about music to write a song. With a twist of a couple of knobs, the flick of a switch or two and with just one finger on the keyboard, it was possible to come up with sounds never before heard by the human ear. And with the use of two or more synthesizers or a cheap multi-track tape machine, it was possible to record a full album literally in one's bedroom.

That's exactly what Daniel Miller did. Throughout the 70s, he played guitar in a procession of bands, all of which went nowhere. When he wasn't trying to establish a music career, he worked as a DJ at a Swiss resort, which is where he was exposed to Kraftwerk, the cold, electronic sounds of David Bowie's *Low* and the electronic pulse of disco artists like Donna Summer. When he got home, he purchased a synthesizer and put together a couple of songs, one of which was based on the J.G. Ballard novel *Crash*. "Warm Leatherette" ended up as a hit in the U.K., allowing Miller to form Mute, a record label dedicated to the promotion of post-punk electronic music.

Within two years, the Mute roster had grown to include Fad Gadget, DAF and Miller's greatest asset, Depeche Mode. Martin Gore was fascinated by the synthesizer and saved every penny from his job as a bank teller to buy one. His first keyboard was a monophonic Moog Prodigy, a synthesizer with enough knobs and switches to keep an experimenter happy for hours. Once Gore became bored with making music, he turned to making sounds—which eventually became music. To Gore and partner Vince Clarke, the synthesizer was a very "punk" instrument, an easy-to-use tool that allowed a novice to get out a message without years of formal training.

Other groups agreed. Orchestral Maneuvers in the Dark insisted on being all-electronic, eschewing a live drummer in favor of a reel-to-reel tape machine they called "Winston," while the Human League relied on backing tapes and drum machines. After initially encountering hostility from audiences who weren't keen on bands in which they couldn't see the musicians, these new techno-pop bands, such as Visage, Soft Cell, Blancmange and Ultravox, began to catch on. By 1981, they were everywhere and on December 12 of that year, the Human League made history by becoming the first British techno-pop band to have a number one hit in America with their single, "Don't You Want Me."

Technological developments continued at a furious pace. By the early 80s, synthesizers had moved from being monophonic (meaning they could only play one note or sound at a time) to polyphonic (allowing, for example, a player to form full chords or combinations of several sounds). Manufacturers sprang up all over the world: Korg, ARP, Polyfusion, Oberheim, Roland, Sequential Circuits. The stiffer the competition became, the faster the technology progressed and the further prices fell.

The first electronic revolution in alternative music reached its crescendo in about 1983. Synthesizer-based bands dominated the charts, radio, the video channels and the dance clubs. Even groups who hadn't been into keyboards were incorporating the new technology into their sound, including the Police, the Cure and New Order. Part of the credit goes to Yamaha for their introduction of the extremely versatile DX-7, a keyboard feature 16-voice FM synthesis technology that was so advanced and easy to use that it quickly became the world standard. It also helped that anyone could buy a DX-7 for less than $2,000. Trying to duplicate Yamaha's success, every major manufacturer soon introduced similar models (most notably Roland's D-50), each one more advanced than the one before, and providing extraordinary benefits to musicians who were looking for ways to expand their creativity through technology.

Sampling

Despite the synthesizer's growing capabilities, some musicians were still frustrated and bored with the standard ways of making music. Back in the 50s, Stockhausen had created an entire work featuring nothing but bits of shortwave radio interference. Later, groups like the Beatles and Pink Floyd were constantly looking for new and exciting ways to incorporate sounds and sound effects into their material. By the late 70s, producer Martin Hannett was using the sound of breaking glass to add atmosphere to Joy Division songs. Other groups were experimenting with a technique known as "found sound," the use of a wide variety of recorded sounds in making music. One of the biggest proponents of that approach was the German experimental outfit Einsturzende Neubauten, who used everything from anvils and lead pipes to power tools and shopping carts to make their musical statement.

With the introduction of the VCR, bits of movie and TV dialogue became fair game. Canada's Skinny Puppy began using snippets of dialogue to augment their evolving industrial sound as early as 1983. But the big commercial breakthrough came in 1986, when Big Audio Dynamite released "E=MC^2," a track which was spiced up with dialogue from *Performance* (a 1970 cult film starring Mick Jagger). It became the first worldwide rock hit to feature this new technique, now known as "sampling."

Computer engineers had spent years coming up with new sophisticated ways of manipulating sound. The first attempt at storing real-world sounds for later use was a heavy mechanical piano keyboard device from the early 70s called a mellotron. Pressing a key activated one of a number of ten second tapes that were looped inside a complicated internal tape player. On the front panel were controls that allowed the operator to alter these sounds in a limited number of ways. The mellotron was popular among many prog-rock bands and made a minor comeback in the 90s, when some of the few remaining machines were purchased and used by artists like Billy Corgan of the Smashing Pumpkins.

The first real electronic sampling device was manufactured by an Australian company called Fairlight. The roots of their Fairlight CMI (Computer Musical Instrument) go all the way back to 1971, when a couple of computer engineers figured out a way to digitally store any acoustic sound. Later models could display a sound as a complex waveform on a computer monitor. Then, using a light pen, the sound sample could be altered and manipulated by "drawing" and "erasing" on the screen. The result could then be stored on disk for later use. For the record, the first sound to successfully be sampled electronically was that of a dog barking, which used up all 20kB of the machine's memory.

Early CMIs were huge and hellishly expensive, running anywhere from $25,000 to $36,000. But despite its cost and complexity, Fairlight sold more than 300 CMIs to studios all over the world. Artists like Peter Gabriel explored new territory using a Fairlight on *Security* (1983). Both the Art of Noise and Yello based their entire sound on the new machines. Meanwhile, producer Trevor Horn used a Fairlight to create most of the music for Frankie Goes to Hollywood's *Welcome to the Pleasuredome* (1984). Rumor has it that the snare drum sound for the album was "borrowed" from a Led Zeppelin record.

Once the Fairlight proved itself as a powerful musical tool, other companies started exploring this new marriage of the synthesizer and the computer. In 1980, a company called E-mu introduced the Emulator, a $10,000 keyboard device that could sample and store up to two seconds' worth of material on the then-standard five-inch floppy disk. New Order loved their Emulator, using it to assemble their groundbreaking dance single "Blue Monday," while Paul Hardcastle had a worldwide hit single with the Emulator-generated anti-war opus, "19."

As the electronics improved, prices dropped exponentially. In 1985, a company called Ensoniq unveiled a keyboard sampler that sold for less than $2,000, putting the new technology within reach of the average musician for the first time. Another price break came in 1986, when Akai began selling a sampler that could hold 63 seconds worth of material—and it only cost $1,000. The company's 1988 device, the powerful S1000 sampler, soon became the industry standard.

There were other important developments. In 1983, Sequential Circuits published the specifications for MIDI (Musical Instrument Digital Interface), which set worldwide standards, allowing keyboards, samplers and drum machines to "talk" to each other. As a result of the MIDI standard, it became possible to use home computers to sequence music, and later, using special software, to compose music on the computer. Kaypro, Commodore and Atari all had MIDI-compatible home computers, but none of them had the impact of the Apple, especially after the introduction of the user-friendly Macintosh. Since then, the computer has allowed musicians to create sounds that literally violate the natural physical laws of acoustics, sounds that have no possible equivalent in the real world, all in the comfort of a small home studio.

This new approach to music and technology resulted in another creative breakthrough in 1988. With the help of a couple of London DJs (including one who would later become the manager of Bush), five producers/musicians stitched together a collage that became the musical equivalent of a Frankenstein monster. Using sampled material from several rap groups, Israeli singer Ofra Haza, James Brown and even the Iranian Revolutionary Army Chorus, "Pump Up the Volume" from M/A/R/R/S demonstrated the potential of this new way of composing music.

A Few Legal Matters

As this new technology became more affordable and available, musicians began to go on a sampling rampage, especially in the rap and hip-hop communities where brand new songs were created out of sound collages, and backing tracks were based on material borrowed from other records using two or more turntables and multiple copies of the same record, and sometimes augmented with a drum machine. MCs or "rappers" perform their rhymes over these extended "breaks." However, with the introduction of the inexpensive electronic sample, the quick reflexes of the rap DJ gave way to the much more accurate machine, enabling an artist to excise bits of music from classic records with surgical precision. Following the lead of these rap and hip-hop artists, a large number of alternative performers also began experimenting with samples, using the computer as another musical instrument. The concept proved to be extremely popular with audiences—and with lawyers.

At first, there were no rules regarding what could and could not be sampled: as a result, few artists bothered to seek permission to use what they sampled. But as the technique became more popular, the question of theft and plagiarism came up. How much could a musician sample another artist's song before the original composer was entitled to some sort of credit or compensation? The first serious examination of this issue began when the Turtles filed suit against De La Soul, who appropriated bits of the Turtles' 1969 hit "You Showed Me" for their song "Transmitting Live from Mars." Although the case was settled out of court, it became a turning point for the entire music industry. From then on, it became *de rigeur* to ask permission before using a sample. Depending on the arrangements, the original artist must receive credit in the liner notes and/or some financial payment.

If permission is not sought or denied, then lawyers and judges step into the fray. Soho learned this the hard way when they released their single "Hippy Chick," which featured a sample of the opening riff of the Smiths' "How Soon Is Now." When the matter was taken to court, the judge awarded 50 percent of all royalties to Morrissey and Johnny Marr. Elastica, Bjork and several other big names have been nailed for using uncleared (unauthorized) samples. When preparing the "Discotheque" single for the *Pop* album, U2 had several versions of the song ready to go, including one without any samples—just in case they were denied permission to use them at the last moment. Other artists (including the Chemical Brothers, whose songs have been known to consist of more than 300 individual samples) believe that it's not necessary to seek permission to use some samples, if they've been manipulated and mangled beyond all recognition. In any event, a number of legal cases have made it clear that it's not wise to even *ask* for permission to sample artists like the Beatles or AC/DC, or any Broadway show tune.

The same technology that allows musicians to construct new songs using samples can also help with studio performances. It's quite common for the finished version of a song to contain hundreds of individual edits, all done on a computer, as various studio takes are cannibalized to create the perfect performance. In other cases, a band will go into the studio and record a few songs, and after everyone has gone home, a programmer will come in and dump all the recordings into a computer. Using very sophisticated sampling and sound manipulation software, the programmer will fix all the places where the singer went flat or where the drummer fell out of time. When the band hears the playback the next day, they're blown away by their brilliance. Meanwhile, the producer knows what really happened.

These days, samples are so common that most people don't even notice them anymore. The computer has become an effective and powerful musical instrument, opening new vistas by giving the individual more power than ever. It's composition through deconstruction and with limits beyond imagination.

Familiar Samples and Their Sources

1. "Get Down, Make Love"—Nine Inch Nails
The sample of a moaning woman was lifted from a Japanese porn film.

2. "Closer"—Nine Inch Nails
The opening drum pattern is a modification of the opening bars of the Iggy Pop song "Nightclubbing."

3. "I Am Stretched On Your Grave"—Sinead O'Connor, "Wise Up! Sucker!"—PWEI (and countless others)
The most-sampled drum break in history has to be Clyde Stubblefield's groove in the James Brown song "Funky Drummer." A sample of Stubblefield's drumming can be heard in literally hundreds of recordings from around the world.

4. "Loaded"—Primal Scream
The song begins with dialogue featuring Peter Fonda from a 1966 biker film entitled *The Wild Angels*.

5. "Rocks Off"—Primal Scream
The opening bars of this song are actually a slightly altered sample of the opening from Sly and the Family Stone's "Dance to the Music."

6. "Your Woman"—White Town

Although some people think the hook with the violin sounds like Darth Vader's march from *Star Wars*, it was actually borrowed from a 1932 recording called "My Woman," by Lew Stone and the Monseigneur Band.

7. "Why Is Everyone Always Picking on Me?"—Bloodhound Gang

A good portion of the song is based on "Spooky," the 1968 hit from the Classics IV.

8. "Scooby Snacks"—Fun Lovin' Criminals

This track features large amounts of dialogue from *Reservoir Dogs* and *Pulp Fiction*, two Quentin Tarantino movies. Since they didn't ask for permission to use the samples, Tarantino objected and successfully lobbied to receive a co-writing credit on the song.

9. "Supernaut"—1000 Homo DJs

The anti-rock speech at the beginning is from Art Linkletter.

10. "Stupid Girl"—Garbage

The opening bars appear to be very similar to the opening seconds of "Train in Vain" by the Clash.

11. "Big Time"—Peter Gabriel

The snare drum sound was borrowed from a Police album. Drummer Stewart Copeland is given credit in the liner notes.

12. "Standing Outside a Broken Phone Booth With Money In My Hand"—Primitive Radio Gods

The hook of the song is based on a sample taken from "How Blue Can You Get" by blues singer B.B. King. The title was co-opted from an old Bruce Cockburn song.

13. "Sour Times"—Portishead

The most famous of the six pre-recorded samples that appear on *Dummy* are the strings heard on the album's first single. These were taken from "Danube Incident," a track from an old soundtrack to the TV show *Mission Impossible*.

Six Bands Who Could Really Stretch a Buck

1. *The Ramones*—The Ramones (1976)
From the beginning, Joey Ramone was never one to spend a lot of time in a recording studio. Wanting to keep costs down (so they could keep more of their advance), the group's first album was recorded in less than two weeks for a cost of $6,400.

2. *Spiral Scratch*—The Buzzocks (1977)
The Buzzcocks were probably the first punk group to form their own independent label. New Hormones was financed with a loan from singer Pete Shelley's father. The total cost for setting up the company, recording four songs and manufacturing the record was about $1,000.

3. *Bleach*—Nirvana (1989)
Taking all of 30 hours to record, the final bill from Reciprocal Recording in Seattle was $606.17. Sub Pop couldn't afford to pay it, mainly because they had gone way over budget on the artwork for Green River's *Rehab Doll* EP. Kurt Cobain didn't have the cash either, so he turned to Jason Everman, a commercial fisherman who was a friend of Chad Channing, Nirvana's drummer at the time. In return, Everman was given credit for playing guitar on the album, even though he didn't play a note.

4. "Upside Down"—Jesus and Mary Chain (1984)
When Alan McGee first heard the Jesus and Mary Chain play, he knew he had to sign the group to his fledging indie label Creation Records. He convinced the group to record a single, offering to help pay for at least some of the costs. Jim Reid had a few bucks saved from his job at Rolls-Royce, while brother William contributed part of his salary from his job at a cheese plant. The resulting single sold 35,000 copies, establishing the Jesus and Mary Chain as one of the most radical new bands in Britain, and also giving Creation its first hit. Total cost to record and manufacture: $350.

5. *The Trinity Session*—Cowboy Junkies (1988)
Fascinated by the natural acoustics of the Church of the Holy Trinity in Toronto, the Cowboy Junkies arranged to use the nave on November 27, 1988. Using a single four-capsule ambisonic microphone (originally developed by the British navy to find Soviet submarines), the group took 14 hours to record 12 tracks on a portable DAT machine. The band hoped that the resulting album would sell 5,000 copies, but when RCA picked it up, *The Trinity Session* went on to sell more than a million. The total cost for that one-day recording session was $125—plus the cost of pizza for dinner.

6. "Money"—The Flying Lizards (1978)

The Flying Lizards were an Irish group consisting of conceptual artist David Cunningham and session singer Deborah Evans. Fascinated by minimalist sounds, Cunningham released a radically altered version of Eddie Cochrane's "Summertime Blues" in 1978. The follow-up single, Barrett Strong's "Money," was recorded using an upright piano filled with all sorts of debris (rubber toys, phone books) to give it a strange muted sound. Recorded at home, the final cost was $14. The single was picked up by Virgin and sold millions around the world.

Fifteen Great Alt-Rock Producers

1. Steve Albini

A former fanzine writer from Chicago, Albini fronted several very noisy indie bands (Big Black, Rapeman, Arsenal and Shellac), before turning to record production in the late 80s. Eschewing the description of producer, Albini prefers to be known as a "recorder," someone who simply records a band in their natural state, without imposing his influence on the sound of the music. He's also one of the few people who charges a flat fee for his expertise instead of taking a percentage of the gross record sales. Albini feels that if the band is a success, all the money should go to the band, not the producer.

Selected credits: *Surfer Rosa*—The Pixies, *In Utero*—Nirvana, *To Give You My Love*—PJ Harvey, *Razorblade Suitcase*—Bush

2. Jack Endino

As the chief engineer at Reciprocal Recording in Seattle, Endino saw many of grunge's future stars pass through his studio. Having played in a local indie band called Skin Yard, Endino knew the importance of being able to record on a tight budget. As a result, he produced virtually every recording issued by Sub Pop between 1988 and 1990. And because Endino was a big fan of cheesy effects pedals which give guitars a big, fat, chunky sound, Endino must be considered one of the main architects of grunge.

Selected credits: *Bleach*—Nirvana, *Touch Me I'm Sick*—Mudhoney

3. Brian Eno

Beginning as a member of Roxy Music in 1973 (and the descendent of three generations of postmen), Eno has become one of the most respected record producers in the world. He has worked with everyone from David Bowie in the 70s, to the Talking Heads and U2 in the 80s, and James in the 90s. In addition to his role as a leader in the studio, Eno's solo work helped lay the groundwork for today's ambient techno sounds. Eno is also known as a multimedia installation artist, a sculptor, computer aficionado and philosopher.

Selected credits: Bowie's Berlin trilogy (*Low*, *Heroes* and *Lodger*), *Remain in Light*— Talking Heads, *The Joshua Tree*—U2, *Laid*—James

4. Flood

Flood, whose real name is Mark Price, began his career in the music industry by fetching tea for anyone who happened to be working in the studio. Eventually, he hooked up with Daniel Miller, the head of Mute Records. Recognizing Flood's potential, Miller soon found him work at engineering sessions for groups like the Jesus and Mary Chain, Soft Cell and Depeche Mode. Flood's reputation grew to the point where he was asked by Brian Eno to engineer *The Joshua Tree* for U2. That experience allowed him to move up to producing, which is what he's been doing ever since.

Selected credits: *Songs of Faith and Devotion*—Depeche Mode, *Mellon Collie and the Infinite Sadness*—Smashing Pumpkins

5. Martin Hannett

In the 70s, Manchester's Hannett promoted concerts, played in a couple of bands, managed a musicians' co-operative and did live sound for a number of groups. In 1977, he was asked to produce the Buzzcocks' *Spiral Scratch* EP, a job that led to dozens of other producing gigs. Hannett was a big part of the sound of Joy Division's debut *Unknown Pleasures*, and contributed to New Order's *Movement*. While working as a co-director for Factory Records, Hannett simultaneously gave advice to dozens of other bands, including OMD, the Psychedelic Furs, and U2. And when the Manchester scene heated up again in the late 80s, Hannett produced several important records, including "So Young," the debut single from the Stone Roses, and the Happy Mondays' *Bummed*. Hannett died of a heart attack in 1991.

Selected credits: *Unknown Pleasures*—Joy Division, *The Garage Flowers*—Stone Roses demos, *Bummed*—Happy Mondays

6. Jerry Harrison

Back when he joined Jonathan Richman's Modern Lovers in the early 70s, Harrison didn't expect to end up producing multi-platinum albums 20 years later. After a decade with the Talking Heads, and of playing in his own band, the Casual Gods, Harrison turned to producing. So far, his biggest successes have been with the Crash Test Dummies and Live.

Selected credits: *The Blind Leading the Naked*—Violent Femmes, *God Shuffled His Feet*—Crash Test Dummies, *Throwing Copper*—Live

7. Trevor Horn

As one half of the Buggles, Horn was responsible for "Video Killed the Radio Star," which ended up becoming the first video to be shown on MTV. Once that band had run its course, he briefly joined Yes before turning to production full-time. Horn became famous as the sonic architect for albums from ABC, the Art of Noise and Frankie Goes to Hollywood. He also helped produce "Do They Know It's Christmas?" for Band Aid.

Selected credits: *Age of Plastic*—The Buggles, *Welcome to the Pleasuredome*—Frankie Goes to Hollywood

8. Dave Jerden

Jerden got his big break when he was asked by Perry Farrell to produce Jane's Addiction's debut album in 1988. Before then, he was part of Brian Eno's studio team, which oversaw the production and engineering of *Remain in Light*. The success of *Nothing's Shocking* has led to work with a great number of bands including Love Spit Love, 54.40 and Alice in Chains.

Selected credits: *Nothing's Shocking*—Jane's Addiction, *Love Spit Love*—Love Spit Love, *Ixnay on the Hombre*—Offspring

9. Daniel Lanois

Born in Ottawa and raised in Hamilton, Ontario, Lanois was operating his own recording studio out of his parents' basement before he was 20. By the time he reached his thirties, *Rolling Stone* was calling him "the most important record producer to emerge in the 80s." His big break came in 1979 when Brian Eno opted to do some work at Lanois' Grant Avenue Studios in Hamilton. There was instant chemistry between them, and when Eno was contracted to produce *The Unforgettable Fire* for U2, Lanois was offered a position as his assistant. Since then, Lanois has worked with everyone from Peter Gabriel to Luscious Jackson as well as pursuing a sideline career as a solo artist.

Selected credits: *So*—Peter Gabriel, *The Joshua Tree*—U2, *Fever In, Fever Out*—Luscious Jackson

10. John Leckie

Leckie's résumé includes work in the 70s with John Lennon and Pink Floyd. In the 80s, he was hired to produce records for New Wave groups like Simple Minds, XTC and, most importantly from an alt-rock perspective, the Stone Roses. Having been unable to find their voice with Martin Hannett and New Order's Peter Hook, the Stone Roses turned to Leckie to help turn their semi-psychedelic sound into something fresh and coherent. The result was one of the best and most influential British albums of the post-punk era. Leckie was also at the controls for Kula Shaker's debut album.

Selected credits: *The Stone Roses*—The Stone Roses, *K*—Kula Shaker, *The Bends*—Radiohead

11. Steve Lilywhite

Lilywhite's first studio job was as a tape operator for Phonogram Records in 1972. As a side project, he helped Ultravox produce a series of demo tapes which ultimately resulted in the band being signed by Island and Lilywhite being offered a position as a staff producer at the label. He became a punk and New Wave specialist, helping many new bands through their first recording sessions. Groups to benefit from his guidance included the Members, Siouxsie and the Banshees, XTC and U2. Other Lilywhite clients have included the Psychedelic Furs, Simple Minds, the Pogues and Peter Gabriel.

Selected credits: *Boy*—U2, *Naked*—Talking Heads, *Peace and Love*—Pogues

12. Gil Norton

Best known as the producer of some of the Pixies' best albums, Norton specializes in alt-rock records that have just the right balance of noise and sheen. Norton is respected by many bands who subscribe to the indie-rock esthetic, partly because he is very good at organizing chaotic arrangements without destroying the song's energy. He's also known as a fierce taskmaster, often demanding that a band go through 50 or more takes until he's satisfied with the performance.

Selected credits: *Doolittle*—Pixies, *Star*—Belly, *The Colour and the Shape*—Foo Fighters

13. Brendan O'Brien

An accomplished musician as well as a producer, O'Brien, a native of Atlanta and former member of the Georgia Satellites, turned to producing in the late 80s. A guitar player himself, O'Brien is known to have a great rapport with acts which rely heavily on guitars for their sound. He also likes to work quickly, capturing the intensity and spontaneity of his clients.

Selected credits: *Vs*—Pearl Jam, *Core*—Stone Temple Pilots, *Blue Sky on Mars*—Matthew Sweet

14. Rick Rubin

Rubin started in the music business as Double RR, the DJ scratching behind the Beastie Boys. Eventually becoming their manager, Rubin also found time to form Def Jam Recordings out of room 203 of the Weinstein residence (at New York University) with partner Russell Simmons in 1984. Selling his share of the label after a string of successful rap albums, Rubin moved into record production, salvaging a Cult album from a difficult series of sessions with producer Steve Brown. The result was *Electric*, one of the best-selling albums of their career. Forming a new indie label called Def American (now American Recordings), Rubin continued to produce records, including *BloodSugarSexMagik* for the Red Hot Chili Peppers. He was also at the controls for albums by Slayer, Danzig and Johnny Cash.

Selected credits: *Licensed to Ill*—Beastie Boys, *Electric*—The Cult, *BloodSugarSexMagik*—Red Hot Chili Peppers

15. Butch Vig

Vig tried to make it as a drummer in several bands (such as the long-forgotten Spooner) before he turned to producing out of Smart Studios in Madison, Wisconsin. He acquired a reputation as someone who liked working with raw indie bands (Killdozer, Laughing Hyenas) and as a producer who could coax out strong performances. When Bob Mould (ex-Husker Du) turned down an opportunity to record Nirvana's major-label debut, the band turned to Vig who helped create *Nevermind*, arguably the most important record of the 90s. Vig is now back playing drums for Garbage.

Selected credits: *Nevermind*—Nirvana, *Hungry for Stink*—L7, *Siamese Dream*—Smashing Pumpkins, *Dirty*—Sonic Youth

Come Out and Play: On the Road

City Scenes: Where to Go, What to See

Canada

Montreal, Quebec

St. Laurent Boulevard and the Main

Along with a fine selection of restaurants, the south end of this strip (locally known as the Main) features clubs such as the Loft (1405 St. Laurent) and Purple Haze (3699 St. Laurent) which tend to feature hardcore punk acts, while the nearby Copacabana and Double Deuce (both at 3908 St. Laurent) are good places to see a variety of smaller indie-rock groups. Many musicians and artists congregate at Le Bifteck (3702 St. Laurent) before and after the show.

Fouf (Les Foufounes Electronique, 87 Ste. Catherine East)

This is the city's most infamous club and live music venue. (A mini-riot once started during a Smashing Pumpkins show, when someone nailed Billy Corgan in the head with a beer bottle.)

Selected Radio

Campus: CISM (89.3), CKUT (90.3)

Toronto, Ontario

Queen Street West

Starting around University Avenue and stretching west beyond Spadina for several blocks to the north and south is the city's coolest district, featuring the highest concentration of clubs, funky restaurants and cool shops in Toronto. This includes live music venues, such as the Horseshoe Tavern (368 Queen Street West), its longtime neighbors, the Rivoli and the Bamboo, and close to a dozen dance clubs like Whiskey Saigon, Oz and Joker, just a few blocks away. Similar to St. Mark's Place in New York City (but cleaner and safer) this strip is a hangout for the terminally trendy.

The El Mocambo (464 Spadina Avenue)

Several blocks north of where Spadina intersects with Queen West, the El Mocambo was once a favorite punk and New Wave venue (Elvis Costello, U2, the Ramones and many others played here), although the club also played host to an infamous Rolling Stones show in 1977. Shows by high-profile acts are few and far between these days, but the ElMo remains dedicated to showcasing new local talent.

Lee's Palace (529 Bloor Street West)

Located in the heart of another funky area of the city, Lee's Palace features live music virtually every night of the week, from new local acts to high-caliber international alternative performers. Everyone from Nirvana to Oasis has appeared on its tiny stage.

Selected Radio

Commercial: 102.1 The Edge

Campus: CKLN (88.1), CIUT (89.5), CHRY (105.1)

Vancouver, British Columbia

Gastown

All the city's best clubs are within walking distance of each other in Gastown. This includes the location of the legendary Commodore (870 Granville), Town Pump (66 Water) and the Hungry Eye (23 West Cordova). Other venues that feature the odd alt-rock act include the Niagara (435 West Pender) and the Starfish Room (1055 Homer).

Selected Radio

Campus: CJSF (93.9), CITR (101.9)

The United States

Athens, Georgia

REM World Headquarters (250-252 West Clayton Street)

In this great old house built some time around 1890, the group maintains their management offices, their official fan club, a rehearsal space and a recording studio.

40 Watt Club (285 West Washington Street)

Not far from the REM building is the location of the band's latest preferred hangout. Several fan club Christmas parties and charity benefits have been held here over the years, no doubt partly because the club is co-owned by Barrie Buck, former wife of REM guitarist Peter Buck. With a capacity of about 1,000, the 40 Watt has hosted some of the biggest names in alternative rock.

The Site of REM's First Gig (394 Oconee Street)

The first time REM played together was on April 5, 1980 at a friend's birthday party. The site was an old Episcopal church that had been turned into a flophouse for students at the University of Georgia. All that remains of the church today is the steeple.

Weaver D's (1016 East Broad Street)

Weaver Dexter's restaurant specializes in down-home southern cooking, including fried chicken and collard greens. Weaver's service motto is "automatic for the people," which inspired the name of REM's 1992 album.

Wuxtry Records (197 East Clayton Street)

Just up the street from REM headquarters is the record store where assistant manager Peter Buck first talked to Michael Stipe, one of his regular customers. Buck tried to take a part-time job at Wuxtry after the release of the Document album, but had to quit because too many autograph seekers prevented him from doing his work. Kate Pierson of the B52s also once worked as a clerk in the store.

Tyrone's (110 Foundry Street)

REM played this club almost every weekend in the first year of their existence. Local alternative bands still account for most of the acts featured here.

Selected Radio

Commercial: 99X (99.7 Atlanta)

Campus: WUOG (90.5 Athens)

Boston, Massachusetts

Fort Apache Studios (1 Camp Street, Cambridge)

This former bare-bones, eight-track recording facility is now a fully-equipped complex, featuring two studios, and the offices of Fort Apache Records. Co-owned by Billy Bragg, the studio has been used by local heroes such as the Pixies, the Lemonheads, Buffalo Tom and Dinosaur Jr. International clients have included Radiohead.

The Middle East Restaurant (472 Massachusetts Avenue, Cambridge)

While the front part of the building is a restaurant, the back room features local bands, while still another room can hold up to 500 people for bigger acts.

The Rat (528 Commonwealth Avenue, Boston)

Officially known as the Rathskellar, the club has figured prominently in the Boston music scene. For almost a quarter of a century, the Rat has featured the city's best local bands and has presented rising alt-rock acts from around the world.

The Paradise (967 Commonwealth Avenue, Boston)

Anyone who's ever seen the U2 concert film Rattle and Hum may remember the sequence featuring the band playing in this club. Just a few blocks from the Rat, the Paradise tends to be the place where international acts start their first U.S. tours.

Selected Radio

Commercial: WFNX (101.7), WBCN (104.1)

Campus: WMBR (88.1), WUMB (91.9), WHRB (95.3)

Chicago, Illinois

Guyville

On the North Side, about a mile from West Lincoln, Wicker Park (known by locals as "Guyville") is one of the city's trendiest areas, thanks to its fine selection of clubs, stores, restaurants and coffee houses. Liz Phair had this area in mind when she came up with the title to her 1993 album, *Exile in Guyville*. The new location of the infamous Wax Trax Records is also in Wicker Park.

Aragon Ballroom (1106 West Lawrence Avenue)

One of the city's most important live music venues, the Aragon has featured everyone from the Smashing Pumpkins to Nirvana.

The Metro (3739 North Clark Street)

The old warehouse next to Wrigley Field was christened as a live music venue by REM in 1982. Since then, the Metro has seen literally hundreds of big names perform, all attracted by the club's good acoustics and great sight lines. Guests have included the Smashing Pumpkins, New Order, Oasis, Silverchair, the Tragically Hip and Ministry.

Selected Radio

Commercial: Q101 (101.1)

Campus: WLUW (88.7), WNUR (89.3)

Cleveland, Ohio

The Rock and Roll Hall of Fame (1 Key Plaza, North Coast Harbor)

A visitor can spend hours wandering through the displays, which include everything from the East German Trabant cars that were part of U2's stage set-up on their *Zoo TV* tour, to one of Sid Vicious's T-shirts, complete with the original blood and vomit stains.

The Flats

At the mouth of the Cuyahoga River is a restaurant and bar area once occupied by a variety of heavy industries. This includes the Odeon Concert Club (1295 Old River Road) and Whiskey in the Flats (1575 Merwin). Another worthwhile club, Trilogy, is a short distance away (2325 Elm Street).

Midtown Recording (2108 Payne Avenue)

Trent Reznor once worked here as a house engineer and producer. When the studio wasn't booked, he used the time to write and record the basic tracks for the album that eventually became *Pretty Hate Machine*. A few years later, he was hired to appear in the background of a Michael J. Fox movie called *Light of Day,* and can be seen in the scenes shot at the Euclid Tavern (11629 Euclid Avenue).

Selected Radio

Commercial: The End (107.9)

Campus: WCSB (89.3), WKSR (730 AM)

Los Angeles

Downtown

Just before U2 began their *Joshua Tree* tour in March 1987, they shot the video for "Where the Streets Have No Name" on the roof of a liquor store at 7th and Main. They had so much fun that they launched into a mini-concert, attracting a large crowd in the streets below before the L.A.P.D. moved in and broke up the party.

Sunset Boulevard

The famous Capitol Records round building at 1750 North Vine Street can be seen from the Hollywood Freeway, while the Sunset Strip (Sunset Boulevard from Crescent Heights to Doheny Drive) features cool clubs, trendy shops, well-stocked record stores, and hotels including the Sunset Marquis, where Dave Gahan of Depeche Mode was clinically dead for two minutes after a heroin overdose on March 28, 1996. The infamous Viper Room occupies a nondescript storefront at 8852 Sunset. Nearby are the Whiskey A Go Go (8901 Sunset) and the Roxy (9009 Sunset).

Melrose Avenue

Running parallel a few blocks to the south is the even more trendy Melrose Avenue with its vast array of stores and cafés. It's one of the best people-watching sites on the West Coast.

10050 Cielo Drive

The house that used to stand on this spot just off Benedict Canyon was the infamous site of the Manson Family murders of Sharon Tate and her friends. In 1993, it was rented by Trent Reznor who converted it into a record studio for the sessions that became The Downward Spiral. The house was destroyed during an earthquake in 1994.

Orange County

To the south of Los Angeles is the vast region of subdivisions, shopping malls and amusement parks that gave birth to southern California punk. Several punk record labels have their headquarters here. The members of No Doubt grew up here as well, naming their 1995 album *Tragic Kingdom* because they lived in the shadow of Disneyland, the Magic Kingdom.

Selected Radio

Commercial KROQ (106.7)

Campus: KLA (530 AM), KSCR (104.7)

Minneapolis, Minnesota

Dinkytown

This is the area along the east shore of the Mississippi, near the University of Minnesota, and is a great place for clubs, cafes and record stores. It's also a favorite hangout for local musicians.

First Avenue (701 North First Avenue)

Co-owned by Prince and featured prominently in *Purple Rain*, this former bus station is where most alt-rock acts play when they come to town. The Foo Fighters, Sonic Youth and Oasis are just some of the bands who love to play the club. An additional attraction is Seventh Street Entry, the smaller adjacent room that features smaller acts along with the occasional British indie band.

Selected Radio
Commercial: The Edge (93.7)
Campus: KUOM (770 AM)

New York

The Chelsea Hotel (222 West 23rd Street)

In business as a hotel since 1905, the guest register at the Chelsea has included everyone from writers and poets such as Mark Twain, Arthur C. Clarke and Dylan Thomas, to Sinead O'Connor and the Red Hot Chili Peppers. A variety of Andy Warhol characters stayed at the hotel, including Holly Woodlawn, Candy Darling and Joe Dallesandro, the three people mentioned in Lou Reed's "Walk on the Wild Side." Longtime punk fans will remember the Chelsea as the place where Sid Vicious allegedly killed his girlfriend Nancy Spungen.

St. Mark's Place (East 8th Street)

No visit to Manhattan is complete without a stroll down St. Mark's Place, poking through the used record stores and the junk shops while doing a little people-watching. One of the many restaurants is the Kiev, one of Beck's old hangouts, mentioned in the song "Detachable Penis" by King Missile. The building at 23 St. Mark's used to be the home of Andy Warhol's Exploding Plastic Inevitable and the Velvet Underground.

CBGB & OMFUG (315 Bowery at Bleeker)

Once a Hell's Angels hangout and country music bar (CBGB originally stood for Country, Blue Grass and Blues and Other Music for Urban/Uplifting Gourmets/Gourmandizers), the legendary club still presents live music almost 25 years after owner Hilly Kristal instituted the "rock only" policy. That change in direction led to the birth of the American punk scene. The Ramones, Blondie, Talking Heads, Television and dozens of other punk and New Wave bands eventually found a home at CBGB, playing before an eclectic mix of neighborhood locals, Times Square freaks and middle/upper class kids slumming it in the Bowery. Today, the club still features up and coming bands, along with the occasional set by a bigger name making a pilgrimage to one of alt-rock's holy shrines. Beware the legendary horror of the bathrooms.

The Bottom Line (15 West 4th Street)

If there's a music industry function or special showcase in Manhattan, chances are that it will take place at the Bottom Line. The club also has regular shows featuring a wide variety of music.

Manny's (156 West 48th Street)

This is probably the most famous musical instrument store in the world. Even a non-musician can have a good time looking at the pictures of famous former and current customers that line the walls.

Selected Radio
Commercial: K-ROCK (92.3)
Campus: WNYU (89.1), WFUV (90.7)

Raleigh, Durham and Chapel Hill, North Carolina
Cat's Cradle (206 West Franklin Street, Raleigh)
This club is the best indie rock venue in the city, attracting students from the area's colleges to see such acts as local heroes Superchunk and Ben Folds Five, as well as a variety of international acts.
Selected Radio
Campus: WKNC (88.1), WXDU (88.7), WXYC (89.3),

San Francisco/Oakland
DNA Lounge (375 11th Street)
The main floor of this club in the SoMa district (South of Market Street) features top-level touring acts, while the second floor is a more quiet place to relax between sets.
Slim's (333 11th Street)
This is a popular SoMa live music club owned by Boz Scaggs. The Screaming Trees played here in March 1997, when singer Mark Lanegan was arrested for possession of drugs. He was later released.
Gilman Street Theater (924 Gilman, Berkeley)
As one of the area's most important punk clubs, this volunteer-run venue was where groups ranging from Operation Ivy, to Rancid, to Green Day got their start. There is no sign, so look for the wicker shop next door.
Selected Radio
Commercial: Live 105
Campus: KUSF (90.3), KSJS ((90.7)

Seattle, Washington and the Surrounding Area
Crocodile Café (2200 2nd Avenue)
Run by Stephanie Dorgan, the wife of REM's Peter Buck, the café is a popular hangout with many of the big-name musicians who call Seattle home. It's not uncommon to run into members of Alice in Chains, Pearl Jam and Soundgarden here.
RKCNDY (1812 Yale Avenue)
With a capacity of about 500, this club was frequented by members of Pearl Jam and Nirvana before they became superstars. Pearl Jam's "Alive" video was also shot here.
Reciprocal Recording (4230 North Leary Way NW)
This tiny studio was founded by Jack Endino, a member of a local band called Skin Yard. Working quickly and often with inferior, out-of-date equipment, Endino helped

shape the grunge sound of Seattle, and worked with dozens of local bands who passed through the doors. Nirvana recorded their *Bleach* album here.

The Sound Garden (7600 Sand Point Way NE)

This huge steel sculpture at Magnusan Park on the shore of Lake Washington looks like four tall weathervanes. As the wind rises and falls, the structures whistle. Artist Doug Hollis calls his 1983 installation a "Sound Garden"—and, yes, this was the inspiration for the name of the Seattle band.

Aberdeen, Washington

Some eighty miles southwest of Seattle is the logging town where Kurt Cobain and Krist Novoselic grew up and formed Nirvana. One of the town's main attractions is the Wishkah River, the inspiration for the title of the Nirvana's live album, *From the Muddy Banks of the Wishkah*. Look for the North Aberdeen Bridge pictured in the liner notes. It often served as a chill-out spot for Cobain. The other attraction is Maria's Hair Design, the beauty shop still owned by Novoselic's mother. Nirvana used to practice there.

Selected Radio

Commercial: The End (107.7)

Campus: KCMU (90.3) , KAOS (89.3 in Olympia WA)

Washington, D.C.

9:30 Club (815 V Street NW)

Formerly at 930 F Street NW, this legendary club has been at this new larger location since January 5, 1996, when it was christened by the Smashing Pumpkins. Since then, the club has hosted performances by Radiohead, Primus and many others.

7-11 (Washington and Q Street NW)

Before he moved west to join Black Flag, Henry Rollins worked at this store.

Dischord House (3819 Bleecher Street)

Although the company's offices have moved to a new location across the river in Arlington, Virginia, this address—the childhood home of Dischord Records founder and Fugazi front man Ian MacKaye—is where all the label's mail is sent.

Selected Radio

Commercial: WHFS (99.1)

Campus: WRGW (540 AM), WGTB (92.3)

The UK and Ireland

London

The Club Scene

London has literally hundreds of dance clubs and live music venues from which to choose. Any visitor who's in the mood for music should start by picking up one of the weekly music papers to scan the pages of upcoming concerts. Some of the better-known live music venues include the Academy (211 Stockwell Road SW 9), the Marquee (105 Charing Cross Road W1), Astoria (157 Charing Cross Road W1), the Forum (9-17 High Gate Road NW 5) and the Rock Garden (6-7 Covent Garden Piazza). The infamous punk venue the 100 Club (100 Oxford Street) has gone back to a jazz-only policy.

Camden

Five minutes northeast of the zoo is a huge market region featuring everything from secondhand clothes to bootleg cassettes. The many pubs in the area are where many musicians have met and subsequently formed bands.

Sex (430 The King's Road)

Malcolm McLaren once operated a fetish shop at this address. It's also where the Sex Pistols were born.

Rock Video Gallery (Denman Street, Picadilly)

This is the world's first gallery devoted entirely to the music video. Visitors can wander through the exhibits wearing wireless headphones which trigger a variety of videos on a series of screens. A typical exhibition will run six months.

Selected Radio

BBC Radio 1 (97.6 and 99.8), XFM (104.9)

Manchester

The Club Scene

Most of the city's club scene is concentrated along an area bordering Oxford Street, the main avenue that runs past two universities out from the center of the city. Live music can often by found at the Academy (Oxford Road), the New Order-owned Hacienda (11-13 Whitworth Street) and Paradise Factory (the former headquarters of Factory Records at 112-16 Princess Street). Oasis made their debut at the Boardwalk (15 Little Peter Street).

Ian Curtis's House

The lead singer of Joy Division hung himself in the house he shared with his wife at 77 Barton Street in Macclesfield.

Morrissey's Boyhood Home

Smiths fans from all over the world still come to see the house where Morrissey grew up at 384 King's Road in Stretsford.

Dublin

Clarence Hotel (6/8 Wellington Quay)

Owned and operated by the real estate wing of U2's empire, this 1930s hotel has been completely refurbished. In a prime location for those looking to take in the local night life, the room rates are surprisingly reasonable.

The Kitchen

Located in the basement of the Clarence, the club has become a place for musicians, fans and tourists to mingle. All Temple Bar club crawls should include the Kitchen.

Baggot Inn (143 Lower Baggot Street)

Many local up-and-coming bands get their first shots at this club. U2 played some of their first shows here.

Rock Garden (3A Crown Alley)

The stripped brick decor of Rock Garden creates the proper ambiance for the local and international acts that perform here. The club is located in the Temple Bar district.

Selected Radio

2FM (90.0-92.2), FM104 (104.4)

Touring Hell: Horror Stories from the Road

Contract Riders from Hell

The rider is the part of the performance agreement that stipulates what the promoter must provide to the performer backstage while on tour. In some cases, if the promoter fails to fulfill every single condition on the rider, the promoter may be considered to be in breach of contract, and the performer may refuse to go on. Most riders feature reasonable demands: bottled water, fresh fruits and vegetables and perhaps some beer and soft drinks.

Some memorable contract riders:

• *On the Smiths' 1985 world tour, the group's contract rider required that the following be provided in the dressing room: salt and vinegar potato chips, a bottle of red wine, corn flakes, Cocoa Puffs or Special K, a pint of milk, two green apples, a packet of cashews, cheese sandwiches and one cupcake. Morrissey was also known to demand that no meat (such as hot dogs) be sold at the concession stands during a Smiths show. These days, Morrissey is apparently happy with just a baked potato.*

• *When Howard Jones was on his 1983 college tour, his rider included demands for eight pounds of brown rice, three green peppers, three pounds of onions, one head of garlic, three baguettes, twelve bananas and one whole pineapple.*

• *L7 demand one box of Midol.*

• *Belly once asked for new socks and underwear.*

• *Obsessed with learning to appreciate "serious" music, Rivers Cuomo of Weezer insisted on one tour that he have access to a grand piano at every stop.*

• *Oasis will periodically ask that their "survival kits" be replenished. These kits include tea, gin, a specific brand of rolling papers, Heinz baked beans and regulation English* soccer balls. They also travel with a cache of Burt Bacharach albums and Beatles bootlegs.

• The Tragically Hip need peanut butter, water, five cases of beer and some blue Gatorade.

• Damon Albarn of Blur requires honey-flavored cough drops.

• Bush saves money by packing their own cans of baked beans and boxes of tea bags. If they run out, they ask the promoter to top things up.

• During the 1992 Lollapalooza tour, the Jim Rose Circus Sideshow required that the following props be provided at each show: four junkyard televisions, two large junked appliances (a washing machine or dryer would do), twenty live crickets, ten jumbo meal worms, ten healthy night crawlers and one pound of maggots.

• During the PopMart tour, members of U2 were very particular about the food they were served backstage. The following was a typical request. Bono: a plate of raw broccoli, cauliflower, celery, carrots and black olives, with a ranch dressing dip, a small loaf of white bread and Naya bottled water. The Edge: mushrooms stuffed with feta cheese and basil, a rainbow pasta salad with a low-fat vinaigrette dressing, a plate of wheat melba toast and a case of Snapple raspberry iced tea. Larry Mullen: three soy-veggie burgers with monterey jack cheese, a selection of potato chips, three large bottles of Perrier and a case of peach-flavoured Snapple. Adam Clayton: tofu spinach salad with whole wheat croutons, dijon dressing and Aquafina bottled water.

Courtney Love on Tour

A Hole show on tour can be an unpredictable thing, thanks chiefly to the antics of Courtney Love. On March 18, 1995, a 17-year-old filed battery charges against Love after he alleged she punched him in the chest when she dove into the mosh pit. About five weeks later, she started a fight in the crowd at a show in Amsterdam when someone dumped beer on her from the balcony. A backstage controversy erupted on July 4, 1995 during the first show of the Lollapalooza tour. Responding to an insult from Bikini Kill's Kathleen Hanna, Love gave her a pretty good blow. Assault charges were filed and Love was later given a suspended sentence and ordered to take an anger management class.

Later in the tour, it was Love who became the target. During a stop in Pittsburgh, she broke down when someone tossed empty shotgun shell casings on stage in the middle of Hole's set. At another show, she jumped into the audience to attack heckling fans twice. Her explanation was that she was upset because it was her daughter's birthday and the crowd didn't sing "Happy Birthday" loud enough.

Nine Inch Nails on Tour

The Nine Inch Nails performance during the very first Lollapalooza show on July 18, 1991, was a disaster. It was so hot in the desert outside of Phoenix that one of the power boxes that provided electricity to the stage literally melted. The result was that every time the PA rumbled with a low keyboard note or a shot from the bass drum, the chord to the power box would vibrate and all the electricity would go out. As soon as the power was off, the rumbling would stop, ending the vibration in the chord and the power would come back on. It was on-off, on-off, every ten seconds. For a band that relied on computers, sequencers and keyboards with delicate electronic memories, this was the worst thing that could happen. After a few minutes of frustration and heckling from the crowd, the band smashed all their instruments and ran for the bus.

The members of Nine Inch Nails have also been known to suffer significant damage. Trent Reznor can be a very violent performer, smashing guitars, tearing the keys off keyboards, body-checking anyone he can find and throwing debris all over the stage—and his bandmates have often found themselves in the line of fire. Guitarist and keyboardist Danny Lohner was hit in the face by a mic stand and had his wrist broken. Keyboardist James Wooley has been hit over the head with the keyboard several times. Drummer Chris Vrenna once required 18 stitches to close a cut on his face that was caused by a flying piece of equipment.

Pearl Jam on Tour

Pearl Jam fans have been known to go a little crazy from time to time. For example, on July 10, 1993, hundreds of people rushed the stage during an outdoor show in Dublin, Ireland, breaking through some crash barriers. Dozens of people required attention in the first aid tent. Fans also broke through a couple of metal fences at a show in Washington State. More than a hundred people were injured. A similar thing happened in March 28, 1994, when 2,000 people without tickets forced their way through some fences, tossing rocks and bottles as they went. Five people were hurt and four others were arrested. There have also been several incidents when the band was sued after someone had been hurt in the mosh pit.

Pearl Jam's biggest impediment to touring has been their long-running feud with Ticketmaster and the service charges the company adds to the price of a concert ticket. When they couldn't negotiate a deal to their liking, they decided to take a stand. On April 17, 1994, after a show at the Palladium in New York, they announced that they were cancelling the rest of their summer tour until they could work out a way to avoid using Ticketmaster. A month later, they filed a complaint with the U.S. Justice Department, accusing Ticketmaster of threatening to sue promoters who sided with the band on creating an alternative arrangement for selling tickets, one that would allow for lower prices and lower service charges. The band's records were subpoenaed and examined by the Justice Department, which heard testimony from Pearl Jam, Ticketmaster and other concerned parties, but the investigation was dropped on July 5,

1995. Determined not to use Ticketmaster to sell tickets to their concerts, Pearl Jam continues to face problems staging North American tours.

REM's Monster Tour

REM fans were ecstatic when the group announced that they were going to tour for the first time in years. Two months after it started, the band was hit with a completely unexpected and near-fatal crisis. On March 1, 1995, the band was 90 minutes into the twenty-seventh show on the tour at the Pantinoire De Malley Auditorium in Lausanne, Switzerland, when drummer Bill Berry began to sing his falsetto part in the song "Tongue." At first, he felt a little light-headed but attributed it to the high altitude (the thinner air made it harder to get all the breath he required to sing falsetto). As he continued with the song, he began to get very dizzy. When it was over, he stood up, ready to play bass on the next song, when he says, "it felt like a bowling ball had hit me." The pain was so intense that he had to be carried from the stage.

The initial diagnosis was a bad migraine, but when the pain didn't abate by the following morning, Berry was given a CAT scan which revealed two brain aneurysms; one had burst and one was about to. With no time to lose and in danger of suffering permanent brain damage, he was immediately rushed into surgery.

The tour was put on hold while everyone wondered if Bill was going to make a full recovery. The surgery had been necessary but risky—and no one could forget the brain surgeon's rhyme: "You ain't never the same after air hits the brain."

Fortunately, Bill did make a complete recovery. Within eight weeks he was playing golf and on May 15, the band returned to the stage in San Francisco. The tour was re-christened "Aneurysm Tour 95" with some editions of the official program featuring the actual CAT scan pictures of Berry's brain.

But more medical problems followed. When the band pulled into Cologne, Germany, in July, Mike Mills had to have surgery to repair an adhesion on his intestine, a leftover from an appendix operation he had in 1994. Seven more dates had to be canceled. Once the tour resumed in Prague a few weeks later, Michael Stipe had to be flown back to the U.S. to have a hernia fixed. The only member of the band to make it back to Athens without being anesthetized at some point was guitarist Peter Buck.

The Trials of Scott Weiland and the Stone Temple Pilots

The first indication that things within the Stone Temple Pilots were not going well came in May 1995 when singer Scott Weiland was arrested at 3:30 a.m. in the parking lot of a seedy Pasadena, California hotel. Charged with drug possession,

Weiland made the first of several court-ordered trips to rehab over a period of more than a year. Things got worse when Weiland briefly went AWOL from the treatment facility, contravening the judge's orders.

In April 1996, the Pilots were forced to cancel a series of free concerts that had been designed to hype the release of their third album, *Tiny Music: Songs from the Vatican Gift Shop*. They issued this statement:

> The reason for this cancellation is that our lead singer, Scott Weiland, has become unable to rehearse or appear for these shows due to his dependency on drugs. On behalf of the band we would like to apologize for any inconvenience this may have caused.

No one knew it at the time, but the situation was so bad that the other three Pilots began to work on a new album with another singer. Nevertheless, Weiland did successfully complete his rehab program and the band pulled together for a tour in the fall of 1996. However, the last few shows had to be canceled because Weiland had slipped off the wagon.

This affected the band financially, as well as personally. The group had been getting a minimum of $200,000 per show and since the band was big enough to play 150 or more shows on an extended tour, the payoff would have been huge. And who knows? It's quite possible that the group could have sold another ten million albums had their singer been together enough to tour.

Smashing Pumpkins and the *Mellon Collie and the Infinite Sadness* Tour

Just before the Smashing Pumpkins started their world tour in Toronto on January 2, 1996, Billy Corgan had a friend do his astrological chart for the coming year. She told him that he and his friends were going to have to survive some difficult times in the months ahead. The Pumpkins had no idea how right she would be.

The first tragedy occurred on May 11, when 17-year-old Bernadette O'Brien was squeezed to death in the mosh pit during a show at the Point Depot in Dublin, Ireland. Shortly thereafter, drummer Jimmy Chamberlin's father died and several shows had to be canceled while he flew home from New Zealand. Then there was an incident in June when several fans were hurt during a show in San Francisco. That prompted Cincinnati City Council to slap a ban on all Pumpkins shows in that city.

And there was still more. Although it was kept under wraps, the Smashing Pumpkins lived with Jimmy Chamberlin's substance abuse problems for years. The first indication the public had that something was wrong came when Chamberlin checked into a rehab program shortly after the Siamese Dream sessions were completed. Things started to unravel in February 1996, during the second month of the *Mellon Collie* tour. That's when Chamberlin and touring keyboardist Jonathan Melvoin overdosed on heroin in Bangkok. When the rest of the band found out, Chamberlin told them that it was an isolated incident and that it would never happen again. Billy Corgan also warned Melvoin that if he was ever found using heroin again, he would be fired on the spot.

The promises and the warnings weren't enough. In May, both Chamberlin and Melvoin overdosed outside the band's hotel and might have died had they not been quickly rushed to a doctor. Chamberlin was threatened again and Melvoin was fired— but, because the group was on such a tight tour schedule, he was asked to stay on for a few more months.

Then came July 11, 1996. Just as the Pumpkins were to start a triumphant two night sold-out stand at Madison Square Garden, Chamberlin and Melvoin left the Regency Hotel on Park Avenue and headed for the East Village to buy some heroin. A few hours later, they returned to the hotel with a bag of "Red Rum" (its name is 'murder' spelled backwards), a particularly potent form of the drug. By 4 a.m., Melvoin—who, ironically, once worked as an emergency medical technician—was dead of an overdose. Chamberlin was coherent enough to call the police and within three hours, the entire group was down at the police station giving statements.

Five days later, the Pumpkins issued a statement of their own:

> For nine years, we have battled with Jimmy's struggles with the insidious disease of drug and alcohol addiction. It has nearly destroyed everything we are and stand for. We have decided to carry on without him, and wish him the best that we have to offer. We would like to thank everyone for their well wishes and support in this very tragic week.

Twenty-Five Short Tour Stories

1. Blur

In November 1990, a group of women attacked the T-shirt vendor at a Blur show in London. They were upset with a poster that featured a naked woman on a hippo.

2. David Bowie

Bowie used to require that he be provided with a punching bag in his dressing room. No punching bag, no show.

3. Bush

During a Chicago show in late May 1997, guitarist Nigel Pulsford found himself covered in ketchup and mustard after two fans charged the stage and showered him with condiments. No charges were pressed, but the group called the fans' parents and insisted they sign a document that said they would accept responsibility for anything that may go wrong with Pulsford's ketchup-covered guitar in the future.

4. Cause and Effect

On tour in support of their 1992 debut album *Another Minute*, singer Sean Rowley had a severe asthma attack during a show in Minneapolis. He went into full cardiac arrest and died.

5. Cranberries

On May 15, 1995, a free midday concert in Washington, D.C., had to be stopped when the audience rushed the stage. Organizers had planned for a crowd of about 3,000 people; more than 15,000 showed up. When the mob overwhelmed the stage, a large number of people (many of whom were trying to avoid the mounted police patrols) made it backstage. When it was over, some of the Cranberries' equipment was missing.

6. Peter Gabriel

Falling into the audience in Chicago while performing "Lay Your Hands On Me," Gabriel returned to the stage missing most of his clothes, including his underwear.

7. Goo Goo Dolls

The only thing that used to cure singer Johnny Rzeznik of his stage fright was several bottles of beer before the show.

8. Green Day

Bassist Mike Dirnt came down with such a severe case of anxiety about performing in front of crowds that a whole tour in 1996 had to be canceled.

9. Hoodoo Gurus

The Australian band had to cancel an entire world tour after drummer Mark Kingsmill fell from his drum riser during a concert in Sydney in the summer of 1996. He fell on top of a fluorescent light bulb which severed an artery and caused extensive nerve damage to his arm.

10. Jewel

On June 1, 1996, the singer walked off stage in Washington, D.C., after just a song-and-a-half. She had been hit in the head with a frisbee.

11. Marilyn Manson

No one wanted to have Marilyn Manson in their town during their 1997 tour. Outraged at the band's alleged satanist leanings, protesters and civic officials tried to cancel shows in Lubbock, Texas; Utica, New York; Salt Lake City, Utah: Las Cruces, New Mexico; Louisville, Kentucky; Orlando and Jacksonville, Florida; Richmond, Virginia; Wheeling, West Virginia; Saginaw and Kalamazoo, Michigan; Evansville, Indiana; Anchorage, Alaska; Hamilton, Ontario, and a dozen more cities across North America. A few concerts were canceled while the vast majority went ahead as scheduled. On May 9, 1997, a member of the lighting crew fell to his death before a show in Washington, D.C.

12. Oasis

Among the many Oasis concert crises was an occasion on April 10, 1996, in Vancouver, British Columbia, when the group walked off stage after Liam Gallagher was hit in the head with a shoe. Riot police were called in, but the crowd left quietly.

13. Pogues

There are nearly 20 documented occasions when the members of the Pogues got into fights *with each other* during gigs over the years.

14. Porno for Pyros

The group had to cancel a portion of their 1996 tour after guitarist Peter DiStefano was diagnosed with cancer. Subsequent chemotherapy treatments were successful.

15. Pulp

During the group's 1996 North American tour, singer Jarvis Cocker lived in fear of being attacked by roving bands of vigilante Michael Jackson fans seeking revenge for Cocker's infamous crashing of Jackson's performance at the 1996 Brit Awards.

16. The Ramones

Young people went on a rampage in a shopping mall in Buenos Aires on March 13, 1996, after lining up all night at the wrong place to buy tickets to an upcoming show.

17. REM

In its early days, a promoter booked the band to play at a fried chicken restaurant in Nebraska. They were also supposed to perform during a "hot legs" contest at a bar in New Mexico—but when the promoter realized that the drunk cowboys in the audience weren't in the mood for some freaky alternative band, REM was paid *not* to play that night.

18. Revolting Cocks

During a 1990 show in Houston, the stage was surrounded by a metal fence that allegedly had a mild electric charge running through it. Inside the perimeter were a series of flame throwers that shot fire twenty feet into the air. Some witnesses swear that they saw a herd of cattle backstage ready to make an appearance when the band launched into "Beers, Steers and Queers." But before the alleged cows could be ushered onstage, the flame throwers set fire to the building and everyone had to be evacuated.

19. Sex Pistols

In the early 90s, Malcolm McLaren revealed that, on the Pistols' infamous 1978 American tour, Sid Vicious never played a note. Realizing that Sid was too strung out and volatile to play his bass, he was never plugged in. A roadie played all his parts backstage and out of sight. When the band reunited for a live album and tour in 1996, a show in Madrid, Spain, was canceled because the promoter feared "anarchy."

20. Shed Seven

The group was threatened with a lifetime ban from playing in Norway, after they allegedly trashed a dressing room at the So What Club in Oslo. Two couches and a toilet were destroyed in what the band described as a bout of "redecorating."

21. Sparklehorse

When singer Mark Linkous collapsed of a heart attack in the bathroom of his hotel room in January 1996, he lay unconscious with his legs pinned beneath him for 14 hours. He was rescued, but required four months in hospital and nine operations in order to walk again.

22. Stone Temple Pilots

The group paid $8,500 to cover damages to Eliot Hall of Music at Purdue University after a show on April 13, 1997, when more than 5,000 fans obeyed singer Scott Weiland's instructions to tear the place apart. There was significant damage to the tiles and walls and 73 seats were destroyed.

23. Suede

Suede has had equipment stolen on two separate North American tours. The first incident occurred in May 1993 in Toronto; the second happened in Boston in May 1997. In each case, the group lost everything, including some irreplaceable vintage guitars. Radiohead was ripped off in a similar way in the fall of 1995 in Denver, during an opening stint for Soul Asylum.

24. 311

In 1993, 311 set off on one of their first tours using a borrowed RV. But when the motorhome caught fire in Missouri, all the band's gear went up in flames.

25. U2

On May 27, 1997, U2's show in Rome on its PopMart tour was so loud that earthquake alarms were set off all over the city. Stringent rules had been set down by the band regarding alcohol on the PopMart tour. The edict declared that no band member could drink hard liquor and that they were limited to two bottles of beer a day and one glass of wine with dinner. On the night of a show, there was no alcohol of any sort allowed beyond dinnertime.

Fifty-Seven Bands Who Have Played on the Main Stage at Lollapalooza (1991–1997)

1. Alice In Chains (1993)
2. Arrested Development (1993)
3. A Tribe Called Quest (1994)
4. Beastie Boys (1994)
5. Beck (1995)
6. Boredoms (first half of the tour, 1994)
7. Breeders (1994)
8. Butthole Surfers (1991)
9. Nick Cave and the Bad Seeds (1994)
10. George Clinton and the P-Funk All Stars (1994)
11. Cypress Hill (1995)
12. Devo (selected dates, 1996)
13. Dinosaur Jr. (1993)
14. Elastica (replaced Sinead O'Connor, 1995)
15. Fishbone (1993)
16. Front 242 (1993)
17. Green Day (second half of the tour, 1994)

18. Hole (1995)
19. Ice Cube (1992)
20. Ice-T and Bodycount (1991)
21. James (1997)
22. Jane's Addiction (1991)
23. Waylon Jennings (selected dates, 1996)
24. Jesus and Mary Chain (1992)
25. Jesus Lizard (1995)
26. Korn (1997)
27. Living Color (1991)
28. L7 (1994)
29. Lush (1992)
30. Julian and Damian Marley and the Uprising Band (1997)
31. Metallica (1996)
32. Mighty Mighty Bosstones (1995)
33. Ministry (1992)
34. Nine Inch Nails (1991)
35. Sinead O'Connor (first few shows, 1995)
36. Orbital (1997)
37. Pavement (1995)
38. Pearl Jam (1992)
39. Primus (1993)
40. Prodigy (selected dates 1997)
41. Psychotica (1996)
42. Rage Against the Machine (1993 and selected dates in 1996)
43. Rancid (1996)
44. Ramones (1996)
45. Red Hot Chili Peppers (1992)
46. Rollins Band (1991)
47. Screaming Trees (1996)
48. Siouxsie and the Banshees (1991)
49. Smashing Pumpkins (1994)
50. Snoop Doggy Dogg (1997)
51. Sonic Youth (1995)
52. Soundgarden (1991 and 1996)
53. Jon Spencer Blues Explosion (1997)
54. Tool (1997 plus a few main stage appearances in 1993)
55. Tricky (1997)
56. Violent Femmes (1996)
57. Wu-Tang Clan (selected dates, 1996)

Equipment List for U2's PopMart Tour

1. The world's largest television, a 150-by-56 foot video screen using twenty-two miles of cable, 21,000 circuit boards, 120,000 connectors and 150,000 pixels made up of one million LEDs. The screen covered 833 square yards and weighed 65,000 pounds. It was manufactured specifically for U2 by a company in Montreal.

2. A main stage of 181-by-71 feet

3. A 100-foot runway to a secondary stage

4. Thirty tons of PA equipment (all in mono), generating over a million watts of power. The system included 149 speaker enclosures of various designs, and incorporated 298 eighteen-inch woofers, 428 10-inch midrange drivers and 604 high frequency tweeters.

5. One 100-foot golden arch inspired by the arch in St. Louis (not McDonald's) that could be broken down into 100 separate sections

6. One lemon-shaped mirror ball, 30-feet high

7. A 12-foot illuminated stuffed olive and a 100-foot toothpick

8. One thousand lighting fixtures including 5,000 feet of disco lighting, a Plexiglass dancefloor, 6 lightning machines, 20 Xenon search lights, 100 strobe lights, 6 TV cameras and one headset camera

9. Three power generators which supplied 4 million watts of electricity (enough to supply 1,500 homes) through 13 miles of cable

10. Seventy-five semi-trailers, 15 buses and one customized 50-seat Boeing 727 were required to move the 1,200 tons of equipment and 250 tour personnel from place to place. Up to an additional 200 people were hired at each stop on the tour.

11. Each stage setup took three days and 3,000 man-hours to complete. As a result, two separate stages were needed for the tour.

12. The cost of maintaining this tour? Over $200,000 a day.

Part 7

Oddities, Mysteries and Conspiracies

Artist Eccentricities A-Z

Ash: All the members of the band like to collect rare *Star Wars* memorabilia.

Bono: This U2 singer is allergic to whiskey.

Corgan, Billy: After the death of touring keyboardist Jonathan Melvoin in July 1996, Corgan admitted to taking so much LSD during the *Gish* sessions that he developed a stutter.

Dando, Evan: This Lemonheads singer is an avid birder and can imitate the songs and whistles of several species. His poster-boy image inspired the fanzine *Die, Evan Dando, Die!*

Elastica: The father of singer Justine Frischmann from Elastica is a very wealthy architect in London, England.

Firley, Matt: The keyboardist from Gravity Kills can simultaneously write forwards with his right hand and backwards with his left. Meanwhile, drummer Kurt Kerns wants everyone to know he can touch the tip of his nose with his tongue.

Green Day: Singer Billie Joe Armstrong has been known to take off all his clothes during a show.

Harvey, PJ: As a young tomboy, PJ wanted everyone to refer to her as "Paul."

Ice-T: The leader of Bodycount has one of the most profitable Internet web sites in the world because it's run by a company that specializes in pornography. Anyone who wants to access it must pay up to $10 a day.

James: Singer Tim Booth dances so hard when the band performs that he has an almost permanent case of whiplash.

Kula Shaker: Concerned about his place in the world from an astrological point of view, singer Crispin Mills refused to sign a contract with Columbia until the stars were exactly right. The original date had Mercury in conjunction with Jupiter, apparently an unwise time to commit to a business relationship. Columbia, determined to have Kula Shaker on their roster (and obviously used to accommodating strange requests), re-scheduled everything to a date and time that were to Mills's liking. The contract was eventually signed at exactly 5:05 p.m., September 29, 1995.

Love, Courtney: Not only does she share a publicist with Tom Cruise and hang out with the daughter of New York mayor Rudy Giuliani, but Love also has a big fan in Vaclav Havel, the President of the Czech Republic. He was one of the people who urged director Milos Forman to cast her in the role of Althea In the movie *The People Vs Larry Flynt*.

Marilyn Manson: According to Manson himself, one of the things he remembers most from his childhood was when a neighbor exposed him to bestiality-based porn. He has also spoken of a neighborhood boy who abused him when they played a game called "prison." His father, a furniture salesman, is a Viet Nam vet who was exposed to Agent Orange: for years after he got out of the army, he and his family were given genetic tests to determine the aftereffects of the chemical. There is a newspaper report from October 1996 which states that during an autograph session at a record store in Vancouver, Manson obliged a fan by signing the fan's testicles.

Nine Inch Nails: Trent Reznor played the tuba in his high school marching band.

Oasis: The living room of Noel Gallagher's mansion in the Belsize Park area of London features a fish tank that is 35-feet long. It is so heavy that the foundations of the house had to be reinforced to support it.

Pixies: Black Frances (now Frank Black) is an astronomy buff.

Queers: This New Hampshire-based hardcore band has released songs with such titles as "Ursula Finally Has Tits" and "I Can't Stop Farting." In 1994, the Queers released an album that covered the entire *Rocket to Russia* album from the Ramones.

REM: Singer Michael Stipe is afraid of mice.

Suede: Brett Anderson's father (a taxi driver) tried to force Brett to become a classical pianist.

Tucker, Moe: When the group broke up for good, the Velvet Underground drummer eventually found work at a Wal-Mart in Georgia to help support herself and her five children.

U2: In Spain, the band is known as "U-Dos."

Velvet Underground: When the group broke up, guitarist Sterling Morrison found a job as a tugboat captain.

Weezer: After the group's first album sold in the millions, singer Rivers Cuomo took some time out from Weezer to study classical music at Harvard.

XTC: Singer Andy Partridge suffered from such a severe case of stage fright that he once wet himself during a gig in Paris. Fortunately, he was able to hide his embarrassment behind his big guitar.

Yorke, Thom: The Radiohead singer was born blind in one eye. As a child, he required several major operations to fix the problem.

Ziffel, Arnold: The Hoodoo Gurus dedicated their 1983 debut album, *Stoneage Romeos,* to Arnold Ziffel, the pig from the 60s TV show *Green Acres*.

101 Strange But True (and Sometimes Useless) Facts

1. In 1997, the one-time punk fashion designer Jean Charles De Castelbajac, who once dressed Johnny Rotten of the Sex Pistols, was hired by the Vatican to update the robes and vestments of Pope John Paul II.

2. *Legend*, Bob Marley's posthumously-released greatest hits collection and the most influential reggae album in history, has quietly sold more than 12 million copies since it was released in 1984. It still sells in the neighborhood of 50,000 copies a month in the U.S.

3. After he drove the band's car into the back of a truck on a highway, Longpigs singer Crispin Hunt fell into a coma for three days. When he regained consciousness, he went on a songwriting blitz, which resulted in the group's 1996 album *The Sun is Often Out*.

4. After playing more than 2,200 shows over their 23-year career, the Ramones' last performance took place at the Billboard Live club in Hollywood on August 6, 1996.

5. In addition to fronting the Rollins Band, Henry Rollins writes books and runs his own small publishing company 2.13.61 (his birthdate).

6. The soundtrack for the best-selling computer game *Quake* was written by Trent Reznor of Nine Inch Nails.

7. In April 1996, 311 had their T-shirts banned in several schools in their hometown of Omaha, Nebraska, because officials made a strange connection between the band and the Ku Klux Klan. Their reasoning went like this: "K" is the eleventh letter of the alphabet, therefore 3-11 is code for KKK. Not so, says the band; "311" is police code for "indecent exposure."

8. Noel Hogan of the Cranberries owns a restaurant in Limerick, Ireland, called Café Nero.

9. Courtney Love was in therapy by the age of 2. At age 14, she started working as a stripper, doffing her clothes to her favorite Fleetwood Mac songs. Her first TV appearance was a bit part in an episode of *Quincy*. Courtney is also no stranger to plastic surgery. She used the money she made playing a junkie in the 1986 film *Sid and Nancy* to get a nose job. Once Hole made it big, she tried some breast implants, but later had them removed.

10. The voice that counts off the beginning of the song "Moonshine" on L7's *The Beauty Process: Triple Platinum* belongs to Lionel Ritchie.

11. When it was announced that U2's *Pop* album wouldn't be ready in time for Christmas 1996, the parent company of the band's label suffered an immediate drop in the price of its stock on markets around the world.

12. Soundgarden was managed by Susan Silver, the former operator of a used clothing store in Seattle, and also the wife of Soundgarden singer Chris Cornell.

13. There really is a Solsbury Hill. Peter Gabriel wrote the song about a hill near his home in Bath where he used to walk and jog. "Games Without Frontiers" was based on a European TV game show featuring contestants from different countries competing for big prizes.

14. The brother of Filter's Richard Patrick played the evil T-1000 in *Terminator II*.

15. The father of Kula Shaker's Crispin Mills is 60 years older than his son.

16. As part of a medical study looking at the connections between Prozac and creativity, Bernard Sumner agreed to write a good portion of Electronic's *Raise the Pressure* album while taking the drug.

17. Love and Rockets had to completely re-record their *Sweet F.A.* album after a fire destroyed their recording studio. All that was left was the charred remains of the guitar that appears on the front cover.

18. The Butthole Surfers were asked to change the name of their 1996 album to *Electriclarryland* from *Oklahoma!* because label executives were worried about being sued by the estate of Rogers and Hammerstein, the people who wrote the musical by the same name. Other people have suggested that the name change came about to avoid charges of bad taste after the bombing of a federal building in Oklahoma City.

19. According to an interview in the spring of 1996, Pearl Jam guitarist Stone Gossard said that when he dies, he wants his body thrown to the sharks.

20. On March 18, 1996, Princess Diana declined an offer of economic aid from the newly reunited Sex Pistols. Concerned for her well-being following her divorce from Prince Charles, Johnny Rotten had proposed a special benefit concert.

21. *Entertainment Monitor*, a monthly newsletter designed to inform parents and teachers about the content of contemporary music, wrote this track-by-track description of White's Zombie's *Astro-Creep: 2000* album in late 1995:

    Themes: Abstract religious-themed songs about the devil taking over someone's thoughts. Pondering life after the Apocalypse. A song critical of war. Sensory overload of pleasure. A song using Las Vegas gambling metaphors as a way to describe God's power. Proclamation of one's zombie-like state. The stranger one is, the more human one is. A song about having sex, in a violent way, with an "angel" or virgin. Beauty never dies.

    The newsletter also describes "Lump" by the group Presidents of the United States of America as "a song about a woman named Lump who possesses the singer's thoughts."

22. REM's 1996 contract with Warner Brothers Records is worth an estimated $80 million. The deal included a $10 million signing bonus, plus a $20 million advance

on royalties from the future sales of the group's six albums on Warner. REM was also guaranteed a 24 percent royalty on the retail price of each record they sold, which works out to about $2.50 per record. Sources say that the 1996 deal signed between Oasis and Creation/Sony could be worth up to $150 million (an $18 million advance, a possible $90 million from worldwide sales for four albums, plus an addition $23 million from any greatest hits package or live album.) Noel Gallagher has a $3 million publishing deal on top of everything else.

23. Veruca Salt chose the title *Eight Arms to Hold You* for their second album because that was the working title of the Beatles' *Help!*

24. There's a strange story about where techno star Aphex Twin got his name. His real name is Richard James and he had an older brother, also named Richard, who died on November 23, 1968, before Aphex Twin was born. When James was born in 1972, his mother gave him the same name, perhaps in the hope that in this way, her first-born would live on. This explains the cover of the 1996 Aphex Twin single "Girl/Boy." The younger James considers himself to be the dead brother's "twin."

25. One of Beck's biggest fans is Crown Prince Frederick of Denmark.

26. Producer Brian Eno was so frustrated with U2's attempts to record "Where the Streets Have No Name" during the *Joshua Tree* sessions that he actually tried to erase the master tape. An assistant engineer stopped him from doing it.

27. Kurt Cobain was Courtney Love's second husband. In 1988, she married James Moreland, the transvestite lead singer for a group called Leaving Trains. Although they lived together for eight months before their quickie wedding in Las Vegas, they divorced exactly one day after they got married.

28. By the time Rivers Cuomo of Weezer was full grown, his right leg was two full inches shorter than his left. Determined to finally get rid of his orthopedic shoes, he took some of the money he had earned from Weezer's first album and gave it to a specialist who promised he could even things out. The doctor broke Cuomo's leg at the thigh and fitted him with a metal frame. Every day, Cuomo would crank the frame another four notches, slowly stretching the leg, forcing the bone to knit together at a longer and longer length. Unfortunately, the technique didn't work, so a piece of his hip bone was ground up and used to connect the two pieces of leg bone together. Cuomo had to walk with a cane for a while and his leg still doesn't bend quite right—but it's a whole lot better than it used to be.

29. Radiohead recorded part of their *OK Computer* album in the library and ballroom of an English mansion in Bath, England, owned by actress Jane Seymour. St. Catherine's Court is a real fourteenth-century castle that was once the property of Henry VIII. It has eight bedrooms, six-and-a-half bathrooms, stables, a tennis court, a full church and is surrounded by fourteen acres of gardens that are literally fit for a king. By the way, anyone can rent St. Catherine's Court—for

$13,000 a week. Radiohead lived there for two months. The Cure also recorded parts of *Wild Mood Swings* in the castle.

30. An unused ticket for a show on Nirvana's uncompleted final European tour can be worth $3,000 or more to a collector. Meanwhile, a signed discharge form from one of his stays at a rehab center can fetch up to $1,500. Another collector tried to sell a bottle of Cobain's acne medicine for $300. Organizers of a 1996 memorabilia auction declined to accept a spoon that was allegedly used by Cobain to prepare his heroin fixes.

31. Members of Rage Against the Machine maintain close ties with the Zapatista rebels in rural Mexico. They've even visited several times.

32. In September 1996, *Hustler* magazine claimed to have purchased four photos of Courtney Love and STP's Scott Weiland having sex. No one ever saw them because publisher Larry Flynt says he destroyed them out of respect for Love.

33. The cover photo of Oasis's *(What's the Story) Morning Glory?* album was actually shot at 4:30 in the morning. The daylight was added later (if you look closely, you'll see that the streetlights are glowing). Here's something else to look for: in the background and to the left, a man is holding a diamond-shaped object above his head. That's producer Owen Morris with the box containing the master tape of the album.

34. REM sued Hershey (the chocolate bar people) when they ran a Kit Kat contest that allegedly exploited the group's name without their permission.

35. Gavin Rossdale of Bush loves his dog, a pouli named Winston, so much that he's insured him for $6 million. Chris Cornell has five dogs, while Trent Reznor still chokes up when he thinks of Maise, the golden retriever who died when she jumped over a railing at a tour stop in Columbus, Ohio. Reznor was so upset by her death that he canceled the rest of the tour.

36. Jill Cuniff, singer for Luscious Jackson, is the voice of a Sega video game called *Enemy Zero*. On the same subject, the Sega Saturn game called *NBA Jam: Tournament Edition* features a "cheat code" that will let you turn some of the players into the Beastie Boys. (Hold down the left and right shift buttons while entering the following initials, months and dates: Ad-Rock ADR APRIL 6, Adam Yauch MCA APRIL 9, Mike D M_D JULY 1.)

37. Blondie singer Deborah Harry was nearly a victim of notorious serial killer Ted Bundy. One night, back in the 70s, she was hitching a ride home from a show at CBGBs at 2 a.m. when a man stopped to give her a lift. She opened the door and had actually sat down, when she decided that something felt wrong and left the car. Harry didn't realize who the driver was until she saw a photo of Bundy after his arrest years later.

38. Sarah McLachlan's Lilith Fair festival was one of the most successful tours of 1997. But who, exactly, is "Lilith?" According to Jewish legend, she was the first

wife of Adam in the Garden of Eden. But when she refused to take orders from Adam, she was banished from the garden and replaced by Eve. So this makes Lilith the proto-typical feminist, right? Not quite. The legend goes on to tell of how she stalked Adam and Eve and eventually killed a few of their descendants while they slept.

39. Country singer Johnny Cash recorded a version of Soundgarden's "Rusty Cage."

40. Lux Interior of the Cramps was hired by Francis Ford Coppola to provide Dracula's screams for his production of *Bram Stoker's Dracula*.

41. REM has performed under a variety of pseudonyms over the years, including Hornets Attack Victor Mature, Worst Case Scenario, The Community Trolls, It Crawled from the South, Bingo Hand Job and Automatic Baby (a one-off performance at Bill Clinton's inauguration in January 1993 which also featured Adam Clayton and Larry Mullen of U2.)

42. Patsy Kensit was married twice before she married Liam Gallagher of Oasis. Her first husband was Dan Donovan of Big Audio Dynamite and her second was Jim Kerr of Simple Minds (who, by the way, was briefly married to Chrissie Hynde of the Pretenders).

43. It took more than $200,000 a day to keep U2's PopMart tour on the road. The show required 75 semi-trailers to carry 1,200 tons of equipment. Sixteen buses and a 50-seat Boeing 727 jet carried personnel and the band from gig to gig.

44. James singer Tim Booth was once so hard up for cash that he volunteered to be the subject of some medical experiments. The researchers declined his services, saying that he was "too strange."

45. Even as *Tragic Kingdom* was selling millions of copies around the world, No Doubt singer Gwen Stefani was still living with her parents in Anaheim, California.

46. The sister of Bush guitarist Nigel Pulsford is Jan Pulsford, one of Cyndi Lauper's co-writers and a keyboardist in her backup band.

47. The idea of recording an album in Iceland came to Blur singer Damon Albarn in a dream. That led to the group recording their fifth album in Reykjavik.

48. The OMD song "Enola Gay" takes its title from the name of the B29 bomber that dropped the atomic bomb on Hiroshima on August 6, 1945. Pilot Paul Tibbets, Jr. named the plane after his mother.

49. "Love Spreads," by the Stone Roses, was used as the theme music for the soccer match of the week on Albanian state television.

50. After seeing the film *The Exorcist* as a kid, Trent Reznor spent weeks fearing that *he* was the Antichrist.

51. The packaging for Pearl Jam's *Vitalogy* album was based on a real book of the same name published in 1899 by a doctor famous for dispensing advice on healthy lifestyles. In its day, the book was very popular, selling close to two million copies. Once the Pearl Jam album came out, the book was reissued and started selling once again.

52. When Belly opened for U2 at a show in Germany in front of more than 65,000 fans, they sold exactly two T-shirts that day—and one of them was purchased by the vendor selling U2 souvenirs.

53. When it came time to choose an outfit for the 1995 Academy Awards, Courtney Love went with a dress she found in a second hand store for $15.

54. All the members of Weezer are susceptible to headaches from loud music. That's why they all wear earplugs on stage.

55. Morrissey and guitarist Billy Duffy of the Cult once played together in a band called the Nosebleeds.

56. Rob Dickinson of the Catherine Wheel is the cousin of Bruce Dickinson, singer for the British metal group Iron Maiden.

57. Tori Amos was the inspiration for Delerium, a character in Neil Gaiman's comic book creation *The Sandman*.

58. The Stone Roses spent 3,470 hours recording their second album. One track took more than six weeks and $60,000 to produce.

59. One rumor that Rancid fans like to trade is that Madonna was once so anxious for the group to sign to her Maverick Records that, in addition to offering them lots of money and phoning them in the middle of the night, she sent the band a nude Polaroid of herself. Rancid stayed with Epitaph.

60. In the beginning, KMFDM was part of a performance-art collective, dedicated to making music that was as far removed from the mainstream as possible. Their first show featured the group playing nothing more than 16 vacuum cleaners through a series of distortion pedals and outboard effects.

61. Johnny Ramone has been collecting autographed eight-by-ten glossy photos of major league baseball players for years. At last count, he had more than 4,300 pictures, the largest known personal collection in the world.

62. Lenny Kravitz's mother was Roxie Roker, the actress who played Helen Willis on *The Jeffersons*.

63. Anthony Kiedis of the Red Hot Chili Peppers was once in a Sylvestor Stallone movie. When he was 16, he had a tiny part as Stallone's son in the 1978 film *F.I.S.T.* Flea, meanwhile, has had roles in almost 20 movies.

64. The original inspiration for the Ramones' "Blitzkrieg Bop" was "Saturday Night" by the Bay City Rollers.

65. Rancid guitarist Larks Fredericksen has a tattoo on the inside of his lower lip that reads "beer."

66. The "Echo" in "Echo and the Bunnymen" was the group's drum machine. The Sisters of Mercy never had a live drummer, preferring to use a drum machine which leader Andrew Eldritch called "Doktor Avalanche."

67. There's a conspiracy theory that the CIA assassinated Sid Vicious in an effort to demoralize the punk movement, thereby blunting its anarchistic influence.

68. The voice that says "You gotta keep 'em separated" in Offspring's "Come Out and Play" belongs to Jason Whittaker, a forklift operator from Orange County, California. The band gave him the part as a way of saying thanks for being one of Offspring's most serious long-time fans.

69. Shannon Hoon of Blind Melon, then an unknown singer, contributed backup vocals for Guns 'n' Roses on their *Use Your Illusion* albums.

70. The name of the dog on Alice In Chains' self-titled 1995 album is Sunshine and he really does only have three legs.

71. Al Jourgensen of Ministry worked as a rodeo clown before he got into music.

72. Courtney Love used to carry around the ashes of Kurt Cobain in a knapsack shaped like a teddy bear.

73. Tori Amos touches up her hair with Miss Clairol's "Torrid Touch of Crimson."

74. Brad Graffin of Bad Religion has a degree in evolutionary biology from Cornell University. Dexter Hollard of Offspring has his degree in virology, while Rage Against the Machine's Tom Morello went to Harvard and graduated with honors and a degree in social studies.

75. No one knows for sure, but it very well might be Iggy Pop playing drums on the old Shangri-Las classic "Leader of the Pack." Iggy was hanging around the studio in Detroit that day and asked to play drums on that song. Once he was done, he was paid and sent home. A few days later, Billy Joel, who was working as a studio musician at the time, laid down his piano parts. Iggy Pop and Billy Joel on the same record?

76. Shirley Manson was asked to join Garbage after drummer Butch Vig saw her on MTV in a video with her old band Angelfish.

77. Chris Cornell of Soundgarden was kicked out of school twice—in seventh grade and again in eighth grade.

78. Gavin Rossdale of Bush didn't speak a word until he was four years old.

79. When Pulp is on tour, singer Jarvis Cocker often checks in using the name "Mr. Sheffield." Courtney Love has been known to use "Neely O'Hara" (the drugged-out egomaniac character in *Valley of the Dolls*), "Mary Magdalene" and "Blanche DuBois."

80. When Dolores O'Riordan of the Cranberries was a child, her older sister burned down the family house. The home was rebuilt, thanks largely to a collection gathered by the other citizens of Ballybricken, Ireland.

81. Even though at age sixteen, the guys in Silverchair were selling millions of records around the world, they were still required to take music class in their high school.

82. Tracey Bonham is a classically-trained violinist. She won scholarships to both the University of Southern California and the prestigious Berklee School of Music in Boston.

83. The lyrics to track 10 on Tool's *Ænema* album are actually a recipe for cookies. "Die Eier Von Satan" means "the eggs of Satan." If you choose to bake these cookies, note that ingredient number three is a "knifetip of Turkish hash."

84. Green Day bassist Mike Dirnt says he came up with the beat for the song "Longview" while he was tripping on acid. Elvis Costello wrote "Pump It Up" on a fire escape at his hotel while blitzed on vodka and amphetamines.

85. Kurt Cobain didn't think "Smells Like Teen Spirit" was any good, because it sounded too much like the old Boston song "More Than a Feeling." Nirvana's record company didn't think much of it either—they thought the big single from the album was going to be "Come As You Are."

86. The Sex Pistols' classic "God Save the Queen" was originally entitled "No Future." Manager Malcolm McLaren changed it to "God Save the Queen" because he knew it would stir up some controversy during Queen Elizabeth's Silver Jubilee.

87. When Eddie Vedder, Stone Gossard and Jeff Ament played members of Matt Dillon's band Citizen Dick in the film *Singles*, all of Dillon's clothes came directly of out their closets. The movie also featured appearances by Tad, Alice In Chains, Chris Cornell of Soundgarden and other Seattle music scene characters.

88. One of Billy Corgan's first bands was a death metal outfit called the Marked. Their name was inspired by the fact that both Billy and the drummer had big birthmarks.

89. Rob Zombie of White Zombie had a one-eyed pet rat named "Sammy" (named after Sammy Davis Jr.).

90. The "Elsa" mentioned in the lyrics of Oasis's "Supersonic" was actually the flatulent dog that hung around the studio. She became significantly more fragrant when she somehow got into a box of Alka-Seltzer. The incident inspired Noel Gallagher to immortalize Elsa in the song.

91. Bono had to improvise most of the lyrics on U2's *October* album because someone had stolen his notebook. As far as anyone could tell, three girls took a briefcase out of the band's dressing room after a show in Portland, Oregon, on March 22, 1981.

92. Damon Albarn of Blur is one of eight owners of Honest Guv, a greyhound racing dog often seen at Walthanshow Dog Stadium in London.

93. When Husker Du broke up, bassist Greg Norton became a chef in a Minneapolis restaurant.

94. Page Hamilton of Helmet has a master's degree in jazz guitar.

95. Drummer Bill Berry was the first member of REM to release a solo project. He issued a 1989 single called "My Bible Is the Latest TV Guide" under the name 13111 on Dog Gone Records, an indie label owned by then-REM manager, Jefferson Holt.

96. Before he decided on Nirvana, Kurt Cobain thought about calling his group Throat Oyster, Pen Cap Chew, Skid Row and Fecal Matter.

97. The Ramones were once booked as an opening act for Toto.

98. The Jesus and Mary Chain almost made it onto *The Barbara Mandrell Show* when the talent coordinator thought she was getting a gospel group.

99. According to a music business legend, the Pogues signed with Stiff Records only when the label agreed to give the band half a case of beer as a signing bonus.

100. When he was 16, Henry Rollins had a part-time job working in a gay movie theater. His nickname at the time was "Henrietta."

101. Inspired by the story of Waldo and Marcia in the Velvet Underground song "The Gift," 26-year-old Scott Harner climbed inside a wooden crate and mailed himself to a friend one hundred miles away in May 1997. The delivery charge for the 400 pound parcel was $180.

A Word About Surveys

On Dancing: According to a study conducted by the University of Manchester in 1996, the urge to dance may be a biological response. Researchers concluded that when the sacculus (a structure in the inner ear) is stimulated by sounds of more than 90 decibels, it tells a specific set of nerves to move muscles along the spine. Since the brain finds that sequence of nerve stimulation to be pleasurable, people often involuntarily begin to dance to enhance the effect.

On Exercise: A number of studies suggest that working out to music is not such a good idea because the music may actually sap a person's strength. Everything the body does requires energy, including processing sound. The more intense the music, the more intense the sound. This implies that a person may not be getting maximum workout because so much of their strength is being diverted to the brain.

On Hearing: Several European and American studies have revealed that the performer most likely to suffering hearing loss because of high sound levels is the musician who plays in a symphony orchestra.

On Intelligence: The Institute of Education in London, England, conducted a 1996 study of the effect of music on 11,000 children from 250 schools. They divided the children into three groups and allowed the first group to listen to nothing but classical music. Group two spent their time listening to talk radio, while the third group listened to nothing but Blur and Oasis. While the music was playing, all the children were given tests involving spatial reasoning. Scientists were astonished to learn that the kids who were given steady doses of Blur and Oasis scored an average of 4 percent higher than the classical and talk radio groups. Meanwhile, a test carried out in California suggested that adults performed better while listening to Mozart. Researchers believed this might mean adults process music differently.

On Oasis: In 1996, a British magazine surveyed people between the ages of 15 and 45 in seven U.K. cities. They were asked to name their favorite group of all time. When all the results were in, Oasis finished first with more than twice as many votes as the Beatles.

On Pearl Jam: In 1995, a group of American doctors determined that listening to Pearl Jam can make a person depressed and irritated. They played a Pearl Jam CD (they didn't say which one) for a group of people and then asked them how they felt when it was over. Eighty-five percent said they felt a "decrease in their feeling of peace." The study was commissioned by a company that produces stress-relieving New Age CDs.

On Sex: Nine Inch Nails' "Closer" finished first in the "Big Bonking Poll," a survey conducted by an Australian radio station in 1995. Listeners said that they would rather have sex to "Closer" than to any other song.

On Weirdness: A British metal magazine determined that Marilyn Manson was the weirdest and craziest musical dude of all time. The 1996 poll ranked Jonathan Davis of Korn number two, Al Jourgensen number five and Shirley Manson number seven. Courtney Love finished a disappointing eleventh.

Did Sid Vicious Really Do It?

The breakup of the Sex Pistols in January 1978 left Sid Vicious with nowhere to go. Immediately following the final show at San Francisco's Winterland Theater, he disappeared, turning up comatose in a closet in the Haight-Ashbury area of the city. On the way back to London, he managed to overdose on the plane, which resulted in a hospital stay in New York.

Once he went through detox, he returned to using drugs while in Paris filming with Malcolm McLaren for the movie *The Great Rock 'n' Roll Swindle*. When he and girlfriend Nancy Spungen finally made it home, they were evicted from their London flat by their roommates, one of whom chased them out waving an ax.

With nowhere else to go, the couple moved back to New York, checking into Room 100 at the Chelsea Hotel. For the next month, Nancy attempted to act as Sid's manager, scaring up one or two gigs around the city. However, Sid's reputation preceded him and no record company or musician would have anything to do with either him or Nancy. With $3,000 from a recent gig at Max's Kansas City and a recently-cashed personal cheque from Malcolm McLaren, neither of them were really motivated to do anything. Sinking into a hazy stupor of marijuana, methadone, Tuinols, heroin and Dilaudid (a synthetic form of morphine), they did little with the money but feed their drug habits.

No one really knows what happened on the night of Wednesday, October 11, 1978. Earlier in the day, Sid had gone to Times Square with Stiv Bators of the Dead Boys, Steve Leckie of the Viletones and Neon Leon, another person who was staying at the Chelsea. Sid, feeling a little paranoid, decided to purchase a 007 knife, which he then took back to the room, occasionally toying with it throughout the evening. Some time after supper that evening (maybe as late as 1:30 a.m.), there was a visitor to Room 100, probably Rockets Redglare, a friend who often supplied the couple with Dilaudid. He left around five, later saying that he saw another drug dealer loitering in the lobby.

What actually happened then is unclear. Sid said he awoke the next morning between 9 and 11:15 and found Nancy in a pool of blood with his new knife sticking out of her side. Frightened because he didn't remember a thing, he called the front desk and asked for an ambulance. When it arrived, Sid was taken to the East 51st Street Police Station and questioned. They told Sid they were charging him with second degree murder.

Sid died of a heroin overdose on February 2, 1979, before he could come to trial. When he died, the police closed the case, positive that they had found their murderer. Other people weren't so convinced and believe that Sid (who was totally devoted to Nancy) was, in fact, innocent. Some point a finger at Neon Leon, whose room down the hall was found filled with Sid's stuff, including his leather jacket and some Sex Pistols gold records. Others suggest that the mystery drug dealer is to blame. One story had Nancy and the dealer getting into a fight over drugs after Sid had passed out on the bed. In the struggle, Nancy was stabbed with Sid's knife and the dealer left with the remaining drugs and the couple's cash. This theory is particularly attractive since no one has ever been able to account for the missing money.

After the murder and Sid's death, Room 100 became a ghoulish stop for curiosity seekers. Tired of the disturbances, the hotel gutted Room 100, knocked down the walls and expanded the adjoining rooms into the space.

Was Kurt Cobain Murdered?

At 8:40 a.m., on Friday, April 8, 1994, Gary Smith of Veca Electric arrived at one of the large mansions on Lake Washington Boulevard in Seattle. Employees from the company had been on the grounds all week, working on the installation of a new alarm system. Although the house was eerily quiet, no one suspected anything unusual. Getting no answer at the main house, Smith moved to the carriage house in the back and peered through the glass doors. At first, he thought he was looking at a mannequin on the floor. A second later, he saw the blood. Smith called the police and paged his boss, who promptly phoned a local radio station. By the time two officers arrived at 8:56 a.m., the word was out that something tragic had happened at the Cobain house.

On April 9, Dr. Nikolas Hartshorne of the King County medical examiner's office declared that Cobain's death was a suicide, specifically a "self-inflicted contact perforating shotgun wound to [the] head." Two hundred invited guests attended the funeral at the Unity Church of Try in Seattle on April 10. The body was cremated on April 14.

There were those, however, who weren't satisfied with the verdict of suicide. One of the first was Tom Grant, the private detective hired by Courtney Love to find her husband during his last days. Grant is a former cop who believes that Cobain was murdered after being drugged by someone who either had something to gain or something to lose from Cobain's death. His suspects range from Courtney Love (furious at the prospect of a divorce and angry at Cobain's decision not to have Nirvana play the 1994 Lollapalooza tour) to an unknown local drug dealer (settling a drug debt?) to someone connected with the music industry (believing that a dead Cobain would send the sales of Nirvana records through the roof?).

Grant points to other unanswered questions. Did Cobain purchase the Remington M11 20-gauge shotgun because he thought he was being stalked? If he shot himself on April 5 or 6, who had tried to use Cobain's canceled Mastercard in the early morning hours of April 8? Grant also believes that the rambling letter found at the scene is not a suicide note because it does not specifically mention death anywhere. Instead, it should be read as a statement indicating Cobain's retirement from the music industry. To make things even more suspicious, Grant contends that the last five lines of the note were written in someone else's handwriting—and he has found two handwriting analysts who agreed with him. There's also the alleged existence of a second note that only Courtney Love has seen. According to Grant, that letter (which apparently was never booked as evidence by the police) mentions a divorce but nothing about suicide.

Then there was the matter of the suicide scene itself. Several people—including Gary Smith, the electrician who discovered the body—made statements saying that it looked like Cobain's hair had been combed, a strange thing for someone who had just taken a shotgun blast to the head. Why did Cobain load the gun with three cartridges? How did someone with 1.52 milligrams of heroin in his blood have the presence of mind to even pull the trigger? Although Cobain's hands bore the imprint of a shotgun stock, where were the powder marks? And speaking of the fatal shot: why was there no exit wound? Even the medical examiner admitted this was a "quirk."

Other people stepped forward with theories. A Seattle man named Lee Remington devoted his public-access TV show *Was Kurt Cobain Murdered?* to speculation about the case. He disputed a lot of what has been said about the nature of the fatal head wound, saying that even though the gun featured a light load, the damage should have been much greater. This raises questions about the absence of an exit wound. Two Montreal writers, Max Wallace and Ian Halpearn, planned to reveal the conspiracy in a book entitled *Love & Death: The Story of Kurt and Courtney*. In the April 1996 issue of *High Times* magazine, and soon after in the supermarket tabloid *The Globe*, El Duce (pseudonym for Eldon Hoke), drummer and singer with an L.A. band known as the Mentors, alleged that Courtney Love offered him $50,000 in 1993 to assassinate her husband. El Duce later formed a Mentors side project called "Courtney Killed Kurt." Conspiracy theorists are also intrigued by the fact that El Duce died in a bizarre train accident in Mira Lom, California, on April 19, 1997. Apparently while drunk, he was dismembered by a speeding freight train. Although the deputy coroner stated that it was a "routine train versus pedestrian accident...when [Hoke] disregarded the barriers at a local railway crossing," the Internet chatter about the "real" cause of his death began almost immediately.

The most bizarre entrant into the conspiracy sweepstakes is Hank Harrison, Courtney Love's biological father. Commenting on an interview with Harrison, *Esquire* magazine wrote in March 1996 that "though he cited no evidence, he said he wouldn't be surprised if she was behind Cobain's death." Harrison mounted a pseudo-crusade in the fall of 1996 with a rambling multimedia show entitled *Who Killed Kurt Cobain?* That tour was cut short after Jack Palladino, the San Francisco attorney hired by Love, began to apply serious legal pressure. The highlight of the tour came on November 14, when Nick Auf der Maur (father of Hole bassist Melissa Auf der Maur), along with *Montreal Gazette* music critic Juan Rodriguez, crashed a presentation at the Rialto Theatre in Montreal. He stormed the stage, grabbed the microphone and berated Harrison for being such a traitorous father before he was escorted out.

Despite all lingering questions and constant Internet banter, Seattle police maintain they are not interested in reopening the case.

Text of Kurt Cobain's Suicide Note

To Boddah

Speaking from the tongue of an experienced simpleton who obviously would rather be an emasculated, infantile complain-ee.

This note should be pretty easy to understand.

All the warnings from the punk rock 101 courses over the years, since my first introduction to the, shall we say, ethics involved with independence and the embracement of your community has proven to be very true. I haven't felt the excitement of listening to as well as creating music along with reading and writing for too many years now. I feel guilty beyond words about these things.

For example when we're backstage and the lights go out and the manic roar of the crowd begins, it doesn't affect me the way in which it did for Freddy Mercury, who seemed to love, relish in the love and adoration from the crowd, which is something I totally admire and envy. The fact is, I can't fool you, any one of you. It simply isn't fair to you or me. The worst crime I can think of would be to rip people off by faking it and pretending as if I'm having 100% fun.

Sometimes I feel as if I should have a punch-in time clock before I walk out on stage. I've tried everything within my power to appreciate it (and I do, God, believe me I do, but it's not enough). I appreciate the fact that I and we have affected and entertained a lot of people. I must be one of those narcissists who only appreciate things when they're gone. I'm too sensitive. I need to be slightly numb in order to regain the enthusiasm I once had as a child.

On our last 3 tours, I've had a much better appreciation for all the people I've known personally and as fans of our music, but I still can't get over the frustration, the guilt and empathy I have for everyone. There's good in all of us and I think I simply love people too much, so much that it makes me feel too fucking sad. The sad little, sensitive, unappreciative, Pisces, Jesus man! Why don't you just enjoy it? I don't know!

I have a goddess of a wife who sweats ambition and empathy and a daughter who reminds me too much of what I used to be, full of love and joy, kissing every person she meets because everyone is good and will do her no harm. And that terrifies me to the point to where I can barely function. I can't stand the thought of Frances becoming the miserable, self-destructive, death rocker that I've become.

I have it good, very good, and I'm grateful, but since the age of seven, I've become hateful towards all humans in general. Only because it seems so easy for people to get along and have empathy. Only because I love and feel sorry for people too much I guess.

Thank you all from the pit of my burning, nauseous stomach for your letters and concern during the past years. I'm too much of an erratic, moody, baby! I don't have the passion anymore, and so remember, it's better to burn out than to fade away.

> Peace, Love, Empathy.
> Kurt Cobain

Frances and Courtney, I'll be at your altar.
Please keep going Courtney, for Frances.
For her life, which will be so much happier without me.

I LOVE YOU, I LOVE YOU!

The Disappearance of Richey Manic

At 7 a.m. on February 1, 1995, Richey James Edwards, guitarist with the Manic Street Preachers, simply vanished.

Richey had long been known as the Welsh group's most volatile member. Although he had been a happy, quiet child, he became angry and alienated as a teenager and even though he graduated with high marks in political history from Cardiff University, he continually suffered from a serious lack of self-esteem. In an effort to deal with a growing sense of paranoia and isolation, he began to drink, skip meals and cut himself. The only thing that made him feel good was music.

In December 1989, he joined the Manic Street Preachers, replacing the band's original rhythm guitarist. Although he loved being in the group, the almost ritualistic self-mutilation continued. While most people are content to pass the time watching TV or reading a book, Richey would absent-mindedly carve up his arms with a knife. After a gig at the Norwich Arts Center on May 15, 1991, Richey—determined to shock an *NME* journalist who questioned the Manic's punk authenticity—calmly carved the words 4 REAL in his left forearm with a razor blade. The incident made national headlines.

Richey's self-abuse continued over the next few years. The arm-carving continued; he'd put cigarettes out on his skin; his drug use and alcohol intake increased. There were rumors that Richey was so strung out that he wasn't able to play a note on the Manic's 1992 album *Generation Terrorists*. Two trips to a rehab center yielded only temporary results and he eventually sank back into a deep depression.

After moving out of his parents' house in 1994, Richey's drinking increased to a bottle-and-a-half of vodka a day. His paranoia was so severe that he was afraid to fall asleep at night. While on tour in Bangkok, a fan presented him with a set of knives and he obliged her by slashing his torso before going onstage. By the summer, fearing that he was going insane and suffering from anorexia, he had checked into Cardiff Hospital and then transferred to a private clinic. Three months later, Richey re-emerged, looking better than he had in years. Doctors had prescribed Prozac for what was diagnosed as manic depression, and he was attending a 12-step recovery program. Things were looking up.

In mid-January, Richey began to withdraw £200 a day from his bank account. On February 1, 1994, the same day he and Manics singer James Bradfield were scheduled to leave for a promotional tour of North America, Richey checked out of his room at the Embassy Hotel in West London. The following morning, Martin Hall, the Manics' manager and someone well-acquainted with Richey's destructive tendencies, filed a missing persons report with the police, who discovered Richey's passport, credit cards and Prozac in the hotel room. Two weeks later, Richey's silver Vauxhall Cavalier (license number L519 HKX) was found near Severn Bridge, an infamous site of many suicides over the Bristol Channel. There was no trace of Richey.

Although the Manics decided to carry on, the riddle of Richey's disappearance has never been solved. No one—not his family, nor his bandmates, nor any of his friends—has any idea where he might have gone and, with the absence of a body, the case remains open. There were several alleged sightings of Richey in late 1996 at a hippie commune outside of Goa, India, but a subsequent investigation failed to turn up any new leads. Meanwhile, a British band called Ideal created some controversy when they released a single called "Richey is Dead."

A Quick Guide to New Rock on the Net

As anyone who has purchased an expensive printed directory knows, the exponential growth and amorphous nature of the Internet makes it impossible to keep track of what really is out there on the Net. Fan-based sites come and go while commercial sites are constantly being moved and upgraded.

Nevertheless, there are a few sites that are worth the risk of including in a book. Record companies have figured out how to use the Net and are now reliably maintaining web sites. Other commercial sites with steady advertising revenue seem to have staying power and offer material that is consistently useful. There's even the odd university music site that seems to survive, despite being handed over to a new group of students year after year. This chapter lists some of those addresses.

Where to Start

If you're looking for information on a new group, the first place to check is the web site of the group's record company. Many labels post biographies, discographies and interviews on officially-sanctioned web pages long before they are sent out to the media. A record company site is often most helpful when you're looking for information on a brand new performer.

Another option is to read through the liner notes of a CD. Many performers are now building and maintaining their own private web sites, often containing far more detail than the page provided by their label. Groups such as the Offspring, Live, the Tragically Hip, Seven Mary Three and dozens more have spent considerable time and effort creating entertaining and appealing sites.

However, if you're looking for something a little juicier, then it's time to search through band sites maintained by fans. Although you can use any of the popular search engines (Yahoo!, Lycos, Excite, and so on), there are several sites that provide easy links to hundreds of other sites.

Internet Music Resource Guide: www.teleport.com/~celinec/music.shtml
This is a well-equipped site that includes pages with links to general music sites, artist sites, on-line music stores, e-zines, record labels and USENET groups. It also includes a handy search engine.

Rolling Stone Rock Guide: www.rockguide.com
Operated by Excite, the people behind the search engine of the same name, Rock Guide is a dedicated music search tool that can lead you to official and unofficial band sites, concert tickets, album release dates, fan clubs and more.

Tunes.Com: www.tunes.com
This information database features reviews, biographies and recommendations.

Ultimate Band List: www.ubl.com
A repository of links for thousands of band sites, both official and unofficial. If you're looking for information on a certain artist, this is an excellent place to start.

WOW: Where on the Web: www.ecliptic.com/wow/wow_art.htm
Another site than can provide a variety of music-related links.

Your Personal Network: www.ypn.com/music
This site links you to record stores, radio stations, concert information, lyrics and more.

Record Labels

2.13.61: www.two1361.com/
550 Music: see Sony
4AD: www.4ad.com/

A&M: amrecords.com
American Recordings: american.recordings.com
Amphetamine Reptile: amphetaminereptile.com/
Atlantic: www.atlantic-records.com/

Beggar's Banquet: www.beggars.com/
BMG alternative: www.bugjuice.com

Cargo Records: www.cargorecords.com
Columbia: see Sony
Creation: see Sony

DGC: see Geffen
Dischord: www.southern.com/dischord/
Dreamworks: see Geffen

Elektra: www.elektra.com
EMI (Canada): www.emimusic.ca
EMI (US): www.emirecords.com/
The Enclave: www.the-enclave.com/
Epic: www.epiccenter.com
Epitaph: www.epitaph.com/

Factory: www.u-net.com/factory/home.html

Geffen: www.geffen.com
Go! Discs: www.godiscs.co.uk/godiscs/
Grand Royal: www.southern.com/grandroyal/

Hollywood: www.hollywood.com

Island: see Polygram
Interscope: www.interscoperecords.com/

Kill Rock Stars: www.tweekitten.com/tk/labels/k/kill.rock.starsN.html
K Records: www.olywa.net/kpunk/

Mammoth: www.mammoth.com/
Matador: www.matador.recs.com/
MCA: www.mcarecords.com/
Mercury: see Polygram
Mint: mintrecs.com
Mute: www.mutelibtech.com/mute/

Nettwerk: www.nettwerk.com
Nothing Records: www.nothingrecords.com
Nude: www.nuderecords.com

One Little Indian: www.indian.co.uk/

Polydor: see Polygram
Polygram: www.polygram.com

Radioactive: radioactive.net/

RCA: www.rcavictor/com/

Reprise: www.repriserec.com

Restless: www.restless.com/

Rhino: rhino.com

Rykodisc: www.rykodisc.com

Scratchie Records: www.scratchie.com/

Sonic Unyon: www.sonicunyon.com/

Sony: www.sony.com

Sub Pop: www.subpop.com

Taang!: www.research/digital.com/CRL/Boston/Music/labels/taang.html

Triple X: www.triple-x.com

TVT: www.tvtrecords.com

Universal (Canada): www.universalcanada.com

Universal (International): www.mcamei.com

Virgin (Canada): www.virginmusiccanada.com/

Virgin (UK): www.vmg.co.uk

Virgin (US): www.virginrecords.com

Warner Bros: www.wbr.com

Wax Trax: waxtrax.com/waxtrax.html

Way Cool Music: www.waycoolmusic.com/

If you're looking for a label that's not on this list, there are several excellent archives of record company addresses on the web. One of the most comprehensive can be found at:
www.friendware.com/Record_Companies_Coast_to_Coast.html

Music News Headlines

When it comes to keeping up-to-date, you have two choices: you can search through the individual music news web sites, or you can use one of several tools that collect the material for you. These are three of the best sites in the latter category.

iMusic News Agent: imusic.interserv.com/newsagent

Interserve can also link you with record labels and the latest chart information.

RapidFAX Entertainment News: www.muchmusic.com/rapidfax/

One of the most user-friendly music news collection points, RapidFAX often provides links that no other sites provide, such as to stories in daily newspapers and e-zines.

unfURLed: www.unfurled.com

A co-production of MTV and Yahoo! that sources out gossip, sound samples, chats and more.

Music News Sites

Daily News: All of the following e-zines and news sites are updated five or more times a week and also offer additional links, interviews, on-line chats, music charts, opinions, reviews and various bits of industry news. Take your time with each of them, because the more you browse, the more you'll understand what each e-zine has to offer.

- *Addicted to Noise: www.addict.com*
- *Allstar Music: www.allstarmag.com/news*
- *Billboard Daily Music News Update: www.billboard-online.com/daily*
- *Daily Alternative Music News: www.chartnet.com/damn/*
- *Jam! Music: www.canoe.ca/JamMusic/home.html*
- *Microsoft Music Central: www.musiccentral.msn.com/TotallyLive#tln1*
- *MTV Online: www.mtv.com/index2/html*
- *Q Magzine: www.erack.com/qweb*
- *Rolling Stone: www.rollingstone.com/Home.asp*
- *Select Magazine: www.erack.com/select/*
- *Sleaze: metaverse.com/vibe/sleaze/00latest.html*
- *SonicNet: www.sonicnet.com*

Weekly News: These sites are updated at least once a week. Some will add updates when necessary.

CMJ Online: www.cmj.music.com/

NME: www.nme.com/

Time Off Magazine (Australia): www.peg.apc.org/~timeoff/

Other Great Sites (Web and USENET)

alt.music.bootlegs
*Although bootlegs are illegal in most countries, they're still big business. This
USENET site features the latest messages from fans who want to trade material.*

alt.music.canadian
This newsgroup provides a forum for fans of Canadian music.

alt.radio.college
*Staff at campus radio stations all over the world meet here to exchange playlists and
to swap stories.*

CDNow!: www.cdnow.com/
*Along with operating a full-service record store on the web, CDNow! also provides
links to a number of useful Internet resources, including the All Music Guide album
archive.*

Concert Web: www.theconcert.web.com
A good resource for tracking down bands on tour. See also Pollstar.

International Lyric Server: www.lyrics.ch
An archive of lyrics to more than 50,000 songs.

International Underground Music Archive: www.iuma.com
*Carefully maintained on a server at the University of California at Santa Cruz, this site
offered one of the first free, high-fidelity music archives. People from all over the
world regularly access IUMA to check out music from hundreds of unsigned bands.
The site is so deep that it's best to start with the special guided tour.*

Lollapalooza: www.lollapalooza.com
*Although very graphics-heavy (and thus slow to load on many machines), the
organizers of the yearly music festival give you lots to look at. The site is re-launched
every summer.*

The Vibe (Metaverse): www.metaverse.com
*A number of useful music resources dwell here. It also offers links to various music
news and chat pages.*

MP3 search engine: www.mp3search.base.org
There are now literally thousands of gigabites' worth of MPEG-3 encoded soundfiles
available on the Internet and downloads are a snap once you have the appropriate
software. This search engine will help you find where these files are. But beware—not
all of this stuff is legal. Bootleggers have come to love MP3 technology.

Online newspaper archives from Editor and Publisher:
www.mediainfo.com/ephome/npaper/online.htm
If you're headed for a particular city and you want to check out the concert scene, a
quick glance through the local paper may be all you need. A continuously updated list
of online papers is available here.

Pollstar: pollstar.com
Pollstar is the bible of the live music industry and hosts one of the most useful music
sites anywhere on the Internet. This is where you'll not only find out who's on tour,
but also when and where they're going to perform, often long before there's an
official announcement to the media. Pollstar's internal search engine makes finding
individual bands and dates of performances a snap. If you want to know if your
favorite band is on the road and coming to your town, all you have to do is consult
the Pollstar page. The site also offers the latest news from the road.

Radio and Records: www.rronline.com and MIT's radio list:
www.wmbr.mit.edu/stations/list.html
Based out of Los Angeles, Radio and Records is the most widely-read of all the radio
industry trade magazines. Although the site is directed mainly at radio professionals,
everyone can benefit from their web site's collection of links to radio stations which
maintain an Internet presence. If you're going on vacation and you want to know if
there are some cool stations (commercial, campus and non-profit in North America
and around the world) in the area, this is the only place that you need consult. Some
radio station sites also offer real time broadcasts through their web pages.

The MIT site is even more comprehensive, archiving more than 3,000 radio
stations around the world. There's also an easy-to-use search engine for finding
specific radio stations in Canada and the United States.

Real TV: www.radiotv.com/realalph.htm (radio)
          www.radiotv.com/realtv.htm (for television)
A list of North American web sites of both radio and TV stations.

Supersonic Guide to British Music: www.freestyle.com/supersonic
With one of the world's best collections of links to British performers, Supersonic has
half a dozen mirror sites around the world. Start with this address, and if you find the
download time to be too slow, try one of Supersonic's other URLs.

Ticketmaster: www.ticketmaster.ca (Canada)
     www.ticketmaster.com (USA)
Both sites allow you to purchase concert tickets online with a credit card. A search
function allows you to browse the site for specific shows in different cities. The sites
also feature databases on various venues and cities.

Trouser Press Record Guide: www.trouserpress.com
Although this site is a little out of date (it contains the entire fourth edition of the guide
which was published in 1991), it's still an excellent source of information on older alt-
rock releases, many of which were not printed in the fifth edition. The discographics
are especially useful. There's also a continuing open forum for fans who wish to
discuss various aspects of music.

Important Browser Plug-Ins

RealAudio (continuous audio): www.realaudio.com

RealVideo (real time video): www.realaudio.com

Shockwave (graphics and audio plus animation): www.sensory.net

Streamworks (graphics and audio): www.xingtech.com